THE COMPLETE WORKS OF ERRICO MALATESTA

Volume IV

EDITED BY DAVIDE TURCATO

The Complete Works of Errico Malatesta

VOLUME I
"Whoever Is Poor Is a Slave":
The Internationalist Period and the South America Exile, 1871–89

VOLUME II
"Let's Go to the People":
L'Associazione and the London Years of 1889–97

VOLUME III
"A Long and Patient Work…":
The Anarchist Socialism of *L'Agitazione*, 1897–98

VOLUME IV
"Towards Anarchy":
Malatesta in America, 1899–1900

VOLUME V
"The Armed Strike":
The Long London Exile of 1900–13

VOLUME VI
"Is Revolution Possible?":
Volontà, the Red Week and the War, 1913–18

VOLUME VII
"United Proletarian Front":
The Red Biennium, *Umanità Nova* and Fascism, 1919–23

VOLUME VIII
"Achievable and Achieving Anarchism":
Pensiero e Volontà and Last Writings, 1924–32

VOLUME IX
"What Anarchists Want":
Pamphlets, Programmes, Manifestos and Other Miscellaneous Publications

VOLUME X
"Yours and for Anarchy…":
Malatesta's Correspondence

"TOWARDS ANARCHY"
MALATESTA IN AMERICA, 1899–1900

INTRODUCTORY ESSAY BY
NUNZIO PERNICONE

TRANSLATED BY PAUL SHARKEY

The Complete Works of Malatesta, Volume IV
"Towards Anarchy": Malatesta in America, 1899–1900

© 2019 Edited by Davide Turcato
Translation © 2019 Paul Sharkey (except where noted)
Introduction © 2019 Nunzio Pernicone
This edition © 2019 AK Press (Chico, Edinburgh)

ISBN: 978-1-84935-148-5
E-ISBN: 978-1-84935-159-1
Library of Congress Control Number: 2016908957

AK Press   AK Press
370 Ryan Ave. #100   33 Tower St.
Chico, CA 95973   Edinburgh EH6 7BN
USA   Scotland
www.akpress.org   www.akuk.com
akpress@akpress.org   ak@akedin.demon.co.uk

The above addresses would be delighted to provide you with the latest AK Press
distribution catalog, which features books, pamphlets, zines, and stylish apparel
published and/or distributed by AK Press. Alternatively, visit our websites for the
complete catalog, latest news, and secure ordering.

Cover design by John Yates, www.stealworks.com
Printed in the USA on recycled paper

Editor's Foreword

Davide Turcato

Having escaped from forced residence and regained his freedom of movement, Errico Malatesta embarked upon a sojourn in the United States between August 1899 and April 1900, a period of about eight months, which also included a short visit to Cuba. This volume of Malatesta's *Complete Works* contains everything that he wrote between the beginning of 1899—at which point he was still confined on Lampedusa—and the end of his time in North America.

While the *Complete Works* include both his published and unpublished writings (such as his correspondence), this volume is entirely composed of published writings. In turn, these include both Malatesta's own output (articles, open letters, and so on) and writings by others that record his words in an almost direct manner (interviews and reports on his speeches).

Malatesta's own writings have been drawn almost entirely from a single newspaper, *La Questione Sociale* (based in Paterson, New Jersey), which he edited between early September 1899 and his return to Europe.

For this periodical, as for all those edited by Malatesta, we must deal with the problem of attributing unsigned articles. Which of them should be included in the volume and which excluded?

In the case of some articles, inclusion is justified by the fact that they were subsequently reprinted in the anarchist press above Malatesta's signature or were credited to him by knowledgeable commentators such as Luigi Fabbri, Malatesta's comrade, friend, and biographer, as well as editor of the original complete works project, of which he managed to issue three volumes.

Other unsigned articles have been included on the basis of intellectual responsibility, which is to say that, as editor of the newspaper, Malatesta made himself "author" of these articles by assuming responsibility for them and clearly acknowledging them as faithful reflections of his own thinking. There is clear evidence of Malatesta's assertion of intellectual responsibility over these texts in the pages of the newspaper itself. On taking over the reins of the paper—in a clear departure from the previous editorship of Giuseppe Ciancabilla, who had announced that he wanted the paper to provide an "open forum"—the "incoming editors" declared: "[The paper] will not be the mouthpiece of any individual, but will genuinely represent the ideas and desires of the organization on whose behalf it is made. Those who have received the responsibility to write the paper, have willingly accepted the requirement of submitting their articles to the collective for the appropriate review."[1] And a few weeks later, lamenting distorted accounts of his talks, Malatesta wrote: "Anyone wishing to know for sure what my thinking is need only come and listen to me and engage me in discussion; or read *La Questione Sociale* (new series) with which I am in perfect agreement."[2] This standard of intellectual responsibility was also plainly set out by Luigi Fabbri who, in crediting Malatesta with the ideas contained in a certain article in *La Questione Sociale*, made the comment: "I am unsure if this article is by Malatesta himself, since it is not only unsigned, but its arguing style is quite different from his own. Yet the ideas are substantially the same as those of Malatesta. Moreover, being the paper's editor, he would not have published the text as an editorial, unsigned and without comment, had it not matched completely with his own thinking."[3]

However, this standard of intellectual responsibility has been applied to Paterson's *La Questione Sociale* more warily than to other newspapers, such as *L'Agitazione*, which Malatesta had edited in Ancona in 1897–98. The reasons for this increased selectivity can also be clearly found in the paper itself. In response to the insinuation that the paper would cease publication after Malatesta's departure, the group in charge reassured the readers by stating that "from the very beginning of this new series, Malatesta, while busy with his propaganda tour and other tasks, provided us with articles but was not able to serve as our consistent editor and that has never prevented us from maintaining a regular publication schedule."[4] And as he said goodbye to his comrades, Malatesta, assuredly out of modesty but most likely not out of modesty alone, declared that he was "sorry he was unable to achieve more than the smallest part of what he had proposed and hoped to do for propaganda in these lands."[5] On the whole, *La Questione Sociale* cannot be regarded as Malatesta's "child" to the same degree as *L'Agitazione*, whose incubation and birth he had been fully involved with from the beginning. In the case of *La Questione Sociale*—notwithstanding the sharp break with the previous administration, as was emphasized by the creation of a new series—the paper already had an editorial staff and a long history that did not involve Malatesta.

---

1   "What Our Newspaper Will Be [Statement of the New Editorial Board]," p. 42 of this volume.

2   Untitled note of September 30, 1899, p. 87 of this volume.

3   Malatesta: *L'uomo e il pensiero* (Naples, 1951), 127. Although I agree with Fabbri's overall reasoning, I have decided in the end to omit the article in question, "Evolution and Revolution," from this volume.

4   Untitled note, *La Questione Sociale* (Paterson) 5, new series, no. 14 (December 9, 1899).

5   Untitled note of April 7, 1900, p. 249 of this volume.

Based on these considerations, a standard that automatically credited unsigned articles to Malatesta, unless there were good grounds for doing otherwise, would be too loose and would probably "water down" genuine Malatesta articles with a plethora of other articles which, while not at odds with his thinking, would not be a typical expression of it either. Instead, a stricter principle has been employed, which involves focusing on texts that stand out for some specific reason. In addition to those credited to him on the basis of the criteria set out above, most of the unsigned articles that have been included can be classified under the following headings: (i) articles that express a qualifying theoretical-tactical stance; (ii) articles written in the first person plural, when the reference is to the newspaper's editorial group as a body; (iii) articles dealing with topics that are recurrent themes in Malatesta; (iv) articles containing personal remarks unmistakably traceable to him; and (v) articles that are continuations of other articles that either were signed or have been ascribed to him according to some of the previously mentioned criteria.

In deciding whether to include or exclude individual articles, several other contributing factors have been taken into account, such as whether Malatesta was present or not in Paterson when the issue in question was published; or whether the issue in which an article appeared was more or less "dense," that is, it contained more or less articles attributable to Malatesta, thereby attesting to his direct involvement in the editing of that issue. Finally, in sporadic cases we have also relied upon stylistic considerations, when these have stood out with particular emphasis.

In any case, as in all the other volumes, we have left out articles that primarily convey facts, or are re-workings from other papers, or where reflections and commentary are limited to brief notes that reaffirm well-known concepts developed in depth elsewhere. Likewise, regular columns have been left out. In particular, one of these, *"Fatti e Opinioni"* (Facts and opinions), contains interesting remarks, some of which probably come from Malatesta's pen. However, it has been left out on the basis that the column was a regular feature, appearing even during the long periods of time in which Malatesta was absent from Paterson. So, it would have been equally misleading to include the column in its entirety as it would have been arbitrary to make a selection based on some fleeting standards for attribution.

We trust that, based on this set of criteria, the writings that have been included will present a faithful and complete picture of Malatesta's thought during this period: faithful not just in the sense of being consistent with his thinking but above all in the sense of representing his point of view on topics that mattered to him; and complete in the sense that none of these topics have been overlooked.

Finally, in also including brief notes by Malatesta regarding the paper's finances and distribution, the growth of the incipient anarchist federation, his propaganda tour as well as his remarks concerning the personal dispute with Giuseppe Ciancabilla, this volume also intends to provide an insight into the life of the newspaper and the larger Italian anarchist movement during these two years. And we speak intentionally of the "Italian" anarchist movement rather than of the "Italian-American" movement in order to emphasize that a proper study of Italian anarchism must consider it as a single transnational movement that reached beyond Italy's physical borders and to which transatlantic components fully belonged.

The articles that are included here are always reproduced in their entirety. Only when a writing of Malatesta's consists of an editor's note or a comment upon someone else's article, parts of the latter article have been summarized or omitted, as long as this has not adversely affected the reader's understanding of Malatesta's comment. The summaries of the omitted passages are inside square brackets. As a rule, all contents within square brackets indicate interventions by the editor. Instances in which the square brackets belong to the original text have been indicated in footnotes. Similarly, sections that digress from strict reporting have been dropped from other people's accounts of Malatesta's speeches. In every case, such omissions have been indicated through the insertion of three spaced dots (. . .), which differ visibly from the hanging dots (...) used in the author's text.

The texts are generally arranged in the chronological order in which they were published, except in two cases: (i) serialized articles, in which case the installments following the initial section have been attached to it; and (ii) certain speech reports or interviews, especially relating to Malatesta's trip to Cuba. For the reader's convenience, the latter have been laid out in chronological order of occurrence, rather than according to publication dates. Finally, as usual, fragmentary reports and statements which have been dropped from the main body of texts due to their brevity or questionable reliability and whose value is primarily documentary, have been gathered together in the "Press Clippings" section at the end.

Malatesta's works span a period of sixty years and were published in a broad range of publications in many countries and languages. Because of such diversity, we have not attempted to enforce uniformity of stylistic conventions. Rather, in a spirit of documentary editing, we have made an effort to reproduce those works as faithfully as possible. As a rule, unless stylistic changes were required by linguistic or cultural differences between the source language and English (such as, for example, different capitalization conventions), we have preserved typesetting styles from the original sources. Hence what might appear as inconsistencies in the present volume adhere to the original publications.

When an article has a short subtitle, this has been placed after the title proper. Otherwise, lengthier, summative subtitles have been placed at the beginning of the body of the text, in small caps. Rather than indicating in a footnote which articles have been signed, the signatures have been incorporated directly into the text, just as they appeared in the original. Articles without a signature at the foot of the text should therefore be deemed as unsigned. Where a footnote is part of the original text, this has been indicated at the start of the note inside square brackets: for instance, "[Translator's note]." All other notes are by the editor.

I should like to offer thanks to Ivo Giaccheri for the transcription of texts; Tomaso Marabini for his ongoing, expert, and disinterested assistance in the tracing and consulting of texts; Kenyon Zimmer for important bibliographical information; Massimo Ortalli for having afforded me access to a rare first edition; the late Bert Altena for consulting a periodical to which I myself had no access; Marianne Enckell from the *Centre Internationale de Recherches sur l'Anarchisme* (Geneva) for her always prompt responses to my requests for assistance; Sara Wakefield and Daniel Necas from the Immigration History Research Center (Minneapolis) for having tracked down a periodical that would otherwise not have been found; Enrico Brandoli for archival research; Odile Papini, Amparo Sánchez Cobos, and Claudio Venza for their linguistic advice; and Elvino Petrossi for a useful exchange of information.

Publisher's acknowledgments

AK Press would like to thank Davide Turcato for his keen editorial sense and the care and craft he brings to this project, and Paul Sharkey for his time and expertise. And thanks also to Andrea Asali for her translation assistance and Andrew Hoyt for his copyediting help.

Malatesta and *La Questione Sociale*

by Nunzio Pernicone[1]

Malatesta's return to Italy in April 1897 and the publication in Ancona of *L'Agitazione* under his direction were decisive contributors to the resurgence of the anarchist movement in this period. After a year of successful activities, carried out for the most part clandestinely as "Giuseppe Rinaldi," Malatesta was arrested during the bread riots that convulsed Ancona and other cities in the spring of 1898, and was sentenced to a prison term of seven months. With Italy deep in the throes of reaction following the *Fatti di Maggio*, the government was not about to liberate Italy's most feared revolutionary despite the expiration of his sentence, condemning him instead to *domicilio coatto* for a period of four years on the islands of Ustica and Lampedusa.

But the authorities were mistaken in their calculations. As Malatesta's personal friend, the socialist deputy Oddino Morgari, would later write in *Avanti!*, "whoever knew that man never believed for a moment that he would meekly spend his five years' relegation term on the islands."[2] Further noting that "a *coatto* can always escape if he has money and guts," Morgari himself, while visiting Lampedusa on what was purported to be an official parliamentary inspection of the penal colony and its political prisoners, had delivered the funds provided by Malatesta's anarchist comrades to bribe the island's director. Thus, on the night of April

---

1   [Editor's note] Nunzio Pernicone was professor of History at Drexel University in Philadelphia. He is the most important historian of Italian anarchism in North America. His book *Italian Anarchism, 1864–1892*, published in 1993 and reissued in 2009, is the standard textbook on this subject in the English language. He edited the autobiography of Carlo Tresca, about whom he also wrote the biography *Carlo Tresca: Portrait of a Rebel*, which has also reached its second edition. He appeared in three documentaries and a radio program on the Sacco–Vanzetti case. His most important articles include: "Carlo Tresca and the Sacco–Vanzetti Case"; "Luigi Galleani and Italian Anarchist Terrorism in the United States"; "Murder Under the 'El': The Greco–Carrillo Case." His last article was about the case of the Italian anarchist Pietro Acciarito. He died in 2013, while he was working on the book, published posthumously with Fraser M. Ottanelli, titled *Assassins against the Old Order: Italian Anarchist Violence in Fin de Siècle Europe* (Chicago: University of Illinois Press, 2018).

2   "A proposito d'una fuga," *Avanti!*, May 10, 1899. As we mentioned earlier, Malatesta was actually sentenced to four years of forced residence.

26–27, 1899, Malatesta and his comrades Giorgio Vivoli and Edoardo Epifani, escaped from Lampedusa by boat and headed as pre-arranged to Tunisia, where he was hosted by the Dr. Niccolò Converti, the anarchist who had long practiced medicine in the capital. A few days later, Malatesta made his way to Malta, and then to London, where he remained until the end of July, when he departed for the United States. Malatesta's arrival in New York on August 12, 1899, was not unexpected. The anarchists of Paterson—especially the group's leading figure, the Catalan Pedro Esteve, who had toured Spain with Malatesta in 1891–92—had been in contact with him for several years, issuing repeated invitations to join them and help the movement in the United States. Therefore, after coming ashore, Malatesta immediately went to nearby Paterson, New Jersey, where he was housed by comrades belonging to the *Gruppo Diritto all'Esistenza*.[3]

Paterson provided several advantages as a base of operations. Renowned as the "silk capital" of the world, Paterson was home to a thriving community of some 10,000 Italians by the turn of the century, sixty percent of whom were employed in the more than 200 broad silk mills and half-dozen dye houses. The Italians were predominantly northerners who had migrated from Biella and Vercelli in Piedmont, Como in Lombardy, and Prato in Tuscany. Those from Biella, Vercelli, Prato, and their satellite towns, most of whom had previous experience in textile manufacture, were employed as weavers, while those from Como and experienced in silk production were employed as dyers in the large dye works. Southern Italians began arriving in appreciable numbers by the turn of the century, and were employed mainly as dyers helpers, the worst and lowest paying jobs in the industry. Not surprisingly, given the racist attitudes of Anglo-Saxon America, the advent of Italian workers in Paterson was not welcomed by English-speaking workers and their labor unions, so tensions between them remained high for several decades. As one expert on Paterson has written, "Because Italians were conspicuous, they were saddled with every prejudice, stereotype, and animosity typically aimed in America at exotic newcomers."[4]

Paterson's Italian community also included one of the largest concentrations of anarchists in the United States, thereby providing Malatesta with vital support for the propaganda activities he intended to conduct. The majority of Italian anarchists were weavers, although many other

---

3   D. Turcato, "La historia oculta del Atlántico anarquista: Errico Malatesta en America, 1899–1900," *Alcores*, no. 15 (2013): 73–75; G. Berti, *Errico Malatesta e il movimento anarchico italiano e internazionale, 1872–1932* (Milan: Franco Angeli, 2003), 284–86.

4   J. D. Osborne, "Italian Immigrants and the Working Class in Paterson: The Strike of 1913," in P. A. Stellhorn, ed., *New Jersey's Ethnic Heritage* (Trenton: New Jersey Historical Commission, 1978), 14, 16, 22–24.

types of workers and artisans were represented as well. Many of the anar-chists had been radicalized in the course of their previous labor struggles in Italy, but others were converted to the cause after their exposure to the movement in the United States. The hard-core militants of Paterson's anarchist colony had come primarily from Biella and its environs.[5] Many had migrated to Paterson and nearly towns like West Hoboken and Orange Valley in order to earn higher wages than in Italy; others had fled from political persecution. In addition to Italians, Paterson hosted many French and German comrades, and also published the Spanish language newspaper *El Despertar,* edited by Esteve, which was read by the large colony of Spanish anarchists living in nearby New York as well as the Spanish and Cuban cigar makers in Tampa, Florida.

Contemporary newspapers, reflecting America's xenophobia and fear of radicals, exaggerated the size of the anarchist colony in Paterson, plac-ing the number of Italians at between 1,500 and 2,500.[6] More likely, there were around three or four hundred avowed Italian anarchists in Paterson and even more sympathizers at the turn of the century, judging from the fact that 1,000 copies of the 3,000 published weekly by the local move-ment's newspaper were read locally.[7] While these numbers suggest that Paterson boasted the perhaps highest per capita percentage of avowed Italian anarchists and sympathizers of any industrial city in America, it is also noteworthy that in the 1890s Paterson's radical community also included perhaps equal numbers of Italian socialists, both reformist and revolutionary/anti-parliamentarist factions, affiliated with the American Socialist Labor Party, who would establish the autonomous *Federazione Socialista Italiana del Nord America* in 1901. The official voice of Italian-American social democracy, *Il Proletario,* was published in Paterson

---

5   R. Rigola, *Rinaldo Rigola e il movimento operaio del Biellese* (Bari: Gius. Laterza & Figli, 1930), 96–99.

6   *The New York Times,* December 18, 1898; *New York Tribune,* July 31, 1900.

7   William Gallo, son of Firmino Gallo, a local militant, placed the figure at 300–400, in P. Avrich, *Anarchist Voices* (Princeton : Princeton University Press, 1995), 154. See also L. V. Ferraris, "L'Assassinio di Umberto I e gli anarchici di Paterson," *Rassegna Storico del Risorgimento* 55, no. 1 (January–May 1968), 52; G. W. Carey, "'La Questione Sociale,' an Anarchist Newspaper in Paterson, N.J. (1895–1908)," in L. F. Tomasi, ed., *Italian Americans: New Perspectives in Italian Immigration and Ethnicity* (New York: Center for Migration Studies, 1985), 291; G. Cerrito, "Sull'emigrazione anarchica italiana negli Stati Uniti d'America," *Volontà* 22, no. 4 (July–August 1969): 269–276; F. Rigazio, "Alberto Guabello, Firmino Gallo e altri anarchici di Mongrando nella catena migratoria dal Biellese a Paterson, N.J.," *Archivi e Storia,* no. 23–24 (2004): 143–258. Besides Turcato's essay and Kenyon Zimmer's *Immigrants against the State* (Champaign: University of Illinois Press, 2015), one of the most informative studies that focus on Paterson remains unpublished as of this writing: G. A. Vizzini, "Gli anarchici italiani a Paterson: Controversie teoriche e prassi politica," (Ph. D. dissertation: Università degli Studi di Catania, 2007).

from 1898 to 1900, under the editorship of Camillo Cianfarra and, later, of Dino Rondani.[8] Needless to say, the rivalry between anarchists and democratic socialists in Paterson and nearby cities was intense.

The first Italian anarchist group in Paterson, formed in 1892, was the *Gruppo Augusto Spies*, named in honor of the Chicago Haymarket martyr. That same year the group changed its name to the *Circolo Studi Sociali*; in November 1893 it adopted the name of *Circolo Diritto all'Esistenza*. That year the *Circolo* attempted to launch a campaign whereby the movement would acquire its own printing press, an aspiration realized in 1895, when the *Circolo* became the *Gruppo Diritto all'Esistenza* and began publishing *La Questione Sociale* that July.[9] The ideological orientation of the *Gruppo Diritto all'Esistenza* and *La Questione Sociale* was akin to Malatesta's, espousing the *socialismo anarchico* that advocated organizing along federative lines and supporting the labor movement. With a fluctuating membership of 40–100, the majority of them weavers from Biella and its environs, the *Gruppo Diritto all'Esistenza* was exceptionally large for an anarchist group in the United States, rivaled in size only by the groups in major cities, such as the *Gruppo Studi Sociali* in New York City. Weekly meetings of the *Gruppo Diritto all'Esistenza* were held every Wednesday night in a room adjoining the newspaper's operating facilities located in a small office on the third floor of 355 Market Street. Larger and more inclusive meetings of local anarchists were held in Bertoldi Hall at 286 Straight Street or in Mazzini Hall. The group's most notable figures in the *Gruppo Diritto all'Esistenza* included the Catalan typesetter Pedro Esteve, Firmino Gallo, Alberto Guabello, Beniamino Mazzotta, Antonio Cravello, and Giuseppe Granotti. Also included among its members was an important contingent of women, such as Esteve's companion Maria Roda, Ninfa Baronio, Ersilia Cavedagni (Luigi Ciancabilla's companion), and the young Ernesta ("Ernestina") Cravello. Rather than always defer to their male comrades, as was often the case even among anarchists and socialists, Roda and her female comrades formed a *Gruppo Emancipazione della Donna* in September 1897.[10] Inevitably, there were anarchists in Paterson and other nearby cities such as West Hoboken that disagreed with the organizationist orientation of the *Gruppo Diritto all'Esistenza* and *La Questione Sociale*. A minority

8   M. De Ciampis, "Storia del movimento socialista rivoluzionario italiano, *La Parola del Popolo* 9, no. 37 (December 1958–January 1959), 136–138; E. Vezzosi, *Il socialismo indifferente: Immigrati italiani e Socialist Party negli Stati Uniti del primo Novecento* (Rome: Edizioni Lavoro, 1991), 27–29.
9   *Il Grido degli Oppressi* (New York), June 18, 1892; November 25, 1893.
10   *La Questione Sociale*, 15 September 1897. For further information of Roda's work, see J. Guglielmo, *Living the Revolution: Italian Women's Resistance and Radicalism in New York City, 1880–1945* (Chapel Hill: University of North Carolina Press, 2010), 139–140, 155–159.

in Paterson, the *anti-organizzatori* formed the *Società Pensiero e Azione* in 1899. The stronghold of the *anti-organizzatori*, however, was West Hoboken, where opposition to organization was so intense that the local anarchists had no formal group at the turn of the century.

With Paterson constituting a major bastion of the movement in the 1890s, the city and its comrades was visited by all the major figures of Italian anarchism who ventured to North America as temporary sojourners during their periods of exile. Francesco Saverio Merlino, the movement's most original thinker prior to his embrace of libertarian socialism, arrived in 1892. Together with Luigi Raffuzzi and Vito Solieri, Merlino founded *Il Grido degli Oppressi* in New York, the first Italian anarchist newspaper of importance published in the United States, preceded only by *L'Anarchico*, published in New York for six months in 1888 by the *Gruppo Carlo Cafiero*. Merlino wrote eloquently about the poor conditions in which Italian immigrants lived, and undertook a lecture tour in eight states, speaking in Italian, French, and English. After he returned to Europe in January 1893, *Il Grido degli Oppressi* was transferred to Chicago, only to survive for another year after moving back to New York.[11]

Merlino was followed in July 1895 by Italian anarchism's "knight errant"—the poet, dramatist, attorney, and criminologist Pietro Gori. Gori spent three months in Paterson, after which he undertook a proselytizing tour from coast to coast, giving several hundred lectures in Italian, French, and English—sometimes three a day—to audiences that often had never heard of anarchism. Although not its first director, as commonly believed, Gori helped establish *La Questione Sociale* as a major voice of the Italian movement by contributing numerous articles in his beautiful prose. Besides Gori, other important contributors of political and theoretical articles at this early juncture included Antonio Agresti, Edoardo Milano, and Oreste Ferrara. The newspaper's first official director was Agresti. He was assisted by several typesetters and printers who belonged to the *Gruppo Diritto all'Esistenza;* they performed various editorial and administrative functions, mostly on a volunteer basis. After Agresti returned to Europe, the editorship of *La Questione Sociale* was entrusted to another temporary sojourner, Francesco Cini, one of Malatesta's closest comrades. He, in turn, was replaced as *de facto* editor by the multi-lingual typesetter Pedro Esteve, who would also edit the Spanish *El Despertar*. The administrator of *La Questione Sociale* at the end of the decade was Francis Widmar—a Slovenian printer who spoke his native tongue, German, Italian, French, and Spanish, but no English. That a Catalan and a Slovenian performed essential roles for *La Questione Sociale* attested to the multinational nature of anarchism

11   G. Berti, *Francesco Saverio Merlino: Dall'anarchismo socialista al socialismo liberale, 1865–1930* (Milan: Franco Angeli, 1993), 192–201.

in Paterson and the close links that bound them to the same cause. Although constantly under financial duress, *La Questione Sociale* managed to publish 3,000 copies on a bi-weekly basis; 1,000 were read locally, while the rest were distributed throughout the United States and to anarchists in Italy and other comrades in European countries, North Africa, and South America. Moreover, in keeping with the practices of the best anarchist publications, *La Questione Sociale* facilitated the anarchists' strong commitment to self-education by operating the *Biblioteca Sociale Libertaria*, which sold and published a variety of pamphlets and books.[12]

In need of a full-time director, however, the *Gruppo* entrusted the position to Giuseppe Ciancabilla in November 1898, after his arrival in the United States—a decision they would come to regret. Born in Rome to a bourgeois family, Ciancabilla was an active socialist in the early 1890s, and joined the editorial staff of the newly founded organ of the Italian Socialist Party, *Avanti!*, in 1896. The following year, inspired by the Greek insurrection in Crete, Ciancabilla joined the legion of Italian republicans, socialists, and anarchists led by the old revolutionary Amilcare Cipriani, and saw action against the Turks in the battle of Domokos in Macedonia, after which he rejoined *Avanti!* Ironically, it was Ciancabilla's interview with Malatesta for *Avanti!* that was instrumental in his conversion from social democracy to anarchism.[13] Subsequently driven into exile, Ciancabilla settled in Paris in November 1897, after brief stops in Switzerland and Belgium. Under the influence of French anarchists, particularly Jean Grave and the group that published *Les Temps Nouveaux*, Ciancabilla embraced Peter Kropotkin's conception of anarchist communism (he wrote the first Italian translation of *The Conquest of Bread*), with its emphasis on revolutionary fatalism and spontaneous social harmony. It was also in this environment that Ciancabilla acquired his intransigent opposition to any and every form of organization, opting instead for the individual *attentat* as the most efficacious method of struggle. Accordingly, Ciancabilla was the most outspoken defender of Luigi Lucheni's assassination of Empress Elizabeth of Austria, despite the general condemnation of the deed expressed by most anarchists, including Kropotkin. Expelled from Switzerland, where he had voiced his approval of Lucheni's *attentat* in *L'Agitatore*, the newspaper he published in Neuchatel, Ciancabilla took temporary refuge in London, the world capital of anarchist exiles.[14]

12 D. Turcato, "Italian Anarchism as a Transnational Movement, 1885–1915," *International Review of Social History* 52 (2007), 421–4; Carey, *"La Questione Sociale,"* 289–293; C. Molaschi, *Pietro Gori* (Milan: Edizioni "Il Pensiero," 1959), 15.
13 "Evoluzione dell'anarchismo," *Avanti!*, October 3, 1897, reproduced in Volume III of these *Complete Works* covering the years 1897–98, p. 316–323.
14 Surprisingly, there is no police file devoted to Ciancabilla in the Italian

By the time he assumed direction of *La Questione Sociale*, Ciancabilla ranked as one of the movement's principal intellectuals and the foremost spokesman of the anti-organizationist current in its most extreme form. Inevitably, Ciancabilla sought to change the ideological orientation of *La Questione Sociale* to reflect his anti-organizationist views, which may best be described as libertarian individualism. Ciancabilla's interpretation of libertarian individualism ran counter to the ideas of the group's majority, and the pages of *La Questione Sociale* soon raged with fierce polemics, the *organizzatori* represented chiefly by Pedro Esteve and Salvatore Pallavicini on one side, and the *anti-organizzatori/individualisti* championed by Ciancabilla on the other.[15]

Reconciliation between the two tendencies was impossible, according to Ciancabilla:

> It is our belief that the one tendency fatally tends to choke the individual's initiatives, autonomy, and independence, creating also a fertile ground for the pernicious growth of authoritarianism; the other lets the individual be completely free and master of himself and his own initiatives; indeed, those initiatives are positively promoted by the latter tendency, which keeps its libertarian character pure and intact. This is the tendency we support ...[16]

The acrimony that developed between the *Gruppo Diritto all'Esistenza*'s majority and Ciancabilla was further exacerbated by issues of vital importance to local anarchists as industrial workers locked in perpetual struggle with their capitalist employers. Most members of the group and the editorial position of *La Questione Sociale* had always supported strikes in Paterson and other textile centers, as well as the efforts of Italian weavers to establish their own unions, such as the *Lega di Resistenza* and the *Lega dei Tessitori*, which counted more than 500 members while it lasted.[17]

Ciancabilla was adamantly opposed to labor unions and virtually any form of activity that involved even a modicum of organization—anarchist

Interior Ministry's *Casellario Politico Centrale*. Moreover, there has been very little written about him. See U. Fedeli, *Giuseppe Ciancabilla* (Imola: Editrice Galeati, 1965); M. Mapelli, "Giuseppe Ciancabilla," in *Dizionario biografico degli anarchici italiani*, eds. M. Antonioli et al., vol. 1 (Pisa: Biblioteca Franco Serantini, 2003), 393–96.

15   *La Questione Sociale*, December 10, 17, and 31, 1898; January 28, June 24, July 29, and August 5, 1899.

16   "Idee e tattica (Dichiarazioni dei dissidenti)," *La Questione Sociale*, September 2, 1899.

17   *La Questione Sociale*, June 30, October 15, and December 15, 1897. See also A. Guabello, "Un po' di storia," *L'Era Nuova*, July 17, 1915.

federations, congresses, cooperatives, mutual aid societies, formalized programs, permanent committees, etc.[18] He rejected them all as harbingers of authoritarianism. As he succinctly stated, "organization ... is anti-anarchist."[19] "Free initiative" and "free association" were the alpha and omega of Ciancabilla's anarchist philosophy, the same notions that had condemned the anarchist movement in Italy to fragmentation, inertia, and impotence throughout most of the 1890s. But he was oblivious to this reality.

Fed up with Ciancabilla's efforts to impose his ideological orientation on *La Questione Sociale*, which smacked of the authoritarianism he purported to oppose, Esteve invited his good friend Malatesta to come to the United States in the hope that he would assume direction of the newspaper and resolve the conflict threatening to cripple the anarchist movement in Paterson and the rest of the country. The inevitable showdown between Ciancabilla and Malatesta and their respective supporters came just a few weeks after the latter's arrival in Paterson, where he roomed with Esteve and Maria Roda. By a vote of 80 to 3, the *Gruppo Diritto all'Esistenza* declared itself in favor of anarchist party organization, revolutionary propaganda and action, and the greatest possible participation in the labor movement. As Ciancabilla opposed every aspect of this position, he had no choice but to resign as editor of *La Questione Sociale*. Malatesta was immediately chosen as his successor. To compensate Ciancabilla for his loss, the *Gruppo Diritto all'Esistenza* assisted him financially when he began publication of his own newspaper, *L'Aurora*, in West Hoboken in September 1899. Malatesta was not opposed to Ciancabilla's publishing a newspaper that espoused an anti-organizationist point of view. He always believed that even rivals could produce a fecund exchange of ideas beneficial to all concerned. But it was not to be.[20]

The new series of *La Questione Sociale* under Malatesta's direction began with the September 9, 1899 issue. In reality, he was not the newspaper's full-time director in the strict sense of the term, because he was constantly active as a lecturer throughout his eight-month sojourn, speaking regularly in Paterson, West Hoboken, Orange Valley in New Jersey, and during a four-month propaganda tour that began on September 23 and took him to New York, Connecticut, Rhode Island, Massachusetts, Vermont, Pennsylvania, and Illinois. Typical of his lecture topics were the following: "The anarchists' response to the current

18 Fedeli, *Giuseppe Ciancabilla*, 28–29, 38, 42–53.
19 *La Questione Sociale*, January 28, 1899.
20 *La Questione Sociale*, August 5, 19, and 26 and September 2, 1899; Turcato, "La historia oculta del Atlántico anarquista," 76; M. Nettlau, *Errico Malatesta: Vita e pensieri* (New York: Casa Editrice "Il Martello," 1922), 255–6.

situation in Europe"; "Parliamentarism"; "The Twentieth of September Celebration";[21] "Anarchists and what they want"; "The social question"; "The family"; "Anarchists and workers' unions"; "The needs of the working class."[22] By no means were Malatesta's lectures attended solely by anarchists. By now Malatesta was already a legendary figure whose presence anywhere attracted the attention of radicals of every stamp, ordinary apolitical workers, and even elements among the bourgeoisie. This was especially true on the several occasions when he debated local socialists like Antonio Cravello, Arturo Meunier, Camillo Cianfarra, and the socialist deputy and editor of *Il Proletario*, Dino Rondani.[23] Malatesta himself acknowledged that he was not a great orator in the flowery and eloquent mode of Pietro Gori and Luigi Galleani, but he was nevertheless a great communicator, speaking in a conversational style, using simple language easily comprehensible to ordinary workers. It was not mere boasting, therefore, when *La Questione Sociale* reported that Malatesta always bested Rondani in their several encounters.[24]

Malatesta's writings in *La Questione Sociale* were likewise composed in a direct, clear, easily comprehensible style intended for a working-class readership—the perfect style for propaganda. And although he devoted considerable time to his lecture activities, Malatesta's contribution to the newspaper was prodigious: more than ninety articles, commentaries, and messages, covering some thirty or more subjects. The most important themes treated in his articles are discussed below.

Malatesta never considered himself a theorist of anarchism. Yet, as evidenced by several articles in *La Questione Sociale*, Malatesta's contribution to anarchist thought was considerably more important than he ever gave himself credit. He refrained from formulating a blueprint for the future anarchist society, believing that men and women would have to determine its ultimate nature for themselves. However, Malatesta had much to say about the path to anarchy, as superbly expressed in his article "Towards Anarchy."[25]

Always a voluntarist in his approach to revolution and the future anarchist society, Malatesta had no faith in the revolutionary fatalism inspired by Peter Kropotkin, a theory that effectively immobilized so many anarchists in a state of passive expectation. He criticized those anarchists who, because anarchy was not immediately attainable, "waver between an extreme dogmatism which blinds them to the realities of

---

21   [Editor's note] The 20th of September, the anniversary of Rome's annexation to the kingdom of Italy in 1870, was the opportunity for nationalist celebrations in Italy and in Italian communities abroad.

22   *La Questione Sociale,* September 16, 1899, p. 78 of the current volume.

23   *Il Proletario,* August 19, September 2, and December 23, 1899.

24   *La Questione Sociale,* September 23, 1899; *L'Era Nuova,* July 17, 1915.

25   "Verso l'anarchia," December 9, 1899, p. 167 of the current volume.

life and an opportunism which practically makes them forget that they
are Anarchists and that for Anarchy they should struggle." Anarchy,
he acknowledged, could only come about slowly, gradually "growing in
intensity and extension." Therefore, "every blow given to the institutions of private property and to the government, every exaltation of the
conscience of man, every disruption of the present conditions, every lie
unmasked, every part of human activity taken away from the control of
the authority, every augmentation of the spirit of solidarity and initiative,
is a step towards Anarchy."[26]

Malatesta knew that some anarchists would hesitate to participate in
the kind of insurrectionary alliance that he promoted because the overthrow of the monarchy would not result in the immediate creation of
an anarchist socialist society. He insisted nevertheless on the absolute
necessity of anarchist participation:

> We must cooperate with the republicans, the democratic socialists, and
> any other anti-monarchy party to bring down the monarchy; but we
> must do so as anarchists, in the interests of anarchy, without disbanding
> our forces or mixing them in with others' forces, and without making
> any commitment beyond cooperation on military action.
>
> Only thus, as we see it, can we, in the coming events, reap all the
> benefits of an alliance with the other anti-monarchy parties without
> surrendering any part of our own program.[27]

Clearly Malatesta's intent was to have this message sent back to Italy
by the spoken and written word. It is also noteworthy in this regard,
especially in light of later allegations that he was the mastermind behind
Bresci's *attentat*, that in none of his writings or lectures advocating the
overthrow of the Savoy Monarchy did Malatesta recommend the assassination of King Umberto. He believed like his teacher, Bakunin, that
institutions were the enemy, not men.

The more general objectives of Malatesta's revolutionary agenda
were published under the rubric of "Il nostro programma" (Our program) within a few weeks of his arrival in Paterson, essentially itemizing
the same goals the anarchists had embraced since the days of Bakunin
and the First International: 1) abolition of private property; 2) abolition
of government and institutions based on coercion; 3) the organization
of social life on the basis of free association and the will of the people;
4) the guarantee of life and well-being to children and anyone incapable
of providing for themselves; 5) war against religion and other lies and
myths; 6) war on patriotism, the abolitions of frontiers, and brotherhood

---

26   Ibid., 168.
27   "Il compito degli anarchici," December 2, 1899, p. 159 of the current volume.

among all people; 7) the reconstitution of the family on the basis of love and freedom from legal, economic, physical constraints, and religious prejudice.[28]

Malatesta's revolutionary program did not mince words about the necessity of employing force. The government, the church, and the bourgeoisie in general would inevitably defend their property and power by means of force (the army, police, etc.). Malatesta insisted, therefore, that "in order to defeat them, we must of necessity resort to physical force, to violent revolution."[29] The principal target of the revolution was the government—not this or that government, but the institution of government. The material fight against government would ultimately culminate with insurrection—"A successful insurrection is the most potent factor in the emancipation of the people ... The insurrection determines the revolution, that is, the speedy emergence of the latent forces built up during the 'evolutionary' period."[30]

Malatesta specified the role he assigned the anarchist with a phrase expressed countless times in his writings: "We shall have to push the people." In effect, the anarchists were to constitute themselves as a revolutionary vanguard that, by word and deed, would continually spur the people to action on their own behalf. Malatesta knew that revolution against the state could succeed only with the defeat of the government's military and police force; therefore, "we shall have to, above all, oppose with every means the re-establishment of the police and the armed forces, and use any opportunity to incite workers to a general strike that lays the most far reaching demands we can induce them to make." However events might develop, the anarchists should assume of position of permanent revolt, to "continue the struggle against the possessing class and the rulers without respite, having always in mind the complete economic, political and moral emancipation of all mankind."[31]

Of necessity, the revolutionary role Malatesta envisioned for the anarchists required the movement to *organize* its forces for action. Throughout the 1890s and earlier Malatesta had vigorously opposed the prevailing tendency among so many anarchists in Italy and Europe to associate any and all forms of organization with authoritarianism. The same anti-organizationist tendency, as personified by Ciancabilla in the United States, was already deeply entrenched among many Italian anarchists in the United States, who were isolated mainly in small groups and dispersed throughout the country, often in mining camps, literally from coast to

---

28   *La Questione Sociale,* September 9, 1899, p. 43 of the current volume.
29   "Il compito degli anarchici."
30   "Il nostro programma: Lotta politica – Azione rivoluzionaria," *La Questione Sociale*, September 30, 1899, p. 55 of the current volume.
31   Ibid., p. 56 of the current volume.

coast.[32] One of Malatesta's major objectives during his sojourn, therefore, was to counter this self-defeating attitude, again with the hope that his message would influence not only the movement in the United States but reverberate back in Italy, where his hard fought efforts had proved ephemeral because of government repression and intransigent opposition from the *anti-organizzatori*. Addressing the theme of organization, Malatesta insisted that "organization ... should be regarded by us as a matter of principle. And we believe that, far from there being any contradiction between the idea of anarchy and the idea of organization, anarchy cannot exist and is unthinkable as anything other than the free organization of all common interests, by the interested parties themselves."[33] As he had numerous times in earlier publications, Malatesta in *La Questione Sociale* underscored the crucial difference between authoritarian organization and anarchist organization, explaining that the latter "is the agreement of those who, having a common aim to achieve, unite under a common interest and divide the work as they think most appropriate to achieve that goal, each having a moral responsibility only to those agreements that he freely accepted, and only for as long as he accepts them."[34]

Organization, Malatesta argued, was imperative in order for the anarchists to undertake their propaganda mission—"propaganda that must lay the moral foundations for revolutionary action, and for the realization of our ideas."[35] Ever since the days of his paramount role in the Italian Federation of the International Workingmen's Association, Malatesta believed that the form of organization best suited for anarchist activities was a national federation, and in Italy he had campaigned vigorously for its creation in 1883–1884, 1891, and 1897. In this regard, he had achieved an appreciable measure of success with the formation of the *Federazione Socialista-Anarchica* during his clandestine sojourn in Ancona in 1897, but his arrest and the government's suppression of all anarchist activity after the *Fatti di Maggio* in 1898 brought his efforts to naught. Malatesta was more optimistic about the prospects for federating the anarchist groups in the United States because the government was unlikely to interfere. After Malatesta's speaking engagement in Barre, Vermont, where the movement had a major following among the granite quarrymen who had previously worked in the marble quarries of Carrara, the local *Circolo di Studi Sociali* took an initial step toward the formation of the *Federazione Socialista-Anarchica del Nord America*

32 Cerrito, "Sull'emigrazione anarchica italiana negli Stati Uniti d'America," 269–270.
33 "Il principio d'organizzazione," *La Questione Sociale*, October 7, 1899, p. 92 of the current volume.
34 "La nostra organizzazione," *La Questione Sociale*, November 11, 1899, p. 130 of the current volume.
35 Ibid.

SECTION I
From Lampedusa Island to London

government-backed *camorra*, and not out for radical, thoroughgoing changes. They have been easily crushed, with no discernible impact other than slaughter and ferocious persecution mounted by the authorities. And even when broader and more enlightened upheavals have shaken the country, the absence of preparations, agreement, and a specified target have ensured that the government has easily stemmed them and exploited them as the pretext for fiercer reaction.

So, if there is the will to win, rather than face periodical and pointless slaughter, we must lay preparations appropriate for the force we are going to have to confront.

*
**

In Italy, as everywhere else, there are several parties that, while all honestly desirous of the general good, differ radically from one another both about the chief causes of society's woes and about the remedies that might end them.

Some are believers in the inviolability of lawfully acquired private property, and in the intrinsic fairness of profit and interest and these contend that democratic institutions that afford everyone access to property by means of work and economies are possible and desirable; whereas others see private ownership of the land and the means of production as the primary cause of all injustice and wretchedness.

Some believe that, with the monarchy abolished, we should look for society to be changed by laws passed by the representatives of the people, elected by universal suffrage; whereas others hold that any government is of necessity an instrument of oppression in the hands of some privileged class, and these want to see the arrangement of society be the direct handiwork of the freely associated workers.

Some believe in a harmony of interests between property owners and proletarians, whereas others are convinced that there is an irreconcilable antagonism between the two classes and thus that the propertied class must, of necessity, disappear, as all of its members are absorbed into the class of useful workers. And so on.

We need not enter here into which of the various contenders may be right, nor side with any given view. What we do wish to establish here is that everybody suffers from lack of freedom, that they all have a common foe in the Monarchy, and that as none of the parties are strong enough to overthrow it by themselves, there is a shared interest in joining forces in order to rid ourselves of this obstacle in the way of any progress and every improvement.

Not that we mean to suggest that the various parties abjure their own ideas, their own hopes, their own autonomous organization and amalgamate into one; and if we were to suggest any such thing we should most certainly go unheeded since the differences that divide them, one from another, are too serious and too fundamental.

Those who believe in the legitimacy of private ownership, and contend that the establishment of a government is useful and necessary could certainly not countenance expropriation and anarchy. Conversely, the opponents of property and governmentalism would refuse to recognize the acquired rights of owners and defer of their own free will to some new government.

Let each of them therefore remain who they are and let them get on with propaganda on behalf of their own ideas and their own side. But, no matter how great they may be, the differences separating the various parties should not stop them from coming together for a specific purpose, whenever there really is some interest they all share in common.

And what more pressing interest could there be than winning the essential conditions of freedom without which the people slide into brutishness and become incapable of reacting and where the parties have no means of spreading their ideas?

In face of the brutality of certain situations, all discussion is of necessity cut short: what is needed is action.

When a man falls into the water and is drowning, one does not stand around debating why he fell in and what needs to be done to prevent him from falling in again; what matters is getting him out of the water and preventing his death.

When a country is invaded by some savage horde that mistreats, pillages, and massacres the inhabitants, the priority above all else is to drive the invader out of the country, no matter the scale of the grievance that one part of the population may have against the other part or how different the interests of the various classes and the aspirations of the various parties may be.

This is the sort of situation in which Italy finds herself today: that of a country under military occupation, where, save for the *camorra* surrounding the government and supporting it as the spring of its life, all of the inhabitants, no matter to which class they may belong, are threatened and aggrieved in their property and in their freedom and subject to the most unbearable soldierly arrogance.

What party, being in no position to slay the enemy on its own, would doom itself and the entire people to the indefinite continuation of its current slavishness, rather than join with the other parties opposed to the monarchy and seek, through union, the power to win?

Besides, even if, due to some inexcusable sectarianism that would ultimately show its lack of confidence in the validity and practicability of its own program, one of them was to opt instead to let the status quo continue, rather than act in concert with the other parties, necessity would anyway impose union on anyone not content to remain a passive onlooker, and thus effectively let down his own ideas and his own party.

Given the circumstances in Italy and of her government, the fact is that, sooner or later, a fresh eruption of the people's wrath is on its way and it will be drowned in blood if, yet again, it has nothing but stones with which to answer rifles and cannons. The subversive parties, if they have learned anything at all from past experience and have some sense of their duty and their own interest, will throw themselves into the fray and afford the people the aid of resources and plans readied in advance. So, if the various revolutionary parties participate in the struggle and there is no one able, even if he could, to prevent others from helping and thus deny them whatever morsel of influence over the future course of the revolution will accrue to them from the part they played in the victory, would it not be a very grave mistake for each of them to act on their own without any agreement, and run the risk of thwarting each other, with the advantage going to the common enemy? Instead, should they not try, through concerted action, to ensure the sort of material victory that is the essential precondition for any transformation of the established order?

Afterwards, if everybody respects freedom, as they say they do, and affords anyone else the right and the means to spread and try out their own ideas, freedom will bring forth that which it can, and those methods and institutions that best cater for the material and moral conditions of the moment will carry the day. Otherwise, the downfall of the monarchy will still mean that the worst of our enemies has been dealt with—and the fighting will start all over, but in more humane and more civilized circumstances.

***

We are dealing here with a material issue that will prevail with all brute force over the economic and moral problems by which the country is exercised.

The government has its soldiers, cannons, rapid means of communication, and transport; it has a whole mighty organization ready for the task of repression; and it has demonstrated the extent to which it is ready and willing to deploy it.

The government has not hesitated to massacre citizens by the hundreds just to snuff out some agitation that came down to harmless demonstrations and minor disturbances easily assuaged by abolition of some levy or some other anodyne concessions.[19] What might the uni-

---

19   The reference is to the bread riots that spread throughout Italy in 1898. They peaked with the Milan riots of May 6–9, in which hundreds of demonstrators were killed by the soldiers of General Bava-Beccaris.

formed beasts in the king's service not be capable of, if they were threatened by some grave danger?

A city that rises up, in the hope that others might respond to its example, would probably be reduced to rubble before the news could reach the outside world. A populace out to make a vigorous display of its own unhappiness, but lacking appropriate weaponry, would be drowned in blood before its rebellion could get off the ground.

We must therefore strike with consensus, with force, and with determination. Before the authorities can recover from their surprise, the people, or—to be more accurate—groups previously organized for action, will need to have seized as many army and government leaders as possible. Each rebel group, each unruly mob needs to have a sense that it is not on its own, so that, encouraged by the hope for victory, it sticks with the struggle and pursues it to the bitter end. Soldiers need to realize that they are confronted by a genuine revolution and to feel the temptation to desert and fraternize with the people, before the intoxication of bloodletting turns them into savages. Useful intelligence needs to be spread at speed and troop movements obstructed by every possible means. The troops must be attracted away from the places targeted for action by means of diversionary maneuvers, and rapid-fire rifles and cannons must be answered with bombs, mines, and arson. In short, there must be an appropriate response to the enemy's weapons of war, to a determined crackdown that will stop at nothing. A response must be made in the shape of action even more determined. This is war and so everything commended by the science of warfare but applied to the conditions of a risen people that has to face regulars equipped with the most up to date weaponry must be pressed into service.

But none of this can be improvised at a moment's notice: experience should have proved that to everybody. At the moment of truth, arms are in short supply unless they have been prepared in advance and unless the means of seizing them by force and by surprise have been looked into. Agreement on the allocation of roles in the erection of barricades, the bringing of fire-power to bear wherever required, and implementation of some battle-plan—these cannot be done at the drop of a hat, once the fighting is already under way. Synchronization of insurrections in various places or at least such a swift spread of the conflagration as to prevent the government from marshaling its troops and snuffing out the various insurgent centers one at a time—this is not achievable unless the action groups have agreed beforehand to liaise with one another.

We invite all the enemies of the monarchy who are seriously determined to end it to engage with this work of practical preparation.

Let men of good will seek one another out and liaise in the preparation of the insurrection. Their several initiatives will meet and federate with one another, thereby accumulating the strength required to steer the next popular uprising to victory.

The not so distant future will tell if we were mistaken in counting upon the Italian people's revolutionary energies.

August, 1899.

SECTION II
On the Other Side of the Atlantic

The Anarchist Gospel
Explained by Enrico Malatesta

Translated from "Il verbo anarchico spiegato da Enrico Malatesta,"
Il Progresso Italo-Americano (New York) 20, no. 198 (August 20, 1899)

In a lecture given in Paterson, N.J., renowned anarchist agitator Signor Enrico Malatesta explained anarchist theory, as he understands it. A friend has taken the trouble—for which we are sincerely thankful—to send us a brief summary of the lecture, that we are happy to publish, taking into account that the learned lecturer, and the gracious rapporteur, are responsible for the opinions expressed in the following.

*
**

Paterson, N.J. August 17, '99.
On Wednesday evening the renowned anarchist Enrico Malatesta held his first anarchist propaganda lecture at the Teatro Sociale hall in Paterson.[20] There was a huge crowd, even some from New York and other surrounding areas.

Malatesta very effectively expounded upon the topic "The anarchists and the current situation in Europe."

First he explained who are these feared anarchists banished by concerned governments. The anarchists, he said, are people who find that there is poverty in this world because there are too many products; there are those who are hungry because there is too much food, those who have no clothes because there are too many garments; those who lack housing and shelter because there are too many houses.

The anarchists find that this is happening because there is a very large class who does all the work and produces everything, and a tiny class that does not work and yet consumes everything, and when they cannot manage to consume everything they prefer to squander it, rather than share it with those who go without.

The anarchists oppose[21] how stupid and nonsensical this situation is, because even if there was a scarcity of products, logic would dictate that those who consume them should be those who produce them, and not those who have done nothing. Consequently anarchists seek to build a society in which the interested parties, which is to say the entire population, organize themselves to produce, consume, and expand their physical and intellectual abilities, yet happy finally.

As to the situation in Europe, and particularly in Italy, Malatesta demonstrated how it is no longer an issue of class struggle against the bourgeoisie, like

---

20   August 16.

21   The word used here (*contrastano*) may have been used deliberately or it might be a misprint for *constatano* (meaning "observe").

the old socialist schools would have us believe. It involves a resurgence of Medieval relics, such as militarism, clericalism, and imperialism, which champion the interests of their caste even at the expense of bourgeois interests.

In this struggle we must take whichever position seems most useful, ally ourselves with the most progressive factions, and enter into alliances in Italy with republicans and socialists, if today—although there is every reason to doubt this—they have revolutionary intentions to drive out the monarchy with bullets. However we must not follow them. We must remain distinct, separate, at the forefront, without commitments, and not establish a republic, which is to say another government, but take advantage of this situation to tear down every form of government, old and new, and prevent them from being formed.

These intentions of the anarchists gave rise to a lively debate with the socialist republicans, who believe it is more useful to help with the establishment and development of a bourgeois republic, so that tomorrow they will be better able to fight for socialism, as they say. But Malatesta debunked these illusions and these fallacies, showing, through tight and splendid logic, how socialism can only come to pass when, in addition to private property, every form of government and authority is dismantled.

Malatesta will be in New York this coming Saturday and Sunday, and perhaps will give a lecture. He will deliver a series of anarchist lectures in Italian, French, English, and Spanish in as many locations in the United States as he can.

Signor Malatesta Explains

Translated from "Il signor Malatesta si spiega,"
Il Progresso Italo-Americano (New York) 20, no. 200 (August 23, 1899)

Signor E. Malatesta wishes to amend certain views, not reflective of his thinking, carried in the report sent to us by third parties on the talk he gave on the evening of the 16th inst., in Paterson, N.J.

To which end he has sent us this letter in which he asks that we accommodate him, which we are happy to do as follows.

750 Clay St., Paterson, 20/8 '99[22]

Dear Editor-in-chief,

I read in your issue of today's date that I am supposed to have stated in Paterson that "henceforth it is no longer a matter of class struggle against the bourgeoisie as the older socialist schools wished us to believe."

---

22   The address provided by Malatesta is that of Pedro Esteve and his wife Maria Roda, with whom he was staying. Esteve was the Spanish anarchist with whom Malatesta had toured Spain in 1891. Esteve had since emigrated to America.

Since this does not accurately reflect my thinking, allow me to reiterate for your readers what I actually did say.

As I see it, it is not the case that the bourgeoisie forms a single body in the struggle against the proletariat and that government, army, bench, church, etc. have no reason to exist other than the protection of bourgeois interests, just as the various schools of socialism believed once upon a time.

The current position in Europe is there as evidence, even for the most pig-headed, that the bourgeoisie is split into a number of factions competing among themselves, and that the various political, court, military, religious institutions, etc., not only champion the bourgeoisie against the proletariat, but indeed have interests of their own, which they protect even at the expense of placing bourgeois interests in jeopardy.

This situation represents a benefit and a danger as far as the laboring population is concerned; a benefit insofar as the enemy is divided; a danger in that it might lead the workers to forget that "all" bourgeois are its enemies.

So we anarchist socialists should cash in on the divisions within the enemy camp; and, if it can be done to some purpose, ally ourselves with this or that bourgeois faction in order to rid ourselves of the most immediate obstacles such as, in Italy, the monarchy; but we must always remain what we are, namely, implacable enemies of capitalism and authoritarianism, and, insofar as we have it in us so to do, prevent the workers from being used yet again as a footstool for new rulers and new exploiters.

The point is not to give up on the class struggle but rather to prevent the workers from straying from the Polar Star of class struggle in the complex struggles at the present hour and in the near future.

The debate centers on a de facto matter, to wit, the influence, exclusive or otherwise, of the class struggle in a wide variety of historical events. But all socialists, of no matter what school of thought, are—or ought to be—in agreement on the necessity of the proletariat's always being guided by the interests of the working class; given that, as far socialists are concerned, there is no equitable solution to the social question other than the destruction of all parasitical classes through the eradication of private ownership and the conversion of all able-bodied men into useful workers.

In the hope that you will be willing to publish these few lines for the sake of the truth, thanking you in anticipation.

Yours
ENRICO MALATESTA

Malatesta Lectures

Translated from "Conferenze Malatesta,"
La Questione Sociale (Paterson, New Jersey) 5, no. 126 (August 26, 1899)

It would be a difficult task to set out to summarize even in broad terms, in a normal report the lecture by comrade Malatesta delivered here in Paterson last Wednesday, as dense in ideas and concepts as it was.[23] Therefore we will omit or merely mention many parts of it, striving instead to bring out what seemed to us most important and most interesting.

After having explained who the anarchists are, what they want and by which methods they want it, Malatesta immediately moved on to the chief topic of the lecture, which was an explanation of what position the anarchists should take in response to the situation in Europe, and especially in Italy.

An old sociological notion, he said, made us believe that the institutions of the State, the army, the judiciary, etc., had no other function than to defend private property, the bourgeoisie. Therefore the state of the struggle was clear cut: on one side is the owner as such, in other words the possessor of the tools for work, of the land, and the holder of the capital; and on the other side is the worker with zero privilege at the mercy of the former. But now this illusion has subsided. It was, nonetheless, a helpful illusion, as it created the great idea of socialism that, with its notion of abolishing private property and putting it into common ownership, indicates the sole resolution of the conflict.

But then we were left shocked when we saw other factors in the struggle that we thought had disappeared reemerge from the shadows of the Middle Ages; when we saw that, contrary to Marx's claims, the government does not only represent the interests of the bourgeois class, but often sides against them in order to give preference to dynastic, militarist, and other interests, which is to say, to the interests of a special caste. So the political struggle again comes to the fore, as an exclusively economic struggle is no longer enough.

Here Malatesta outlined the current situation in Europe, and especially in France, Spain, and Italy where these caste interests have reemerged more than ever, and are at odds with the same bourgeois interests. He therefore stated his belief that it is a serious mistake to think that we ought to refrain from all action, when our enemies are fighting among themselves. We must, while always aiming to fight for the complete emancipation of the masses of workers, take advantage of the situation, and since the enemies are divided, we can temporarily join with one or the other of them to demolish whichever is the most problematic.

Thus faced with the monarchy in Italy we see that there are some parties that have their own interests in destroying it. So we can unite with them in this

---

23 This refers to the same talk given on August 16, as reported in *Il Progresso Italo-Americano.*

7:10 cm

Malatesta

Source: International Institute of Social History, Amsterdam,
BG A8/785

demolition work, not because that monarchy is worse than any other monarchy or the very republic, but because it exists, it is an obstacle to the realization of our ideas: therefore let us go after it to take a step forward.

Let it be an alliance in the field of action, of gunfire, though; and let us remain ourselves, with our whole program, without compromise and without commitments, and determined to continue the struggle even when the others want to rest, to reach our ultimate goal, which is anarchy. And the more we stand firm in our determination to reach it the quicker we will get there.

What will happen tomorrow if a revolution breaks out in Italy? If we join in, perhaps we will not achieve anarchy, but we may be able to prevent or hinder the formation of a new government by all means: refusing to comply with the draft, to pay taxes and landlords, causing strikes, inciting workers to drive their masters from the factories and the peasants to bring home the grain and every harvest from the field, instead of giving it to their masters. We will ultimately continue, by all means and with greater enthusiasm and activity than at present, the struggle, because now we are dealing with an established, and relatively robust, government, and tomorrow we will instead face a weaker government, because it will not yet have been established.

Therefore an alliance yes, with the socialists and with the republicans if they seriously mean to take up arms and make a revolution, which seems increasingly doubtful; but an alliance without commitments, not for the republic, because entering into a commitment with republicans to consolidate their power means betraying the people's cause. Making revolution for the republic would perhaps be worse, because it would eliminate every source of conflict—so useful to us—among bourgeois interests, as is the case now; therefore we do not recognize monarchy, nor republic, and we will strive to prevent one from being built on the ruins of the other, because it is certain that for people needing bread and freedom, even under a republican regime there will be the same firing squads whose volleys recently echoed through the streets of Milan.[24]

And Malatesta concludes with a warning that when anarchists speak of their own interests, they mean the people's interests, since anarchists, who ask nothing for themselves, neither appointments, nor privileges, nor authority, are the only party to pursue and genuinely care for the interests of the people, from whom they ask for nothing more than to go with them on the barricades and die for the people's cause, unlike socialists and republicans who wish to gain power, and as long as they achieve that, even if poverty and authority continue to prevail, they will still have won their battle.

This lecture, of which we have only provided a feeble summary here, inasmuch as it involves a tight chain of arguments, should be reprinted verbatim to give a precise and complete picture. A lengthy discussion followed, or rather a polite contradictory duel between Doctor Rondani, a socialist, and comrade Malatesta.

---

24   See note 19.

Essentially Rondani, who stated that he accepted as an accurate factual description the portrait that Malatesta had painted of the European situation, reduces the revolutionary question pressing upon Italy to a republican question. He argues that the support socialists and anarchists should give the republicans must be intelligent, not chaotic, which for him means that they must support, aide, and promote the establishment of a republic, obtain guarantees of freedom from it, and then also defend the republic against maneuvers by the defeated monarchy who will resume the fight, as the French socialists are now doing, who defend the republic from assaults by monarchists, even 30 years after the republic was established. After which... everybody will return to their battle stations.

Rondani therefore denies that socialists want to establish a new authoritarian State, but he insists that once the bourgeoisie has been expropriated, government too will vanish. Parliaments are merely transitional conventions for lawmaking, which too must disappear. He then invokes the anarchists for the truce of God in their fight against the socialists, in order to combine common forces to make the republic, which will bring schooling for all, the *nazione armata*, and... universal suffrage, thereby being worthy of the cause of civilization.[25]

Malatesta counters Rondani's arguments with an effective and lively rebuttal. To begin with, anarchists have no intention of following behind the socialists and republicans. It is only a question of entering the garden of desires, and all three together slaughtering the beast defending the entrance. What will the anarchists do after that? This does not concern the socialists, nor the republicans, but only the public. If the circumstances allow, we will take possession of the land, machinery, the instruments of labor, the products; if we can, we will gun down anybody who attempts to govern us, and we will burn the *Montecitorio*, if it is still used to house lawmakers, which is to say the people's masters.[26]

We have had our fill of the guarantees promised by governments! If the people are strong, they will obtain the guarantees by themselves and the government will yield. If the people are weak, with all the guarantees and laws in the world, they will have handcuffs, bullets, and forced residence.

Returning to the concept of State socialism advocated by today's so-called socialists, he insists: and responds to Rondani that even if the conservatives have observed the same thing as the anarchists, is that a surprise? Conservatives are often intelligent people and, if they say some truth, their opinions should be considered.

He then recalls the resolution passed at the London Congress, which Rondani would rather deny, but which Malatesta reads aloud from the official text, which... contradicts Rondani. (See the article "Observations" below).[27]

---

25   *Nazione armata* (armed nation) was the model of army that progressive parties advocated, in contrast to the model of a permanent army at the service of the king. It was based on military education to be given to all citizens since school, rather than on long periods of military service.

26   Palazzo Montecitorio was the seat of the Italian Chamber of Deputies in Rome.

27   The international socialist and labor congress in London, in which Malatesta took part and from where he sent correspondence to *L'Italia del Popolo* (see

What Rondani says is true, that once private property has been eliminated, tyranny will also cease to exist, but precisely for this reason he does not believe Rondani is a socialist, because a socialist cannot conceive of the abolition of property without the joint abolition of the government and the State, what instead the supposed democratic-socialists wish to preserve.

Moreover, now we see them in France defending, through electoral opportunism, small property owners, contrary to the theories of Marx and Engels. Now we see them like Millerand, rising to bourgeois power, as a shoe-shine boy to the butcher Galliffet.

Drawing to a close, Malatesta laments that the popular parties, now that the government of the sword has treaded over everything, laws, statutes, freedom, squander all of their activity into political and administrative elections, sedating the true revolutionary energies of the people. So, to be clear: yes to an alliance, but not one for holding elections, but one for bullets; an alliance with revolutionaries, but not with the soporifics; yes to a truce, but not a naive one to play into your hands, but only an agreement: that you cease your talk of elections and speak only of revolution.

Rondani naturally protests, and argues that anti-monarchy electoral gymnastics is educational, and not soporific work; he wants to vindicate the many voters who lost bread and freedom to cast their votes and carry out anti-government propaganda... Malatesta interrupts him: We have nothing against them, but against those who exploit them by getting them to cast votes so that they can be elected.

And so Rondani remains a parliamentarian, convinced that he is doing courageous work, and he gives assurances that he will defend suffrage even under a monarchical regime; and repeats that he hopes for great things from the republic.

Esteve rightly points out that even if they wanted to, logically speaking, the socialists and republicans cannot offer any guarantees, because by claiming to be the people's governments, they must leave it up to the people to determine how they wish to be governed, under which laws, etc. How, therefore, can they speculate now as to their future conduct?

After a few more remarks from Malatesta who explains to Rondani, who does not wish to understand it, the text of the London resolution, the packed gathering begins to break up at a late hour, leaving everyone with an appreciative feeling and the desire to hold such events more often.[28]

Volume II of these *Complete Works*) took place between July 27 and August 1, 1896 and was the arena for a protracted procedural dispute over exclusion of the anarchists. The aforementioned article, originally titled "Constatazioni," reports the official text of the congress's resolution on political action, which reads as follows: "This Congress understands political action as the organized struggle in all forms for the conquest of political power and its use nationally and locally in legislation and administration by the working class on behalf of their emancipation." On the congress, see also "The 1900 Socialist Congresses in Paris," p. 204.

28   The New York socialist newspaper *Il Proletario* also carried a short report

New Rival for John Most

New York Press (New York), August 28, 1899

MALATESTA COMES TO THIS COUNTRY TO PREACH ANARCHY.

John Most, the anarchist, would better look to his laurels. A rival is in the field in the person of Errico Malatesta, also an anarchist, who arrived here a few days ago to preach the gospel of the social revolution.

Malatesta can speak several languages, and boasts that he has been in prison at least once for anarchist utterances. He addressed about 200 Italians yesterday in Teutonia Hall, at Third avenue and Sixteenth street, and was received with enthusiasm. Malatesta said that the workingmen of Spain and Italy were preparing for revolution.

"They will soon rise in their might and sweep all before them," he continued. "I believe in the economic movement and in strikes. Strikes lead to revolution. I am against all political action, for it keeps up the old order of things. I would have the workingmen keep away from the polls and refrain from voting or taking part in politics. We don't want to do anything that will keep back the social revolution. Let it come."

Malatesta said he was going to establish anarchist "groups" in and around New York. He will try to bring about a community of feeling between the "Reds" of all nationalities who live here.

His friends say he will hustle about in a way that will make John Most feel sick.

Malatesta, Anarchist. A Talk with the Italian Outlaw Who Is Here [by Abraham Cahan][29]

The Commercial Advertiser (New York), September 1, 1899

TO SPEND THE REST OF HIS LIFE IN THIS COUNTRY—HIS VIEW OF CONDITIONS IN ITALY, OF ANARCHY, OF POPULAR GOVERNMENT, OF

on this same talk in its August 19 edition, mainly summarizing Rondani's contribution: "Rondani insisted upon correcting Malatesta's error that the socialists were out to conquer power. No, as the London Congress reiterated, the aim of the socialists was to turn private property into collective property." For Rondani, political action was only a means leading to that end and as such had to come before it. "Regarding the current situation in Italy," *Il Proletario* added, "Malatesta acknowledged that today he is less inclined to follow the socialists into concerted action with all Italians opposed to the Savoy monarchy."

29 This interview is unsigned, but was reprinted in an anthology of Cahan's articles, *Grandma Never Lived in America* (Bloomington, 1985).

STRIKES, OF VIOLENCE IN GENERAL—HEAR HIM NOW, FOR HE SOON WILL BE AS OBSCURE AS MOST ET AL.

Errico Malatesta, the noted Italian anarchist, who arrived in this country a few days ago, is living with friends in Paterson, N.J. The house is crowded every evening with Spanish, French and Italian anarchists, who come there to pay their respects to the great man and listen with religious attention to the expression of his views.

Errico Malatesta is a man of about fifty years of age, his once robust body bears the marks of his prolonged and repeated residences in Italian jails. He is the descendant of an old Italian family and is highly educated. He speaks four languages fluently and has been a frequent contributor to Italian, French and Spanish magazines dealing with economic subjects. He was elected a member of the Italian parliament five years ago and took his seat as an outspoken anarchist. He played, during the bread riots in his land, a part so prominent that he was sentenced (without trial, he says) to four years' exile in the penal colony of the Isla Salvadore, on the African coast. Because of his failing health he was pardoned a few months ago, and has now come to the United States to propagate his ideas.[30]

"The conditions of the people in Italy are in such a terrible state," said he to a reporter, "that one must have lived there in order to believe such misery possible. In spite of the fact that Italy has the forms of representative government every Italian is practically at the mercy of the officials. The constitution guarantees trial by jury in the French sense of the word, but this guarantee amounts to nothing. Years ago Crispi, then in the height of power, "jammed through" (as you say) parliament a little insignificant looking law, which introduced into Italy the Russian method of administrative dealing with political offenders. It was maintained in the beginning that this law was intended expressly for the repression of the anarchists, but later it was extended to include the socialists also, and to-day it is not rare that the government invokes these paragraphs whenever it finds it expedient to rid itself of some opponent. This state of affairs alone would, perhaps, be sufficient to drive an English population to open revolt, but the Italian does not feel so greatly oppressed by it. The him the enormous burden of taxes is the one thing he will not submit to.

"And do you wonder that this is so, when I tell you that human ingenuity has been exerted to the utmost to increase the number of taxes and to take more and more from the poor laborer in the name of the state? The immense army and the costly navy which Italy has to maintain for the sake of the triple alliance have brought about a condition where fully two-thirds of the earnings of every Italian

---

30   It cannot be ruled out that this short biographical outline may have been based in part on a number of misleading details furnished by Malatesta himself. As a general rule, though, this piece is typical of the degree of accuracy and understanding of anarchism that characterized Malatesta biographies in the American press right up until he died.

are taken by the tax collector. The rich, and Italy has her share of very rich people just as much as you have here, evade payment of taxes by various loopholes and subterfuges, but the poor have to pay them. Everything you can conceive of is taxed. The government has a monopoly on salt, which it sells at exorbitant prices to the poor, and they have the mill tax, the most oppressive tax ever invented. Think of it, every time the poor man brings his wheat or corn to the mill he has to pay to the government about 10 per cent of its value for the privilege of transforming his wheat into flour. This is the monument Crispi erected for himself. Then there is the compulsory military service, which takes the young man from his work for three years—is there in all this no reason for a revolt?

"And once in a while the Italians do revolt. An especially obnoxious prime minister is killed or they rise in their hunger and help themselves to food from the stores. Then, of course, the government sends its soldiers, and the killing is done legally and is applauded by every 'upholder of law and order.'

"How did I come to be an anarchist? I have studied the social question for a number of years. I had firmly believed that popular government was the salvation of the race. I learned that parliament is a sham in Italy and I went to England and to the United States to study the workings of popular government in its highest developments, and in both countries I saw that misery is ever on the increase. Then I became convinced that nothing short of a complete revolution would be of any avail."

Malatesta became here very enthusiastic, and he left no doubts as to where he stands in regard to violence.

"Much has been said about we anarchists being bomb-throwers, assassins, cutthroats and so on. In a sense these accusations are true. I, personally (and no real anarchist can speak for anyone but himself), regret very much that deeds of violence are committed from time to time. But it seems to me that in the natural order of evolution human violence has as much place as has the eruption of the volcano. All great progress has been paid for by streams of blood, and I cannot see how the present conditions, based upon brutal force, can be changed in any other way but by force. Did it ever occur to those in power to stop the use of force on their part? Oh, no. The state and all government is based upon force, and as long as they are going to use force against us, we, in self-defense, must necessarily employ violent methods. Show me one anarchistic deed and I will point out to you the brutal oppression, the terrible crimes, which were responsible for it. Moreover, it is easy to raise the cry 'Another anarchistic dastardly outrage,' but how many take the trouble to investigate all the circumstances connected with the act. Not one in ten millions."

Malatesta intends to stay in the United States permanently. He does not fear that the authorities will interfere with him; he is not afraid of being sent back. "I have been convicted and sentenced a number of times, but never for a felony. All my crimes were of a political nature, and I understand that as a political offender I am not barred from this country.

"I have already addressed a few meetings of workingmen in this country and will go on to do so. I want to impress upon them the folly of all political actions. They only perpetuate the existing order of things, while the only hope lies in the absolute abolition of the system. I can see some good signs of progress here. Strikes are increasing in number and while they are lost in most cases they are very valuable. A strike is a sort of revolt and it prepares the workingman for more serious fighting; every lost strike leaves a great bitterness in the hearts of the defeated workingmen. They learn to look upon the capitalist as their enemy, and once they become enlightened on this subject they will be ready to deal with their enemies as the Washington government deals with the Philippines."

Mr. Malatesta said that he is not a rival of John Most nor of Emma Goldman.[31] He believes they will work in harmony, though he admits that the so-called individualistic anarchists will have nothing in common with him. In due time he expects to go on an extended lecture tour over the country and to organize anarchistic groups wherever possible.

Parting of the Ways

Translated from "Separazione,"
La Questione Sociale (Paterson, New Jersey) 5, no. 127 (September 2, 1899)

For some time ideological differences have emerged between the group responsible for managing LA QUESTIONE SOCIALE and the comrades who edited it. An attempt was made to satisfy all sides, turning the newspaper into a sort of open forum, in which anyone calling himself an anarchist might set out and defend his ideas even if they contradicted those held by other collaborators.

The attempt satisfied no one; and everyone agreed that if the paper was to be able to make effective propaganda it needed unity of direction and to be the organ of a specific tendency.

The issue was brought before the group and the various competing principles were widely discussed, the group declared itself in favor of organizing as a party for propaganda and revolutionary action, as well as the widest possible participation in the labor movement.

The old editorial team did not agree with the group's decision and resigned; and stated that it would produce another newspaper.

The group appointed another editorial team in perfect harmony with its leanings; and at the same time, convinced that all ideas are entitled to be explained and that the cause of truth can only profit from a discussion

---

31   See article "New Rival for John Most," p. 35. Reporting Malatesta's arrival in America, the *New York Sun's* August 28 edition also carried the headline: "Rival for John Most."

conducted with civility and in good faith, stated that they were pleased with the plans of the old editorial team.

Readers will find below an explanation from the two parties of the principles which will guide the two newspapers.[32]

⁂

To avoid any misunderstandings let us note that we are not dealing here with a *crisis*, or rather a new anarchist crisis. These two tendencies have always existed within the anarchist movement, and after having been confused and concealed by the dominance of one or the other for a long time, went their separate ways already several years ago in Italy and elsewhere.

The Italian comrades in the United States had thought they could overlook these differences in view of common ideals. The facts have shown that even here only people who agree can work together, and on matters upon which they all agree.

Nothing to lament for that matter: every vibrant idea is destined to differentiate itself and divide in various ways, and the greater the diversity, the livelier and more fertile it is.

To work, everyone: and divided, we can do more good for the common cause than we can amongst the inevitable friction when we do not agree.

What Our Newspaper Will Be [Statement of the New Editorial Board][33]

Translated from "Ciò che sarà il nostro giornale [Dichiarazioni della nuova redazione]," *La Questione Sociale* (Paterson, New Jersey) 5, no. 127 (September 2, 1899)

With the next issue the newspaper LA QUESTIONE SOCIALE (in a bigger format and with a new masthead) will begin a new series and will serve as the organ of an anarchist organization with a specific program.

---

32   For the incoming editorial team's statement, see the next article. It followed the article "Idee e tattica [Dichiarazioni dei dissidenti]," signed "on behalf of the *Aurora* Editors and Administrators: G. Ciancabilla, G. Della Barile, A. Guabello." The latter was republished in *L'Aurora*'s November 4 edition.

33   The part in square brackets is part of the original title.

This program will be set out methodically in issue no. 1 of the new series, and discussed and defended in all aspects in the following issues.[34]

Now we will discuss the general principles that will guide the action of the organization and the newspaper that will represent its ideas.

We are convinced that no one holds a monopoly on the truth, that nobody possesses the whole truth and that only through free discussion and free experimentation can we move towards an ever wider and more detailed understanding of social problems and their solutions.

We therefore believe that everyone has full and unlimited rights to completely express their ideas, even those that may seem absurd or wicked to us, and that the progress of humanity depends upon this unlimited freedom. But indeed we believe that anybody who has fully developed convictions, must defend their convictions, and cannot, under penalty of being condemned to impotence and futility, forever hover between yes and no, and wrap themselves up in continual contradictions.

Certainly any conviction, that isn't stubbornly obstinate, is susceptible to modification and change when it comes into contact with fresh facts and new arguments; but for as long as it exists it has to be defended as it stands; nor could it have any impact upon the world and become an objective reality unless it assumes a concrete shape, liable to change as the conviction changes, but always fixed during the period in which it is intended to be carried out.

We can for example—it has already been said a thousand times—continually follow the progress of engineering and mechanics, in matters of railway construction; but if it is a question not of discussion and study, but a question of *building* a railway, we have to take engineering and mechanics as they stand at the time when we begin our project, and build the line as best we can, given the current state of the art, and equip ourselves with the best materials available at the time when we need them.

But maybe tomorrow we will learn to do better!… Well, tomorrow we will do better: but in the meantime we must do what we know how to do. Otherwise, always waiting for a better future, we shall remain forever without a railroad.

We are not dabblers in sociology who amuse themselves with intellectual exercises that lack any practical purpose. We are workers who suffer from the injustices of which we and our comrades are victims: and from this day forward we want to fight for our emancipation and for the emancipation of others. And to do so we need to know the causes of the evils we denounce and the means by which they can be eliminated: we need to decide the objective to achieve and the route by which we mean to get there.

---

34   See "An Anarchist Programme," p. 43.

If we did not yet understand the evils to destroy nor how we can destroy them, then clearly we could do nothing but study, observe, and investigate: but then we could not insist on making propaganda, since we would not know what to propagate; and much less make revolution, which is to say, push the people to overthrow existing institutions; since we would not know whether these are good or bad, and whether, and by what means, they might be replaced with better institutions.

But we do make propaganda; we prepare ourselves and strive to prepare the popular masses for revolution: therefore we need to have fully developed ideas; that we know what we want to destroy and why we want to destroy it; what we want to do and how we want to do it.

This is called having a program.

We could change our program, if we become convinced that we are wrong; and at such a time we will have the duty to honestly admit this to our comrades. Meanwhile, since we are inviting people to embrace our ideas, we must clearly tell others what we want, and require those willing to work with us to clearly state what they want.

Therefore the first characteristic of our newspaper, as well as of our organization, is that it shall have a set program.

We shall keep our readers informed of all interesting opinions that come to our notice, and we will discuss them in order to broaden our own intellectual horizon and that of our comrades and benefit from every new idea that comes along: but the primary purpose of the newspaper will not be to search for new truths (this being a matter for *Journals* and other learned publications) but propaganda of established truths, as is appropriate for the organ of a party of action.

And the second characteristic of our newspaper will be to speak to the masses, the huge masses of the oppressed and exploited. And, given our convictions and our purpose, this is only natural.

We seek the good of all, and we are convinced that this good could only be attained through the efforts of all. Good foisted upon others by one man, by one class or by one party, were such a thing possible, would have a disheartening effect on dignity, on capacity for initiative, on self-confidence of the recipients, and would therefore cease to be a good, and even its material effects would not last long.

Therefore to reach our goal, we need to awaken within the people, within every man of the people, the awareness of their rights, the feeling of love and solidarity towards all men, the hatred of injustice and oppression, and the faith in the strength that the oppressed can generate when they achieve agreement and unity with their comrades. And to do this we must not look upon ourselves as superior beings who deign to stoop to the people's level, but as comrades who offer and seek help from comrades for the common good; remembering the great truth, that by coming into contact with the people, even the most ignorant part of the people, we receive intellectually and morally a lot more than we give.

Finally, the last characteristic of our newspaper which we wish to draw attention to in this article, is that it will not be the mouthpiece of any individual, but will genuinely represent the ideas and desires of the organization on whose behalf it is made. Those who have received the responsibility to write the paper, have willingly accepted the requirement of submitting their articles to the collective for the appropriate review; and they find this requirement perfectly compatible with their freedom, because they know that they and all comrades of the organization share the same program and aim to fight for the same goal using the same methods.

And now an appeal to all comrades in the United States and beyond. We intend to develop and publicize the newspaper to enable its propaganda to penetrate the mainstream public; with the idea that producing a newspaper that is read only by the already converted or few more, is nearly useless. We therefore ask everyone who finds our work useful to promptly take an interest in diffusing the newspaper: find us retailers in every location, or, better yet, make agreements in various groups to order the largest number of papers from us that can be sold and find a comrade to volunteer his services as a vendor; send us addresses in locations as yet unreached by the newspaper, find us lots of subscribers... and let everyone bear in mind that the newspaper is entering its new life phase burdened by a fairly substantial deficit and needs comrades to help with generous oblations.

On behalf of the anarchist-socialist group of Paterson
IL DIRITTO ALL'ESISTENZA
THE NEW EDITORIAL TEAM

Anarchists Divided Among Themselves

New York Herald, no. 23021 (September 2, 1899)

BUT ALL AGREED, AT A MEETING LAST NIGHT THAT THE "SOCIAL REVOLUTION" MUST COME.

About sixty anarchists met last night, in a hall in East Broadway, for the double purpose of harmonizing the various groups and to agree on some policy for the fall and winter.

Harmony was soon found to be impossible. The Russian anarchists have some grievances against the few English speaking ones, who, in turn, do not care to be identified with the Russians. None of the followers of Emma Goldman was present. Herr Most was denounced in vehement language and was branded as "a renegade who had sold himself."

Errico Malatesta, an Italian anarchist, saved the meeting from breaking up in disorder. He was listened to with great attention. He declared that political action is barren of results and the social revolution must be ushered in in some way or other.

"Meet violence with violence, if need be," he said, "but do not throw away your lives in killing nobodies. As a matter of simple expediency I should advise against any extreme deeds, for we are few and our opponents are many. Leave it to each individual to decide whether he is ready to throw his life into the balance. If he has special reasons to commit an act of violence it is his own concern. I will not condemn him for it. But neither I nor any one else should give advice in such matters."

For the immediate future he advised an active propaganda. This is to be confined to foreigners, as Americans do not become converts.

An Anarchist Programme

In *Errico Malatesta: His Life and Ideas*, compiled and edited by Vernon Richards (London: Freedom Press, 1965; reprinted in 1993), 182–198. Originally published as "Il nostro programma," parts 1–4, *La Questione Sociale* (Paterson) 5, new series, nos. 1–4 (September 9, 16, 23 and 30, 1899)[35]

We have nothing new to say.

Propaganda is not, and cannot be, but the incessant, tireless repetition of those principles that must guide our conduct in the diverse circumstances of life.

Hence we will restate, with more or less different words but along the same lines, our old revolutionary-anarchist-socialist program.[36]

---

35   In 1920 this program was adopted by the Italian Anarchist Union (UAI) and reissued, with modifications, as the pamphlet *Programma Anarchico, accettato dall'Unione Anarchica Italiana nel Congresso di Bologna del 1–4 Luglio 1920* (Bologna: Commissione di Corrispondenza dell'UAI, 1920). Richards's translation, which we have preferred to earlier ones as more faithful, is from the 1920 edition. Where the two Italian editions substantially differ, we have modified the main text so as to reflect the original 1899 edition and we have shown the translation of the 1920 edition in the notes.

36   In the 1920 edition, the whole foregoing preamble is replaced by the following paragraph (omitted in Richards's translation): "The programme of the *Unione Anarchica Italiana* is the revolutionary-anarchist-communist programme that fifty years ago was already upheld in Italy within the 1st International under the name of socialist programme, was later identified by the name of anarchist-socialist, and finally, after the increasing authoritarian and parliamentarian degeneration of the socialist movement and in reaction to it, was simply called anarchist." The rest of this first section, which was originally untitled, bore the title "What we Want" in the 1920 edition and "Aims and Objectives" in Richards's version.

We believe that most of the ills that afflict mankind stem from a bad social organisation; and that Man could destroy them if he wished and knew how.

Present society is the result of age-long struggles of man against man. Not understanding the advantages that could accrue for all by cooperation and solidarity; seeing in every other man (with the possible exception of those closest to them by blood ties) a competitor and an enemy, each one of them sought to secure for himself, the greatest number of advantages possible without giving a thought to the interests of others.

In such a struggle, obviously the strongest or more fortunate were bound to win, and in one way or another subject and oppress the losers.

So long as Man was unable to produce more than was strictly needed to keep alive, the conquerors could do no more than put to flight or massacre their victims, and seize the food they had gathered.

Then when with the discovery of grazing and agriculture a man could produce more than what he needed to live, the conquerors found it more profitable to reduce the conquered to a state of slavery, and put them to work for their advantage.

Later, the conquerors realised that it was more convenient, more profitable and certain to exploit the labour of others by other means: to retain for themselves the exclusive right to the land and working implements, and set free the disinherited who, finding themselves without the means of life, were obliged to have recourse to the landowners and work for them, on their terms.

Thus, step by step through a most complicated series of struggles of every description, of invasions, wars, rebellions, repressions, concessions won by struggle, associations of the oppressed united for defence, and of the conquerors for attack, we have arrived at the present state of society, in which some have inherited the land and all social wealth, while the mass of the people, disinherited in all respects, is exploited and oppressed by a small possessing class.

From all this stems the misery in which most workers live today, and which in turn creates the evils such as ignorance, crime, prostitution, diseases due to malnutrition, mental depression and premature death. From all this arises a special class (government) which, provided with the necessary means of repression, exists to legalise and protect the owning class from the demands of the workers; and then it uses the powers at its disposal to create privileges for itself and to subject, if it can, the owning class itself as well. From this the creation of another privileged class (the clergy), which by a series of fables about the will of God, and about an after-life etc., seeks to persuade the oppressed to accept oppression meekly, and (just as the government does), as well as serving the interest of the owning class, serves its own. From this the creation of an official science which, in all those matters serving the interests of the ruling class, is the negation of true science. From this the patriotic spirit, race hatred, wars and armed peace, sometimes more disastrous than wars themselves. From this the transformation of love into torment or sordid commerce. From this hatred, more or less disguised, rivalry, suspicion among all men, insecurity and universal fear.

We want to change radically such a state of affairs. And since all these ills have their origin in the struggle between men, in the seeking after well-being through one's own efforts and for oneself and against everybody, we want to make amends, replacing hatred by love, competition by solidarity, the individual search for personal well-being by the fraternal cooperation for the well-being of all, oppression and imposition by liberty, the religious and pseudo-scientific lie by truth.

Therefore:

1. Abolition of private property in land, in raw materials and the instruments of labour, so that no one shall have the means of living by the exploitation of the labour of others, and that everybody, being assured of the means to produce and to live, shall be truly independent and in a position to unite freely among themselves for a common objective and according to their personal sympathies.

2. Abolition of government and of every power which makes the law and imposes it on others: therefore abolition of monarchies, republics, parliaments, armies, police forces, magistratures and any institution whatsoever endowed with coercive powers.

3. Organisation of social life by means of free association and federations of producers and consumers, created and modified according to the wishes of their members, guided by science and experience, and free from any kind of imposition which does not spring from natural needs, to which everyone, convinced by a feeling of overriding necessity, voluntarily submits.

4. The means of life, for development and well-being, will be guaranteed to children and all who are prevented from providing for themselves.

5. War on religions and all lies, even if they shelter under the cloak of science. Scientific instruction for all to advanced level.

6. War on patriotism.[37] Abolition of frontiers; brotherhood among all peoples.

7. Reconstruction of the family, as will emerge from the practice of love, freed from every legal tie, from every economic and physical oppression, from every religious prejudice.

This is our ideal.

---

37   In the 1920 edition: "War on rivalries and patriotic prejudices."

Ways and Means

We have outlined under a number of headings our objectives and the ideal for which we struggle.

But it is not enough to desire something; if one really wants it adequate means must be used to secure it. And these means are not arbitrary, but instead cannot but be conditioned by the ends we aspire to and by the circumstances in which the struggle takes place, for if we ignore the choice of means we would achieve other ends, possibly diametrically opposed to those we aspire to, and this would be the obvious and inevitable consequence of our choice of means. Whoever sets out on the highroad and takes a wrong turning does not go where he intends to go but where the road leads him.

It is therefore necessary to state what are the means which in our opinion lead to our desired ends, and which we propose to adopt.

Our ideal is not one which depends for its success on the individual considered in isolation. The question is of changing the way of life of society as a whole; of establishing among men relationships based on love and solidarity; of achieving the full material, moral and intellectual development not for isolated individuals, or members of one class or of a particular political party, but for all mankind—and this is not something that can be imposed by force, but must emerge through the enlightened consciences of each one of us and be achieved with the free consent of all.

Our first task therefore must be to persuade people.

We must make people aware of the misfortunes they suffer and of their chances to destroy them. We must awaken sympathy in everybody for the misfortunes of others and a warm desire for the good of all people.

To those who are cold and hungry we will demonstrate how possible and easy it could be to assure to everybody their material needs. To those who are oppressed and despised we shall show how it is possible to live happily in a world of people who are free and equal; to those who are tormented by hatred and bitterness we will point to the road that leads to peace and human warmth that comes through learning to love one's fellow beings.

And when we will have succeeded in arousing the sentiment of rebellion in the minds of men against the avoidable and unjust evils from which we suffer in society today, and in getting them to understand how they are caused and how it depends on human will to rid ourselves of them; and when we will have created a lively and strong desire in men to transform society for the good of all, then those who are convinced, will by their own efforts as well as by the example of those already convinced, unite and want to as well as be able to act for their common ideals.

As we have already pointed out, it would be ridiculous and contrary to our objectives to seek to impose freedom, love among men and the radical development of human faculties, by means of force. One must therefore rely on the free will of others, and all we can do is to provoke the development and the expression of the will of the people. But it would be equally absurd and contrary to our aims to admit that those who do not share our views should prevent us from expressing our will, so long as it does not deny them the same freedom.

Freedom for all, therefore, to propagate and to experiment with their ideas, with no other limitation than that which arises naturally from the equal liberty of everybody.

*
**

But to this are opposed—and with brute force—those who benefit from existing privileges and who today dominate and control all social life.

In their hands they have all the means of production; and thus they suppress not only the possibility of free experimentation in new ways of communal living, and the right of workers to live freely by the product of their own efforts,[38] but also the right to life itself; and they oblige whoever is not a boss to have to allow himself to be exploited and oppressed if he does not wish to die of hunger.

They have police forces, a judiciary, and armies created for the express purpose of defending their privileges; and they persecute, imprison and massacre those who would want to abolish those privileges and who claim the means of life and liberty for everyone.

Jealous of their present and immediate interests, corrupted by the spirit of domination, fearful of the future, they, the privileged class, are, generally speaking incapable of a generous gesture; are equally incapable of a wider concept of their interests. And it would be foolish to hope that they should freely give up property and power and adapt themselves to living as equals and with those who today they keep in subjection.

Leaving aside the lessons of history (which demonstrates that never has a privileged class divested itself of all or some of its privileges, and never has a government abandoned its power unless obliged to do so by force or the fear of force), there is enough contemporary evidence to convince anyone that the bourgeoisie and governments intend to use armed force to defend themselves, not only against complete expropriation, but equally against the smallest popular demands, and are always ready to engage in the most atrocious persecutions and the bloodiest massacres.

---

38   In the 1920 edition: "freely by their own efforts."

For those people who want to emancipate themselves, only one course is open: that of opposing force with force.

It follows from what we have said that we have to work to awaken in the oppressed the conscious desire for a radical social transformation, and to persuade them that by uniting they have the strength to win; we must propagate our ideal and prepare the required material and moral forces to overcome those of the enemy, and to organise the new society. And when we will have the strength needed we must, by taking advantage of favourable circumstances as they arise, or which we can ourselves create, make the social revolution, by using force to destroy the government and to expropriate the owners of wealth, and by putting in common the means of life and production, and by preventing the setting up of new governments which would impose their will and hamper the reorganisation of society by the people themselves.

All this is however less simple than it might appear at first sight. We have to deal with people as they are in society today, in the most miserable moral and material condition; and we would be deluding ourselves in thinking that propaganda is enough to raise them to that level of intellectual development which is needed to put our ideas into effect.

Between man and his social environment there is a reciprocal action. Men make society what it is and society makes men what they are, and the result is therefore a kind of vicious circle. To transform society men must be changed, and to transform men, society must be changed.

Poverty brutalizes man, and to abolish poverty men must have a social conscience and determination. Slavery teaches men to be slaves, and to free oneself from slavery there is a need for men who aspire to liberty. Ignorance has the effect of making men unaware of the causes of their misfortunes as well as the means of overcoming them, and to do away with ignorance people must have the time and the means to educate themselves.

Governments accustom people to submit to the Law and to believe that Law is essential to society; and to abolish government men must be convinced of the uselessness and the harmfulness of government.

How does one escape from this vicious circle?

Fortunately existing society has not been created by the inspired will of a dominating class, which has succeeded in reducing all its subjects to passive and unconscious instruments of its interests. It is the result of a thousand internecine struggles, of a thousand human and natural factors acting indifferently, without directive criteria; and thus there are no clear-cut divisions either between individuals or between classes.

with brute force, constitutes a barrier to human progress, which must be beaten down with force if one does not wish to remain indefinitely under present conditions or even worse.

From the economic struggle one must pass to the political struggle, that is to the struggle against government; and instead of opposing the capitalist millions with the workers' few pennies scraped together with difficulty, one must oppose the rifles and guns which defend property with the more effective means that the people will be able to find to defeat force by force.

Political Struggle—Revolutionary Action[44]

By the political struggle we mean the struggle against government. Government is the *ensemble* of all those individuals who hold the reins of power, however acquired, to make the law and to impose it on the governed, that is the public.

Government is the consequence of the spirit of domination and violence with which some men have imposed themselves on other, and is at the same time the creature as well as the creator of privilege and its natural defender.

It is wrongly said that today government performs the function of defender of capitalism but that once capitalism is abolished it would become the representative and administrator of the general interest. In the first place capitalism will not be destroyed until the workers, having rid themselves of government, take possession of all social wealth and themselves organise production and consumption in the interests of everybody without waiting for the initiative to come from government which, however willing to comply, would be incapable of doing so.

But there is a further question: if capitalism were to be destroyed and a government were to be left in office, the government, through the concession of all kinds of privileges, would create capitalism anew for, being unable to please everybody it would need an economically powerful class to support it in return for the legal and material protection it would receive.

Consequently privilege cannot be abolished and freedom and equality established firmly and definitely without abolishing government—not this or that government but the very institution of government.

As in all questions of general interest, and especially this one, the consent of the people as a whole is needed, and therefore we must strain every nerve to persuade the people that government is useless as well as harmful, and that we can live better lives without government.

But, as we have repeated more than once, propaganda alone is impotent to convince everybody—and if we were to want to limit ourselves to

---

44   In the 1920 edition, this section is simply titled "The Political Struggle."

preaching against government, and in the meantime waiting supinely for the day when the public will be convinced of the possibility and value of radically destroying every kind of government, then that day would never come.

While preaching against every kind of government, and demanding complete freedom, we must support all struggles for partial freedom, because we are convinced that one learns through struggle, and that once one begins to enjoy a little freedom one ends by wanting it all. We must always be with the people, and when we do not succeed in getting them to demand a lot we must still seek to get them to want something; and we must make every effort to get them to understand that however much or little they may demand should be obtained by their own efforts and that they should despise and detest whoever is part of, or aspires to, government.

Since government today has the power, through the legal system, to regulate daily life and to broaden or restrict the liberty of the citizen, and because we are still unable to tear this power from its grasp, we must seek to reduce its power and oblige governments to use it in the least harmful ways possible. But this we must do always remaining outside, and against, government, putting pressure on it through agitation in the streets, by threatening to take by force what we demand. Never must we accept any kind of legislative position, be it national or local, for in so doing we will neutralise the effectiveness of our activity as well as betraying the future of our cause.

*
**

The struggle against government in the last analysis, is physical, material.

Governments make the law. They must therefore dispose of the material forces (police and army) to impose the law, for otherwise only those who wanted to would obey it, and it would no longer be the law, but a simple series of suggestions which all would be free to accept or reject. Governments have this power, however, and use it through the law, to strengthen their power, as well as to serve the interests of the ruling classes, by oppressing and exploiting the workers.

The only limit to the oppression of government is the power with which the people show themselves capable of opposing it. Conflict may be open or latent; but it always exists since the government does not pay attention to discontent and popular resistance except when it is faced with the danger of insurrection.

When the people meekly submit to the law, or their protests are feeble and confined to words, the government studies its own interests and ignores the needs of the people; when the protests are lively, insistent, threatening, the government, depending on whether it is more or less understanding, gives way or resorts to repression. But one always comes back to insurrection, for if the government does not give way, the people will end by rebelling; and if the government does give way, then the people gain confidence in themselves and make ever increasing demands, until such time as the incompatibility between freedom and authority becomes clear and the violent struggle is engaged.

It is therefore necessary to be prepared, morally and materially, so that when this does happen the people will emerge victorious.

*
**

A successful insurrection is the most potent factor in the emancipation of the people, for once the yoke has been shaken off, the people are free to provide themselves with those institutions which they think best, and the time lag between passing the law and the degree of civilisation which the mass of the population has attained, is breached in one leap. The insurrection determines the revolution, that is, the speedy emergence of the latent forces built up during the "evolutionary" period.

Everything depends on what the people are capable of wanting.

In past insurrections unaware of the real reasons for their misfortunes, they have always wanted very little, and have obtained very little.

What will they want in the next insurrection?

The answer, in part, depends on our propaganda and what efforts we put into it.

We shall have to push the people to expropriate the bosses and put all goods in common and organise their daily lives themselves, through freely constituted associations, without waiting for orders from outside and refusing to nominate or recognise any government, any body that claims the right to lay down the law and impose its will on others.[45]

And if the mass of the population will not respond to our appeal we must—in the name of the right we have to be free even if others wish to remain slaves and because of the force of example—put into effect as many of our ideas as we can, refuse to recognise the new government and keep alive resistance and seek that those communes where our ideas are received with sympathy reject all governmental interference and insist on wanting to live their own lives.[46]

---

45   In the 1920 edition: "... recognise any government or constituted body in whatever guise (constituent, dictatorship, etc.) even in a provisional capacity, which ascribes to itself the right to lay down the law and impose with force its will on others."

46   In the 1920 edition: "... and seek that those localities where our ideas are received with sympathy should constitute themselves into *anarchist communities*, rejecting all governmental interference, establishing free agreements with other communities, and wanting to live their own lives."

We shall have to, above all, oppose with every means the re-establishment of the police and the armed forces, and use any opportunity to incite workers to a general strike that lays the most far reaching demands we can induce them to make.[47]

And however things may go, to continue the struggle against the possessing class and the rulers without respite, having always in mind the complete economic, political and moral emancipation of all mankind.

Recapitulation[48]

What we want, therefore, is the complete destruction of the domination and exploitation of man by man; we want men united as brothers by a conscious and desired solidarity, all cooperating voluntarily for the well-being of all: we want society to be constituted for the purpose of supplying everybody with the means for achieving the maximum well-being, the maximum possible moral and spiritual development; we want bread, freedom, love, and science for everybody.

And in order to achieve these all-important ends, it is necessary in our opinion that the means of production should be at the disposal of everybody and that no man, or group of men, should be in a position to oblige others to submit to their will or to exercise their influence other than through the power of reason and by example.

Therefore: expropriation of landowners and capitalists for the benefit of all; and abolition of government.

And while waiting for the day when this can be achieved: the propagation of our ideas; unceasing struggle, violent or non-violent depending on the circumstances, against government and against the boss class to conquer as much freedom and well-being as we can for the benefit of everybody.

---

47   In the 1920 edition: "... incite workers in non anarchist localities to take advantage of the absence of repressive forces to implement the most far reaching demands that we can induce them to make."
48   In the 1920 edition, this section is titled "Conclusions."

La Questione Sociale

Periodico Socialista-Anarchico

Entered at the Post-Office
at Paterson, N. J., as second-
class matter.

Per lettere, comunicazioni,
ecc., dirigersi alle
QUESTIONE SOCIALE
Box 631.
PATERSON, New Jersey, U. S. A.

Abbonamenti
Anno $1.50
Semestre . . . 0.80
Trimestre . . . 0.45
Estero spese postali in più
Numero Separato e Soldi
Gli abbonamenti si pagano
anticipati.

ANNO V.　　　　　PATERSON, N. J., SABATO 9 SETTEMBRE 1899.　　　　　NUOVA SERIE No. 1.

IMPORTANTISSIMO

Riteniamo necessario di avvisare ancor una volta tutti i lettori della "Questione Sociale" che tutto ciò che concerne il giornale, sia redazione che amministrazione, non deve essere indirizzato a nessun individuo personalmente, ma semplicemente:

LA QUESTIONE SOCIALE

Box 639

Paterson, New Jersey

(Stati Uniti)

Il nostro programma

Noi non abbiamo novità da dire. La propaganda non è, e non può essere, che la ripetizione continua, instancabile di quei principii, che debbono servirci di guida nella condotta che dobbiamo seguire nelle varie contingenze della vita.

Ripeteremo dunque, con parole più o meno differenti, ma con fondo costante, il nostro vecchio programma socialista-anarchico-rivoluzionario.

Noi crediamo che la più gran parte dei mali che affliggono gli uomini dipende dalla cattiva organizzazione sociale; e che gli uomini, volendo e sapendo, possono distruggerli.

La società attuale è il risultato delle lotte secolari che gli uomini han combattuto tra di loro. Non comprendendo i vantaggi che potevano venire a tutti dalla cooperazione e dalla solidarietà, vedendo in ognuno altro uomo (salvo al massimo i più vicini per vincoli di sangue) un concorrente od un nemico, han cercato di accaparrare, ciascun per sè, la più grande quantità di godimenti possibile, senza curarsi degli interessi degli altri.

Data la lotta, naturalmente i più forti, o i più fortunati, dovevano vincere, ed in vario modo sottoporsi ed opprimere i vinti.

Fino a che l'uomo non fu capace di produrre di più di quello che bastava strettamente alla sua mantenimento, i vincitori non potevano che fugare o massacrare i vinti ed impossessarsi degli alimenti da essi raccolti.

Poi, quando colla scoperta della pastorizia e dell'agricoltura un uomo potette produrre più di ciò che gli occorreva per vivere, i vincitori trovarono più conveniente ridurre i vinti in ischiavitù, e farli lavorare per loro.

Più tardi, i vincitori si avvisarono che era più comodo, più produttivo e più sicuro sfruttare il lavoro altrui con un altro sistema: ritenere per sè la proprietà esclusiva della terra e di tutti i mezzi di lavoro, e lasciar nominalmente liberi gli spogliati i quali poi, non avendo mezzo di vivere, erano costretti a ricorrere ai proprietari ed a lavorare per costo loro, ai patti che essi volevano.

Così, man mano, attraverso tutta una rete complicatissima di lotte di ogni specie, invasioni, guerre, ribellioni, repressioni, concessioni strappate, associazioni di vinti uniti per la difesa e di vincitori uniti per l'offesa, si è giunto allo stato attuale della società, in cui alcuni detengono ereditariamente la terra e tutta la ricchezza sociale; mentre la grande massa degli uomini, diseredata di tutto, è sfruttata ed oppressa dai pochi proprietari.

Da questo dipende lo stato di miseria in cui si trovano generalmente i lavoratori, e tutti i mali che dalla miseria derivano: ignoranza, delitti, prostituzione, deperimento fisico, abbiezione morale, morte prematura. Da questo, la costituzione di una classe speciale (il governo), la quale, fornita di mezzi materiali di repressione, ha il mestiere di legalizzare e difendere i proprietari contro le rivendicazioni del proletariato; e poi si serve della forza che ha, per creare a sè stessa del privilegi e sottomettere, se può, alla sua supremazia anche la stessa classe proprietaria. Da questo, la costituzione di un'altra classe speciale (il clero), la quale con una serie di favole sulla volontà di Dio, sulla vita futura, ecc. cerca d'indurre gli oppressi a sopportare docilmente l'oppressione, ed al pari del governo, oltre di fare gl'interessi dei proprietari, fa anche i suoi propri. Da questo, la formazione di una scienza officiale che, in tutto ciò che può servire agl'interessi dei dominatori, la negazione della scienza vera. Da questo, lo spirito patriottico, gli odii di razza, le guerre e le paci armate, più disastrose delle guerre stesse. Da questo, l'amore trasformato in tormento o in turpe mercato. Da ciò l'odio più o meno larvato, la rivalità, il sospetto fra tutti gli uomini, l'incertezza e la paura per tutti.

Tale stato di cose noi vogliamo radicalmente cambiare. E poichè tutti questi mali derivano dalla lotta fra gli uomini, dalla ricerca del benessere fatta da ciascuno per conto suo e contro tutti, noi vogliamo rimediarvi sostituendo all'odio l'amore, alla concorrenza la solidarietà, alla ricerca esclusiva del proprio benessere la cooperazione fraterna per il benessere di tutti, alla oppressione ed all'imposizione la libertà, alla menzogna religiosa e pseudo-scientifica la verità.

Dunque:

1.° Abolizione della proprietà privata della terra, delle materie prime e degli strumenti di lavoro, perchè nessuno abbia il mezzo di vivere sfruttando il lavoro altrui; e tutti, avendo garentiti i mezzi per produrre e vivere, siano veramente indipendenti e possano associarsi agli altri liberamente, per l'interesse comune e conformandosi alle proprie simpatie.

2.° Abolizione del governo e di ogni potere che faccia la legge e la imponga agli altri: quindi abolizione di monarchie, repubbliche, parlamenti, eserciti, polizie, magistrature, ed ogni qualsiasi istituzione dotata di mezzi coercitivi.

3.° Organizzazione della vita sociale per opera di libere associazioni e federazioni di produttori e di consumatori, fatte e modificate secondo la volontà dei componenti, guidati dalla scienza e dall'esperienza e liberi da ogni imposizione che non derivi dalle necessità naturali, a cui ognuno, vinto dal sentimento stesso della necessità inevitabile, volontariamente si sottomette.

4.° Garentiti i mezzi di vita, di sviluppo, di benessere ai fanciulli, ed a tutti coloro che sono impotenti a provvedere a loro stessi.

5.° Guerra alle religioni ed a tutte le menzogne, anche se si nascondono sotto il manto della scienza.

Cose a posto

[INTORNO ALLE DICHIARAZIONI DEI "DISSIDENTI"]

Come sanno i lettori della QUESTIONE SOCIALE, le differenze d'idee tra chi ultimamente redigeva il giornale ed il gruppo che ne ha la gestione e la responsabilità erano tali che non si è ritenuto necessario separarsi.

Il gruppo decise di cominciare una nuova serie non dei redattori che fossero concordi in perfetto accordo e l'antica redazione ne dichiarò che farebbe un nuovo giornale. Si conveniva di fare intanto un numero a metà tra vecchia e nuova redazione, perchè le due parti potessero, indipendentemente l'una dall'altra, esporre le ragioni della separazione: poichè da questo giudicare tutti coloro che hanno letto, negli ultimi tempi, la QUESTIONE SOCIALE. E non ho parliamone menomente, non avendo che da raffigurarsi veder che le discussioni che han preceduto la divisione non sono restate senza effetto.

Ma non vorremmo però che altri, vedendo come fra i "dissidenti," e come in opposizione a noi, delle idee che noi abbiamo sempre propagate e difese, fosse indotto in errore nel nostro pensiero; ne vorremmo che certi giudichi di parte condannassero chi non è affatto a aver cogliere l'idea che si nasconde sotto l'oscurità della frase; e perciò crediamo necessario fare i commenti che seguono.

I "dissidenti" dicono che hanno un concetto del movimento diverso dal nostro, e, se si deve giudicare da ciò che dicono, non parrebbe davvero.

Essi dicono che "di fronte alla massa ignara ed incosciente la nostra azione di anarchici non può essere che una; quella di formar coscienze anarchiche". È chi dunque in noi detto contro o fatto il contrario!

Non è evidente che, perchè gli anarchici il possano rimire ciò organizzare a necessario studiarlo che vi siano degli anarchici!

Quando si trovano uno individui o collettività vergini, o nostre idee o nostre idee non incominciano forse col cercar di far loro la propaganda, cioè col tentare di formare coscienze anarchiche!

Solamente i nostri contraddittori dimenticano, o questo pare, che la coscienza, la convinzione non è cosa assoluta fissa ed assoluta; dimentichano che vi può essere coscienti e convinti in una infinità di gradi, e che nel contatto continuo coi compagni e col lavoro in comune la convinzione e allargarsi e rinforza. E dimentichano pure che l'organizzazione forma quel mezzo di propaganda di cui non possono disporre gl'individui isolati.

Ma noi non vogliamo l'aclamento prestare i nostri contraddittori. "Quando—noi dicono—dalla massa incosciente si stacche ranno, spingendosi alla lotta contro la compagnie del sistema borghese, gl'individui divenuti anarchici, questi, per necessità di iniziativa e di utilità pratica studeranno tutto all'interno le mani in fraterna amore, si anarchico ad anarchico, da compagno a compagno, da gruppo a gruppo, e riunirà se

Se gl'individui sono deboli, l'unione non potrà dar loro la forza di fare quello che da soli sono impotenti a fare?! Ma v'è bisogno di rispondere a tali paradossi? L'esperienza generale, costante dell'umanità non insegna forse il contrario?

I nostri contradittori dicono che la nostra organizzazione non è libera, quantunque nessuno c'entra per forza, ed entratovi resta libero di ritirarsi; e citano in prova le organizzazioni dei socialisti-democratici le quali ammettono le stesse condizioni di libertà nell'entrata e nell'uscita dei membri, e pure sono autoritarie.

La verità è che le organizzazioni dei socialisti-democratici sono autoritarie perchè autoritario è il loro programma. In quanto all'organizzazione in sè stessa, per quanto infetta da metodi autoritarii, pure essa è un freno anzichè un incentivo all'autoritarismo. Infatti, chi vorrà a sostenere che gli uomini prominenti del partito socialista avrebbero meno autorità di fronte ai loro compagni socialisti, se questi fossero disorganizzati?

Così è fra noi. L'organizzazione di tutti è il rimedio contro il prevalere di pochi. La disorganizzazione è, in pratica, la dittatura, senza controllo e senza responsabilità, di quelli fra noi che possono fare un giornale, dire delle conferenze, o in altro modo accapparrare a vantaggio delle proprie tendenze le forze di tutti.

* * *

In fondo a tutto questo si nasconde un equivoco.

I nostri contradittori, grazie all'educazione autoritaria che tutti subiscono nella società attuale, non sanno immaginare un'organizzazione senza pensar subito a tutta una gerarchia di capi e sottocapi a centri direttivi, consigli legislativi, regime burocratico, ecc.

Noi proponiamo invece che coloro i quali vogliono la stessa cosa ed intendono conseguirla con gli stessi metodi, si uniscano, non già per rinunziare alla loro volontà ed alla loro iniziativa, ma per educarsi ed aiutarsi nell'opera comune, per coordinare allo scopo comune le varie iniziative che, isolate, potrebbero neutralizzarsi a vicenda; e per trovare nell'unione quei mezzi senza di cui il diritto alla libera iniziativa è una semplice ironia.

Noi ammettiamo, ed abbiamo sempre ammesso, il principio dell'autonomia degl'individui nei gruppi, e dei gruppi nelle federazioni: ma vogliamo che sia vincolo, solo vincolo obbligatorio, il programma comune. E contro quest'idea del programma si ribellano i nostri contradditori.

Ma è seria la loro ribellione?

Lasciamo stare la frecciata poco spiritosa del "programma dettato da un individuo." Se vi fosse un individuo, il che ci pare impossibile, dotato di genio sufficiente per dettare da solo un nuovo programma che ci persuadesse e convenisse, noi non ci priveremmo dei suoi vantaggi per il fatto che l'iniziativa ne sarebbe partita da un individuo solo... ed è strano che siamo spinti a dichiarar questo da coloro che hanno sempre in bocca l'iniziativa individuale! Il fatto si è che il programma socialista anarchico è frutto di un'elaborazione collettiva durata, anche trascurando i precursori, parecchie diecine di anni, e che nessuno potrebbe rivendicarne la paternità.

Ma la questione è questa: accettano o no i nostri contradittori quel complesso d'idee che costituisce il socialismo anarchico?

Noi intendiamo che essi vogliano lasciare al programma la massima larghezza, la massima elasticità possibile; ma infine, dei limiti debbano ammetterli pur essi, oltre dei quali non sarà permesso andare senza vedersi negare da loro il titolo di anarchico. Altrimenti, al *siamo tutti socialisti* di tanti reazionari, dovremo aggiungere uno di questi giorni il *siamo tutti anarchici* di reazionarii eguali.

I nostri contradittori vogliono "l'abolizione della proprietà privata e la socializzazione dei mezzi di produzione e di scambio"; vogliono "l'abolizione di fatto di ogni e qualunque forma di Stato, di governo, di legge, di autorità"; sappiamo che respingono i metodi elettorali e parlamentari ed ammettono i metodi rivoluzionari... che diavolo ci vengono dunque a dire che non hanno programma! Potranno differire più o meno dal programma nostro, e stanno nel loro diritto; ma dire che non hanno programma significa semplicemente giuocar sulle parole.

Come pure è una logomachia (guerra di parole) quella che fanno sulla parola partito. "*Partito* — essi dicono — per noi significa chiesuola." Padronissimi essi di cambiare il senso delle parole; ma allora non v'è più modo d'intendersi.

Partito propriamente ha un significato più largo di *organizzazione*. Partito significa l'insieme di quelli che lottano per un dato scopo; mentre in una data organizzazione entrano quelli che, avendo lo stesso scopo, vogliono unire le proprie forze per lottare di consenso; e perciò in uno stesso partito vi possono essere, e vi sono ordinariamente, varie organizzazioni.

I nostri contradittori potranno dir quanto vogliono che non appartengono a nessun partito: ma fino a quando vorranno l'abolizione di ogni forma di governo, la gente dirà che appartengono al partito anarchico.

Le guerre contro il dizionario son difficili a vincere.

* * *

Con le osservazioni che precedono noi siam lungi dal credere di aver esaurita la questione dell'organizzazione, e non mancheremo di tornarvi su.

Vorremmo soltanto aver ottenuto che i nostri contradittori lascin da parte, per quanto è possibile, le questioni di parole, e discutano con noi i punti sui quali realmente divergono dal nostro programma.

Partecipazione alla lotta economica

L'unione fa la forza.

Su quest'argomento dovrebbe parere inutile la discussione; dappoichè noi Anarchici che sosteniamo non essere l'ideale nostro una vaga utopia ma un'aspirazione seria e cosciente, che nasce dai bisogni dell'epoca moderna, non possiamo certo prescindere dal movimento di quella classe i cui interessi maggiormente ci proponiamo di tutelare.

Non è certo ai proprietari di terre, agli industriali, agli uomini politici, ai funzionari dello Stato, a coloro insomma che hanno tutto l'interesse di conservare l'attuale posizione, che noi andremo a propagare le idee nostre; ma agli operai, ai contadini, a quelli insomma che tutto producendo, ricevono inadeguata partecipazione al benessere economico.

E posta questa sacrosanta verità, ne discende logica conseguenza l'attivo nostro concorso al movimento operaio, siccome quello che, mosso dagli stessi interessati, reclama soddisfazione ai loro bisogni; partecipazione che non dev'essere semplicemente passiva, ma anche attiva, nel senso di dare alla lotta operaia quell'indirizzo più conforme all'ideale nostro e più atto al raggiungimento del buon esito.

Una tesi così chiara non andrebbe neppur dimostrata; ma dal momento che fra noi sono corse polemiche aspre in proposito — di cui questo giornale fu lungamente eco — taluno, e con ragione secondo me, virilmente sostenendo la partecipazione alla lotta economica, tal'altro accanitamente combattendola e chiamando indegno del nome di anarchico il proprio avversario, è bene spendere ancora qualche parola.

Svolgerò quindi le ragioni importantissime che assolutamente impongono la nostra adesione alle associazioni economiche ed al movimento operaio; ed in una serie di articoli successivi scenderò ad esaminare minutamente le singole specie di società operaie, per vedere in quali casi convenga applicare praticamente il principio.

* * *

Una prima ragione importantissima, per cui conviene che i Socialisti Anarchici partecipino alle associazioni operaie, è la necessità di porsi a contatto colla classe lavoratrice. Non completamente a torto fummo rimproverati di trascurare la propaganda pratica dalle idee, limitandoci invece ad astruse discussioni fra noi sull'*amorfismo*, il *libero amore*, l'*ateismo* ecc. Occorre figgersi bene in mente che le nostre idee hanno ragione di essere solo in quanto rappresentano un'aspirazione dell'umanità in genere e dei lavoratori in ispecie, verso lo stato d'uguaglianza e di libertà; e che essa, separata dal movimento operaio, non costituirebbe altro che una vana declamazione filosofica, un'astrazione metafisica. Specialmente gli operai debbono comprendere il socialismo-anarchico, e per giungere a questo risultato occorre spiegarlo loro in tutte le occasioni; occorre trovarsi a contatto continuo con essi, occorre occuparsi dei loro affari e dei loro interessi immediati. Quando l'operaio che richiede la soddisfazione di un immediato bisogno, si sente rispondere con una dissertazione filosofica magari mirabile, egli, nel suo naturale buon senso, chiamerà utopista l'interlocutore e darà invece ascolto a coloro che, forse meno sinceri di noi nelle intenzioni, gli dimostrano di prendere a cuore la sua posizione. D'altronde lo studio dei bisogni della classe operaia non può farsi se non entrando nelle associazioni degli operai.

Ma, ci si dice, la partecipazione alla lotta operaia è una transazione da non accettarsi perchè contraria al principio anti-autoritario e rivoluzionario del nostro partito.

Anzitutto è da notarsi che, di transazioni nell'attuale ordinamento sociale, noi siamo costretti a subirne parecchie. Ad esempio: sebbene noi tutti quale caposaldo dei nostri principii proclamiamo l'abolizione della moneta, niun di noi la getta in mezzo alla via o mangia nelle trattorie senza pagare. Se lo facesse, finirebbe in manicomio o in prigione. Adunque, la parola *transazione* non è tale che a priori debba farci abbandonare l'intrapresa; occorre invece esaminare se la transazione sia tale da doversi accettare o meno, se sia assolutamente inconciliabile colla nostra idea, se sia utile al suo incremento.

Ora, non mi pare che, entrando nelle associazioni operaie, noi veniamo volontariamente a riconoscere alcun principio di autorità; poichè, salvo rare eccezioni, le società di lavoratori non hanno cariche con poteri eccessivamente autoritari. Ed anzi la nostra presenza nel loro seno, contribuirà non poco ad allontanare gli operai, per quanto è fattibile, dal concetto di rappresentanza e ad abituarli a gerire essi medesimi i propri interessi.

Non credo nemmeno che si contravvenga alla massima rivoluzionaria, poichè l'agire sul terreno delle riforme immediate non significa rinunziare alla rivoluzione, come non significherebbe rinunziarvi se perdessimo qualche anno di tempo a preparare armi e coscienze. Tutto dipende dall'opera che i compagni nostri presteranno; se essi, anche in una lieve lotta economica sapranno far prevalere il metodo e la forma rivoluzionaria, avranno anzi tante pratiche dimostrazioni della bontà della nostra teoria.

* * *

Secondo importante beneficio delle associazioni operaie è quello di abituare i lavoratori a scorgere nel proprio padrone, non un superuomo benefico, ma un vero nemico, sfruttatore della loro opera. E' una lotta che s'ingaggia fra padrone ed operaio, e certo in quest'ultimo viene man mano sviluppandosi lo spirito di combattività.

* * *

Terzo beneficio è quello di avvezzare gli operai a fare a meno dei padroni. Essi che in tutto l'anno seguono supinamente la dispotica volontà dei loro capi, nelle associazioni imparano a pensare colla testa propria ed infine si accorgono che il padrone è un vero vampiro che nulla dà ai suoi sottoposti ma invece succhia il loro sangue.

* * *

Ma un risultato davvero capitale, che si ottiene dall'associazione economica, è lo sciopero: lotta davvero importante per l'idea nostra, dacchè bene spesso essa è il principio d'una rivoluzione.

E qui, intendiamoci. E' indubitato che se lo sciopero si limita ad una lotta di denaro fra il padrone e gli operai, il primo avrà indubbiamente vittoria; poichè se è vero che le sue macchine si deteriorano ed i suoi capitali restano inerti, d'altra parte è pur vero che l'operaio esaurisce prestissimo gli scarsi fondi all'uopo accumulati, e, vinto dalla fame, deve soccombere. Lo sciopero gigantesco dei meccanici inglesi di due anni fà, dà la conferma più chiara di questo principio.

Quindi la nostra condotta nel caso di uno sciopero sarà quella di consigliare agli operai l'uso dei mezzi violenti quando la lotta finanziaria apparirà con auspici a loro sfavorevoli; e la nostra parola sarà tanto più ascoltata quanto più noi ci saremo dimostrati assidui nell'occuparci dei loro bisogni e delle loro rivendicazioni. Il grande sciopero dei *docks* scoppiato a Londra nel 1891, dimostra se io ho ragione; poichè mentre gli operai erano agli estremi e la fame stava per dominarli, bastò che essi minacciassero di saccheggiare il ricco rione di Londra perchè i loro padroni si affrettassero a cedere.

* * *

Altra opera proficua che noi dobbiamo compiere nelle associazioni operaie, è quella di sottrarle all'influenza che i socialisti legalitari in esse esercitano. I socialisti democratici intendono trasformarle in tante associazioni elettorali e non nascondono davvero questo loro intendimento, giacchè apertamente sostengono che le armi dell'operaio sono due: lo sciopero e la scheda.

Invece, nell'interesse della massa operaia, noi dobbiamo paralizzare questa deleteria influenza; mantenere le associazioni operaie nella lotta strettamente economica e dare a questa l'impronta rivoluzionaria che senza di noi certamente non avrebbe.

* * *

Ed ora una questione importantissima: se dalla lotta economica la classe operaia possa realizzare benefici immediati.

Ma di questo al prossimo articolo.

gh.

Ancona, Agosto '99

Il dovere anarchico

A noi, che, per essere venuti alla chiara conoscenza delle più importanti leggi naturali di Giustizia, accampiamo pretesa a numero maggiore di Diritti, incombono, di conseguenza, Doveri maggiori, sia rispetto all'umanità, per il cui benessere diuturnamente lottiamo, sia rispetto a coloro che, in tutto il mondo, ci sono fidi compagni in questa lotta.

Ed il primo dei doveri riguardanti chi si dice Anarchico, è quello della *Solidarieta' Internazionale*.

Noi siamo, nella teoria e nella pratica, solidali con tutti coloro che, per l'ingiustizia dell'attuale sistema di società, soffrono oppressione, tirannia e sfruttamento; ma noi dobbiamo essere puranche solidali con i compagni nostri di lotta, con gli anarchici di tutto il mondo, perchè nel mondo noi siamo un partito solo, perchè nel mondo riconosciamo un'unica patria comune.

La solidarietà internazionale è la parte psichica più bella, più elevata, più nobile dell'opera nostra di individui e di partito!

Ed a questo io pensava paragonando, nella mente, le condizioni di schiavitù e di persecuzione fatte, in certi paesi (come in Italia), ai compagni nostri e le condizioni di libertà abbastanza ampia in cui altri compagni, in altri luoghi, si muovono. E mi domandavo appunto se agli anarchici che han fortuna oggi di trovarsi a vivere in luoghi ove i supremi diritti di Libertà e di Giustizia sono un po' meno conculcati, non s'imponesse il dovere di accordare tutto il loro appoggio morale, e materiale sopra tutto, a quei compagni che, dannati a vivere in ambiente assai più maligno, purtuttavia, benchè circondati da minaccie, da insidie e da pericoli d'ogni genere, non cessano dallo adoperarsi, pieni d'amore, d'idealità, di fede tenace e di spirito fortissimo di sacrificio, pel trionfo della causa degli oppressi e dei diseredati.

Sì, a voi, o compagni, che vivete dove il lavoratore è, in tesi generale, un po' meno sfruttato ed alquanto meglio retribuito; a voi che vivete ove è abbastanza libertà che vi permette di propagare, senza ostacoli gravissimi, l'Idea emancipatrice; a voi che potete riunirvi in società per facilitare, con lo scambio delle idee e con l'affiatamento, la soddisfazione della mente e del cuore; a voi che potete associarvi in leghe di resistenza contro la forza bruta del capitale ed a tutela del vostro lavoro; a voi parla alto il Dovere di contribuire con la solidarietà vostra efficace al faticoso e pericoloso lavoro di propaganda e di lotta fatto dai compagni, dai fratelli vostri che sono ed operano, ancora e sempre, in quelle tristi patrie che ci son matrigne e che voi, più fortunati certo, abbandonaste.

Noi proseguiamo imperterriti e indistruttibili l'opera nostra di minatori e di educatori, e non ci fanno paura le repressioni e le leggi liberticide dei governi borghesi, nè l'oltraggio o lo scherno degl'imbelli gaudenti. Ma questo avviene, che se vogliamo riunirci in Società di Pensiero e di Lavoro, se vogliamo associare in lega difensiva i lavoratori, se vogliamo con la parola, col giornale, col libro propagare le idee nostre di Giustizia e Libertà, ci attende la galera, il domicilio coatto, le bastonate del poliziotto, del gendarme e dell'aguzzino, la soppressione del diritto all'esistenza colla negazione del lavoro.

E la ferrea resistenza a tanta persecuzione di un'idea altamente civile ed umana trova ad attinge la sua forza nell'amore immenso che nutriamo per gli afflitti fratelli umani, nella simpatia per le sofferenze infinite dei paria di questa odiosa Società dell'egoismo; attinge la sua forza nella sicura Solidarietà dei lottatori compagni di tutto il mondo che non saranno mai sordi, nè fiacchi.

E così, con l'Anarchia e per l'Anarchia, sempre avanti, o compagni!

Otto ore di lavoro

Un compagno scrive da un paese di Francia:

"Ho proposto a varii compagni di lavoro di abbonarsi al giornale e tutti mi han fatto la stessa risposta: Non ho il tempo di leggere.

"Ed è una risposta desolante perchè vera. Noi lavoriamo infatti dalle 6 del mattino alle 6 1|2 di sera, e molti di noi debbono fare un'ora di cammino la mattina ed una la sera per recarsi dalla casa all'officina e viceversa. Se uno ha qualche piccolo lavoro di casa da fare, appena se gli restano sei ore di riposo. E che riposo! Alzandosi la mattina si è più stanchi di quando si è andati a letto. Dove prendere il tempo e la forza per leggere, studiare e meditare sui problemi sociali?

"Da questo punto di vista io sarei quasi partigiano della legge delle otto ore; poichè se essa, economicamente parlando, non migliora le condizioni dei lavoratori, almeno lascerebbe loro del tempo per studiare ed approfondire la questione sociale. I nostri governanti han compreso ciò al pari di noi, e per questo si guardan bene dal votarla, limitandosi tutt'al più a farne uno specchietto da allodole per gli elettori."

Faremo qualche osservazione.

Noi crediamo che non si possa mettere in dubbio che lavorare per un padrone 8 ore, val meglio che lavorare 10, o 12, o 14, o 16. Certamente non sarebbe l'emancipazione. Oltre che l'operaio continuerebbe sempre ad essere sfruttato e a non contare nel meccanismo della produzione che come uno strumento in mano di padroni, i quali lo adoperano a loro beneplacito per il loro proprio profitto, egli resterebbe esposto al ribasso dei salarii, alla mancanza di lavoro ed a tutti i guai che derivano dalla lotta che, nella società attuale, ciascun uomo è costretto a combattere contro tutti gli altri. Ma non è men vero per questo che vi sono dei gradi nel male; e che fra il lavoratore, il quale lavorando 16 ore al giorno non ha il tempo, nonchè di studiare, nemmeno di lavarsi e di baciare i figliuoli, e quello che lavora 8 ore, vi è una reale e grande differenza di condizione non solo, ma anche di possibilità di comprendere le cause dei mali che lo affliggono e di lavorare alla sua emancipazione.

Deriva da ciò che noi dobbiam mettere nel nostro programma le 8 ore di lavoro?

No. Noi siam convinti — e tutti i fatti confermano la nostra convinzione — che la borghesia non farà alcuna concessione se non obbligata dalla forza, o dalla paura della forza, e che quindi dal momento che per istrappare il poco è necessario diventare i più forti, sarebbe sciocco non utilizzare la propria forza per avere il tutto. E d'altronde, quando si è arrivato a comprendere l'ingiustizia fondamentale dell'attuale organizzazione sociale ed il rimedio che solo può apportare il benessere, la libertà e la pace fra gli uomini, mal si riesce ad appassionarsi per delle riforme che sono lungi dal risolvere il problema. Noi dunque dobbiamo, sempre e dovunque, predicare la necessità della trasformazione radicale della società, ed il diritto che ha ogni uomo alla completa emancipazione da qualsiasi oppressione economica e politica.

Però altro è il programma nostro, altro lo stato di coscienza a cui sono arrivate quelle masse, senza il cui concorso i nostri ideali non possono realizzarsi.

Avviene oggi che la maggior parte dei lavoratori che si ribellano alla loro condizione di schiavi e cominciano a lottare contro i padroni, non comprendono ancora la giustizia e la praticità del nostro programma, e si limitano a domandare un miglioramento più o meno importante.

Ebbene, noi dobbiamo sempre sventolare innanzi ai loro occhi tutta larga la nostra bandiera, dobbiamo spingerli sempre a pretender cose maggiori; ma dobbiamo intanto incoraggiarli e secondarli in quelle lotte che essi voglion combattere, sempre che siano nella buona direzione, cioè che tendano a facilitare le conquiste future e siano condotte in modo da abituare i lavoratori a considerare come nemici i padroni e i governi, ed a voler conquistare da loro stessi quello che vogliono.

Molti operai desiderano di non lavorare più di 8 ore. Niente di più giustificabile.

La riforma è di quelle che tendono a migliorare realmente la posizione dei lavoratori ed a facilitare le conquiste future; e noi, quando non potremo indurli ad esigere di più, dobbiamo secondarli in quella pretensione modesta. Ma, nel secondarli dobbiamo indicar loro qual'è la via per la quale l'operaio può e deve ottenere quello che vuole, e combattere la tendenza nefasta di aspettare i miglioramenti dall'azione governativa: poichè, una cosa sono *le 8 ore di lavoro*, ed un'altra *la legge* delle 8 ore.

Il compagno, di cui abbiamo citata la lettera, non pare abbia ben notata la differenza.

Domandare ai poteri legislativi una legge, che obblighi a non far lavorare e a non lavorare più di 8 ore, è inutile ed è dannoso.

E' inutile poichè il governo non concede mai nulla se non quando è persuaso che non concedendo una cosa il popolo se la piglierebbe da sè; e quando, per gettar polvere negli occhi o per altre speciali circostanze, il governo fa qualche legge favorevole al popolo prima che il popolo la voglia ed abbia la forza d'imporla, la legge non è applicata o è applicata in modo da produrre un effetto diverso da quello che sembrava avere in mira, e fare il danno anzichè il bene dei lavoratori.

E' dannoso, poichè i lavoratori, aspettando che la riforma che desiderano venga fatta dal governo, cessano dal lottare per conseguirla direttamente; e così o non l'ottengono affatto, o l'ottengono solo molto più tardi e quando non sono preparati ad imporne l'esecuzione.

Guardate ciò che è avvenuto nel Colorado. Circa tre mesi fa entrò in vigore la legge delle 8 ore votata dalla legislatura di quello Stato. I padroni dichiararono che ottempererebbero alle prescrizioni della legge, ma che diminuirebbero i salarii in proporzione della diminuzione del tempo di lavoro. In conseguenza di ciò i fonditori (*smelters*) di Denver, Pueblo, Leadville, ecc. si dichiararono in isciopero.

Al principio sembrava che lo sciopero dovesse trionfare, poichè si andava estendendo alle miniere e ad altre industrie, e faceva sperare in uno sciopero generale che avrebbe costretto i capitalisti a cedere; ma il movimento si fermò, e la vittoria restò ai padroni.

Dopo due mesi di lotta i fonditori son ritornati al lavoro accettando tutte le imposizioni delle compagnie: e non è difficile che, non potendo vivere con un salario ridotto, uno di questi giorni domandino l'abrogazione della legge o aiutino essi stessi i padroni ad eluderla.

E' chiaro: se le otto ore fossero state conquistate direttamente dagli operai, questi si sarebbero trovati in forza per impedire la diminuzione del salario. Concesse dal governo, non servono a nulla, o servono a fare del danno, poichè i capitalisti possono sempre, con una forma o coll'altra, fare quello che vogliono.

E v'è altro. Le condizioni economiche e morali dei lavoratori sono molti differenti da una località all'altra, dall'una all'altra corporazione. Quando gli operai lottano direttamente possono ottenere delle riforme mano mano che raggiungono la forza morale e materiale che serve ad imporle. Sperando invece nella legge, siccome questa non si può fare per ogni caso particolare e si deve applicare a tutto un paese, o almeno a tutta una corporazione, gli elementi più arretrati ostacolano i progressi degli altri e servono al governo di pretesto e di forza per non concedere nulla. Così succede in Inghilterra per la legge delle 8 ore in pro dei minatori, dove serve di scusa per non votarla il fatto che una frazione di minatori vi è opposta.

Dunque, quando non è possibile di far meglio, vada pure per le otto ore; ma siano esse imposte ai capitalisti dall'azione diretta degli operai, e non già *concesse* dal governo.

Temo i Danai anche se portan doni!

Triste momento

E' la così detta lotta elettorale che perpetua nel popolo la devozione ai capi, che confida nelle mani di questi privilegiati il destino di tutti, che crea dei nuovi puntelli alle istituzioni. E quando dei proletari hanno mandato alla camera un socialista, credono di aver vinta una battaglia, si fregano le mani contenti, tornano alle loro case pacificamente e aspettano il frutto della vittoria.

Qual'è il frutto? Lo abbiamo visto e lo vediamo ancora: un supplemento di fame, di manette e di piombo.

E se i proletari osano tentare di ribellarsi non incontrano soltanto gli sbirri del governo, ma incontrano ancora i loro deputati che li esortano alla calma e gettano, al popolo in rivolta, l'anatema.

Ma le dure lezioni sembra che non valgono, poichè i cervelli sono ancora più duri.

Una epidemia elettorale si è scatenata in Italia; dappertutto i socialisti ,i repubblicani e democratici si sono coalizzati per vincere i partigiani del governo.

Non si è trovato altro mezzo che le elezioni per rispondere alla manomissione delle ben magre libertà perpetrata dal governo, il quale, ad onta delle vittorie elettorali dei suoi avversari, continua ad opprimere la nazione.

Se ci è mai stato un momento in cui sia stato dimostrato luminosamente la inutilità della lotta elettorale è appunto il presente; se ci è mai stato un momento in cui sia stato altrettanto luminosamente provato che la fede in questi mezzi di lotta, permessi dal governo, tolgono al popolo l'energia e l'audacia per lottare veramente, non colla scheda ma col braccio, è appunto il momento presente.

Se ci è mai stato un momento in cui sia stato necessario, pel partito anarchico, di affermare i proprii principi e di tenersi lontano dalle baraonde elettorali è appunto il momento presente, poichè ora che il popolo è più che mai oppresso è duopo l'esempio del nostro disprezzo per le false lotte, della nostra coerenza e tenacia nella fede professata.

Eppure, chi lo direbbe? Ad onta degli esempi così chiari il popolo si lascia ancora condurre alle urne; ma ciò che è ben più triste e sconfortante è che fra questo popolo di montoni si sono imbrancati degli anarchici.

Sicuro: in diverse provincie della media e dell'alta Italia dei compagni — che io chiamo dei rinnegati — sono andati a votare la lista pei partiti popolari e hanno fatto i galoppini elettorali!

La disorientazione, prodotta dalla reazione presente, ha portato a simile pervertimento.

Pei compagni d'America riescirà inesplicabile questo fenomeno; eppure si è verificato e si verifica.

Quali sono le cause! E' forse la fede che manca?

Io non credo che manchi la fede nell'ideale nostro; ma manca l'energia, manca la tenacia nei propositi, manca il coraggio di affrontare l'opinione pubblica.

Se tutto questo manca, mi si dirà, allora non si è anarchici.

Certo l'anarchico non deve avere nè debolezze nè pregiudizi; ma vi è un numero non indifferente di seguaci che una volta che non possono più leggere il periodico o l'opuscolo che li conforta, che li anima, che non possono più udire la voce del compagno propagandista che li entusiasma, costretti a rincantucciarsi nel silenzio e nell'inerzia per fuggire il carcere, a poco a poco, senza che se ne accorgano, subiscono le influenze dell'ambiente e finiscono per rimanerne vinti.

Allora perdono la percezione giusta della realtà delle cose e si arrestano soltanto alle apparenze superficiali.

Tutto quello che trovavano giusto e buono prima, diventa come impossibile e quasi pazzesco, perchè urta troppo contro l'opinione pubblica creata dalla nuova situazione.

Non si può più fare come prima, essi pensano; bisogna conformarsi alle necessità dell'ambiente.

E' allora che, senza avvedersene, hanno disertato, perchè l'ambiente li ha assorbiti.

Viene allora la lotta fra governo ed opposizione. Il paese considera questa lotta come una vera battaglia fra la reazione e la libertà: così la spiega la stampa.

Il governo ha soppresso tutte le libertà, ma lascia andare a votare; ciò dovrebbe bastare per comprendere l'ironia del voto. I socialisti, coerenti al loro programma, bandiscono la lotta elettorale in nome della libertà e del progresso, si alleano agli altri partiti dell'opposizione e buttano là l'assioma: *chi vota con noi vota per la libertà, chi vota contro di noi vota per la reazione, chi non vota sostiene la reazione.*

Questo assioma fa il suo effetto; molti che hanno morso il freno dell'inerzia e del mutismo forzato hanno bisogno di uno sfogo e non possono far nulla. Viene l'elezione: o pel governo o per la libertà, si grida da tutte le parti; oramai un certo adattamento all'ambiente il nostro soggetto l'ha subito; è titubante, perplesso, ancora un po' d'esitazione, di contrasto colla propria coscienza e poi la resa: l'anarchico diventa elettore.

Ecco come si imbranca colle altre pecore, ecco come diserta il campo, come rinnega i principi.

Tutto ciò proviene dal non avere forza sufficente per resistere agli effetti d'una data situazione, alle tentazioni di un falso ambiente e di falsi assiomi.

E basta che qualcuno si lasci travolgere perchè trascini con se tanti altri.

F. V.

Nostre Corrispondenze

Lettera Francese

Da Parigi

20 Agosto, 1899

F. V.

Quando vi giungerà questa lettera il telegrafo avrà già annunciato avvenimenti che stanno maturandosi e che ora è difficile prevedere.

A giorni il processo Dreyfus sarà già finito e la vittima dello stato maggiore francese sarà liberata o ricacciata all'isola del Diavolo.

Se il tribunale militare si rende solidale coi falsari dello stato maggiore, Dreyfus sarà di nuovo condannato; se si inchinerà dinanzi all'evidenza dei fatti dovrà assolvere.

Ma nell'un caso e nell'altro è difficile prevedere le conseguenze.

Dreyfus assolto significa la condanna dei generali francesi che non hanno rifuggito da nessun mezzo per farlo condannare; e per conseguenza può essere la rivolta in massa degli ufficiali contro il governo, trascinanti l'esercito.

Dreyfus condannato sarà un'offesa terribile alla verità, alla giustizia, una sfida alla parte più vitale della popolazione, la parte rivoluzionaria.

Se condannato, sarà la Francia ricaduta nelle mani dei reazionari, perchè la reazione clerico-militare avrà vinto; se assolto, è la minaccia di una contro rivoluzione che si affaccia.

Il popolo guarda incerto e non è possibile prevedere la parte che prenderà.

I partiti rivoluzionari non sembrano abbastanza affiatati e pronti per un'azione, sebbene i *meetings* si susseguano, gli appelli si ripetano ogni giorno e un lavorio di organizzazione si vada operando.

Ma mentre i rivoluzionari mostrano di prepararsi apertamente e alla luce del sole, i reazionari si preparano nell'ombra.

A quanto pare il governo avrebbe già in mano le fila di un vasto complotto ordito dagli orleanisti, bonapartisti, antisemiti, ecc., i quali non sono che un'amalgama di quanto vi ha di più putrido nella casta clerico-militarista, per rovesciare la repubblica.

Varii arresti sono stati fatti e si dice che altri se ne faranno ancora, alcuni sono riusciti a fuggire all'estero e il direttore dell'*Antijuif* si è chiuso in casa, insieme con una quarantina di accoliti, e rifiuta di consegnarsi alla polizia che ha mandato di arresto.

E' già una settimana che dura questa farsa: una casa bloccata dalla polizia, bloccata una strada e le adiacenze.

Non si vuole procedere violentemente perchè questo signor giornalista ha promesso che risponderà a fucilate se la polizia vorrà far uso della sua forza.

Se si trattasse di una quarantina di anarchici che, armati, opponessero tale rifiuto e facessero tali minaccie, vedreste se a quest'ora non li avrebbero snidati, a costo, magari, di distruggere la casa o una strada intiera; ma si tratta di gente che grida: viva l'esercito e allora si hanno tutti i riguardi.

Vedremo se la commedia dura un pezzo.

Accanto alla commedia la tragedia: la settimana scorsa si tentò di assassinare l'avvocato Labori, il difensore di Zola, ed ora difensore di Dreyfus.

E' certamente una vendetta che parte dalle mene dello stato maggiore. Per perdere Dreyfus si è ricorso a tutti i mezzi, ed ora si è ricorso all'assassinio.

Naturalmente colui che ha commesso l'attentato è salvo, nessuno lo ha potuto arrestare e non sarà certo più ritrovato.

Labori è rimasto salvo per miracolo, perchè la palla tiratagli nella schiena non ha toccato nessun organo interno, per cui ora è già in convalescenza e presto riprenderà il suo posto al processo.

Non è dunque che questione di giorni e poi sapremo se dalla situazione presente ne uscirà la rivoluzione schiacciante i reazionari coalizzati ed estendentesi ad abbattere il sistema attuale o se ne sortirá un pronunciamento militaresco, capace di seppellire la repubblica e d'inaugurare un nuovo regime del terrore contro il pensiero moderno.

Io mi auguro la rivoluzione sociale.

* * *

Per oggi era indetto un grande *meeting* in piazza della Repubblica. Alle tre la piazza era gremita di popolo, Sebastien Faure disse poche parole dai piedi del monumento, poscia polizia e soldati hanno proceduto allo scioglimento. Allora la folla si è riversata per il boulevard Richard e continuando per il boulevard Voltaire si è diretta a piazza della Nazione. Anche là Faure ha arringato il popolo, poi si è continuata la marcia fino all'intervento della polizia, la quale volendo di nuovo sciogliere i dimostranti, questi hanno resistito e ne è venuto un conflitto.

Molti sono i feriti da ambe le parti, e l'eccitazione del popolo è fortissima. In vari punti della città si riproducono conflitti tra la forza e i rivoluzionari, una chiesa è assaltata e, forzatene le porte, viene incendiata. In alcuni punti si è tentato di costrurre barricate.

Anche gli antisemiti hanno tentato di liberare il loro Guerin, assalendo la polizia che lo tiene bloccato, hanno tentato di costrurre una barricata e di uccidere il capo di polizia.

Sebastien Faure ed altri redattori del *Journal du Peuple* sono arrestati. Si dice che i feriti siano circa 500.

I fatti di oggi dimostrano che Parigi non è ancora disposta a sottomettersi al dispotismo. Che l'agitazione si allarghi e la libertà trionferà.

Da Barre, Vermont

E' con sorpresa che abbiamo letto sul *Proletario* una corrispondenza firmata A. C. nella quale si afferma cosa non vera e si getta un insulto agli anarchici di qui.

Lasciando al compagno S. P. la cura di rispondere a quanto lo riguarda personalmente, ci limitiamo a rispondere a ció che il signor A. C. afferma, che cioé non v'é bisogno di spiegare l'attitudine degli anarchici di Barre riguardo al voto politico visto l'atteggiamento da essi tenuto nelle ultime elezioni comunali fatte qua.

Ora facciamo notare al sig. A. C. che dicendo ció egli dice cosa non vera, poiché se vi fu qualche anarchico che agendo sotto l'eccitamento contro il sindaco (il quale aveva vietato alla Goldmann di tenere una conferenza anarchica) andó alle urne, il sig. A. C. non puó dire che gli anarchici di Barre abbiano tenuto un contegno contrario ai loro principii, perché la maggioranza grande di noi ha, come sempre, dimostrata la sua fede astensionista.

Chiudendo la corrispondenza poi, il sig. A. C. dopo aver parlato un po' di tutti noi si permette di insultarci dicendo che non discuterá piú con "questa gente, perché é tempo perso discutere con gente che non vuol saperne di buona fede."

Che il sig. A. C. venga a dir ció mentre poi personalmente si mostra con noi buon amico, é cosa che ci fa cascar dalle nuvole.

Entusiasti, di temperamento impetuoso forse, poco colti, ma non mai in "mala fede," il sig. A. C. se lo tenga per detto.

E se egli mantiene ció che ha scritto, ci dimostri quali degli anarchici di qui non siano in buona fede.

Ci dispiace che con affermazioni non vere o con insulti il sig. A. C. cominci la sua propaganda socialista in Barre.

C. Gattoni, A. Gianni, O. Boffino, A. Piccolo, R. Bettigi.

\+ \+ \+ \+

Nel N° 20 del giornale *Il Proletario* leggo una corta diatriba intitolata "Per la Veritá,, firmata da un certo A. C., socialista, la quale (a mio credere, e potrei quasi asserire anche a quello degli anarchici di Barre,) non merita risposta alcuna.

Il detto A. C. (ispirato evidentemente dalla manía di scorgere fiamme e fuoco colá ove scorre semplicemente acqua pura e limpida) si mostra in quei dieci corti paragrafi aggressivo per tendenza, sconclusionato di natura, e – diró anche, perché mi ci si forza – ignaro parzialmente, o totalmente, del valore esatto delle parole che compongono il vocabolario della lingua che ci é comune.

Comunque siasi, mi affretto a dichiarare ch'io sono uno di "quella gente,, che han saputo esser cortesi cogli avversari e che non han *mai* fatto coro coi borghesi e colle polizie allo scopo di denigrarli o ad essere loro pregiudizievole con stupide suggestioni e con fallaci interpretazioni. Il corrispondente socialista del *Proletario* si é mostrato in questa occasione affetto da quella maledetta infermitá che affligge tutti i "neofiti,, d'ogni nuova idea; vale a dire la biliositá accompagnata da un eccessivo zelo; in piú, esso ha certamente la vista corta ed anche il *comprendonium*... non bene bilanciati. Almeno arguisco ció da quanto mi sono sforzato a comprendere – leggendo con qualche po' di sudore, per dire la veritá – la cinquantina di righe cosí "benevolmente,, pubblicate dal "redattore in capo,, dell'organo massimo dei socialisti italiani negli Stati Uniti. Auguro sinceramente all'A. C. i "disinteressati" servigi del famoso Professor Collins, il Dulcamara che guarisce tutti i mali e che estirpa... i dollari dalle tasche dei lavoratori. Esso deve sapere ove trovare l'indirizzo di quel gran "benefattore,, dell'umanitá. Diavolo! non bisogna lasciare invecchiare il male!

Gió che peró trovo strano, stranissimo, si é che il Dottor Dino Rondani, il conferenziere al quale indirizzai qualche mia critica nella *Questione Sociale*, e che *intese* colle proprie orecchie quanto io gli obbiettai, e che certamente *lesse* quanto io scrissi a suo riguardo, abbia potuto pubblicare una corrispondenza scritta con sí pronunciata animositá e talmente erronea nell'interpetrazione di quanto io tentai (in buona fede, caro A. C.) di relatare. Rondani sa indubbiamente parlare e leggere la lingua italiana cento volte meglio che il sottoscritto, ed avrebbe dovuto accorgersi del granchio preso dal suo corrispondente.

Basta, non intendo suscitare oziose polemiche *and I shut my mouth.*

Aspettiamo Malatesta e Rondani per le conferenze in contradittorie, e posso assicurare l'amico A. C. che il compagno Trentini é risoluto ad "impappinarsi,, di bel nuovo sanza tener conto delle critiche indirizzategli dai suoi avversari: esso non pretende essere avvocato o dottore in legge, ma sempre si è detto un semplice operaio desideroso di veder trionfare la veritá.

Ghio Primo poi rinnovellerá – se fa bisogno – gli elogi ai quali fa allusione il nostro avversario. Boffioo anch'esso – uno di quella gente – si é promesso di chiarir le cose.

Suvvia socialista A. G., invece di perdere il vostro tempo a sprezzare gli anarchici, aiutateli a combattere governi e borghesia: ció sará proficuo alla vostra ed alla nostra idea... Faccio punto.

S. PALLAVICINI.

Leggo nel N° 20 del *Proletario* una corrispondenza da Bridgeport, Conn. firmata dai socialisti, con la quale vorrebbero smentire il conpagno L. I. riguardo alla conferenza Rondani.

Invece io credo che sia verissimo ció che ha scritto il compagno L. I. nel numero 124 della *Questione Sociale*, perché anche qui in Barre, specialmente la seconda sera, Rondani aveva sempre l'orologio in mano e cercava di chiudere la conferenza, e di evitare le discussioni cogli anarchici, scusandosi col dire che doveva assistere all'adunanza dei socialisti e che doveva partire la stessa sera. In realtá poi é partito il giorno dopo.

Ora sfido tutti i socialisti di Barre, e il Rondani stesso a smentire queste cose.

OTTAVIO GRANAI.

Progredendo

Raimondo Mastelloni di Napoli ci prega di pubblicare che egli é diventato anarchico e lavora alla costituzione di gruppi di propaganda nella terra di Masaniello e di Pisacane.

Ci congratuliamo col nuovo compagno, e gli auguriamo feconda di risultati l'opera sua.

Sciopero di Manuali - muratori in Paterson

Lo sciopero incominciato alla Scuola N° 3 si é rapidamente esteso a tutte le grandi fabbriche in costruzione.

I manuali guadagnano ora $ 1.75, e pretendono invece $ 2, allegando giustamente che tutti i generi di consumo sono cresciuti in prezzo.

Gli scioperanti si dicono sicuri della vittoria e si burlano della minaccia che saranno sostituiti dalle macchine, poiché sanno che nel loro mestiere le macchine vengono a costare piú caro degli uomini.

Abbiamo constatato con piacere che i manuali italiani sono perfettamente solidali coi compagni di altre nazionalitá.

MOVIMENTO SOCIALE

Dall'Estero

Austria

Abbiamo da Cilli (Stiria) che dall'Universitá di Praga convennero in quella ridente cittadella 180 studenti universitari allo scopo di passare un pò allegramente le vacanze estive. Ma l'intolleranza tedesca che spadroneggia nelle provincie slave del Sud, aizzò contro di loro tutta la feccia incosciente che abbonda nelle città vicine di Graz, Marburg e Klagenfurt. Piovvero pietre e proiettili d'ogni genere addosso ai malcapitati studenti, e i vetri del Narodni Dom e quelli dell'Hotel ove erano alloggiati, furono mandati tutti in frantumi. La polizia lasció fare perché alla testa della vergognosa dimostrazione si trovavano fra altri anche il podestà di Cilli e suo figlio. Due professori slavi, mentre rincasavano, furono dalla folla avvinazzata assaliti a colpi di forcone e a fatica, difendendosi a colpi di revolver contro i dimostranti, riuscirono a salvare la propria pelle.

Si ebbe un morto e molti feriti, due dei quali ben difficilmente potranno essere salvati a causa delle gravi ferite riportate.

A quando la fine di queste vergognose gazzarre nazionaliste che fanno fremere di sdegno i ben pensanti?

Spagna

In seguito all'agitazione promossa in tutta la Spagna a favore della revisione del processo di Montjuich, l'opinione si fa sempre più strada fra il popolo che gli infelici condannati, quelli che sono tuttora in vita, debbono essere *graziati*.

Ma i nostri bravi compagni non vogliono saperne di *grazia*. In una lettera dalle carceri di Melilla, dove sono rinchiusi, essi protestano contro l'intenzione che si ha di graziarli.

"Il rossore ci sale al viso al pensarci solamente che noi dovessimo riacquistare la nostra libertà per mezzo di un tale atto. Noi non possiamo, nè vogliamo accettare la grazia. Noi non vogliamo essere graziati, vogliamo *giustizia*. Noi vogliamo uscire da questo tenebroso processo allo stesso modo col quale vi siamo stati coinvolti: *senza nessuna colpa*. Tutto il mondo deve saperlo. Noi vogliamo che giustizia sia fatta, affinchè in avvenire non possano più succedere atti così infami e vigliacchi, come questi usati contro le nostre persone.

"Se ciò non è possibile, noi preferiamo morire per anemia in quest'inferno ove viviamo, piuttostochè venire ad un accomodamento coi nostri carnefici. Del nostro sacrificio di dare la vita per la giustizia, non intendiamo farne un mestiere. Il nostro onore lo teniamo più caro che la nostra vita; e al di sopra del nostro capo sta l'umanità e il sublime ideale della giustizia.

Melilla, 26 Luglio 1899.

Francisco Callis, José Pons Villaplana, Jacinto Melich, Jaime Vilella Cristofol.

Germania

Il mondo tedesco festeggia ora il 150 anniversario di nascita di Wolfang Goethe. Se siano però molti coloro fra i festeggianti che abbiano letto Goethe — tacciamo di coloro che possono averlo compreso — è molto problematico. Ai più accade come alla maggior parte dei marxisti, i quali chiacchierano tutto l'anno di Marx, senza avere mai avuto nelle mani, nonchè letto, le sue opere sette volte suggellate.

Se questi entusiasti di Goethe avessero soltanto una pallida idea della sua filosofia, essi voterebbero il suo autore semplicemente all'inferno, poichè tutto ciò che ne forma — dirò così — la quintessenza è semplicemente Anarchismo, Materialismo ed Ateismo.

Ma, naturalmente, la maniera ed il modo di scrivere di Goethe non era tale da essere compreso da tutti, e perció purtroppo il popolo lavoratore non potè mai trovare molto godimento nella lettura delle sue opere, giacchè nei pochi anni di scuola non gli diedero quella istruzione che è necessaria per seguire anche superficialmente i voli sublimi di questo spirito gigante.

Goethe era uno di coloro che Nietzsche chiama "superuomini," un aristocrata del pensiero, il quale scrisse per i buongustai della letteratura. Ma verrá il tempo in cui le sue opere saranno comprese anche dalla massa: ma allora gl'insegnamenti ch'esse contengono non saranno più necessarii, perchè le loro conseguenze saranno giá realizzate in altro modo.

Oggi possono essere innumerevoli *gli entusiasti* di Goethe, ma coloro che lo comprendono veramente sono ben pochi; essi somigliano a quegli *uomini* che Diogene di pieno giorno cercava col lanternino.

Dunque, meno ipocrisia e niente millanteria: abbasso la maschera di erudizione finchè i cervelli sono ottusi e le teste piene di paglia!

La *Deutsche Tageszeitung*, l'organo direttivo degli Agrarii non si vergogna di chiedere che il progetto di legge contro gli operai delle campagne sia allargato in modo che, ogni sciopero di questi sia proibito sotto pena di gravi pene di reclusione *inasprite con la fustigazione* dei colpevoli. Anche altri giornali agrarii osservano che la frusta sia l'unico mezzo per ridurre alla ragione gli operai che con la pretesa di salari più alti cercano di soddisfare la loro brama di ubbriaconi e ribelli.

Per un paese come la Germania, che da trenta anni in qua cerca inutilmente di mettersi alla testa delle nazioni più progredite, non c'è male davvero!

Evviva la frusta dunque!

Inghilterra

Ecco una notizia che fará riflettere profondamente gli operai sulle loro condizioni di vita nella società presente. Una delle più grandi fabbriche di prodotti chimici fece noto che d'ora in poi *non avrebbe accettato nella fabbrica nessun operaio che avesse un'età superiore a 30 anni.* Occorrono degli operai giovani, perchè questi lavorano di più, e di questi si trova sempre un ricco assortimento sul moderno mercato degli schiavi. Dei vecchi ci si sbarazza e li si getta sulla strada come viti smussate o ruote sconquassate che non servono più a nulla. Queste almeno conservano ancora il valore del ferro vecchio, mentre l'energia operaia una volta sfruttata va ramingando nel mondezzaio dei rifiuti, e si vorrebbe piuttosto farla affondare nel mare.

La pratica di accettare soltanto operai giovani non è nuova, ma un'aperta dichiarazione di questo genere la si fece sempre molto raramente, stantecchè con ciò perfino quelli fra gli operai che non sono abituati a pensare ai casi loro, dovrebbero rimanerne stupiti. Con terrore essi s'accorgerebbero d'invecchiare, e conseguentemente avvicinarsi la miseria e le privazioni più crudeli. Ch'essi però a trent'anni siano dichiarati già vecchi e non utilizzabili, è molto significante per lo spaventevole sfruttamento delle giovani forze operaie nel moderno sistema di produzione. Condizioni vergognose, inumane!

Che cosa sia la tanto vantata filantropia e beneficenza borghese lo apprendiamo una volta di più da questa breve notizia che ci giunge da Londra.

Un centinaio di ragazzi educati nella Ragged School [scuola per i ragazzi poveri] di Greenwich erano andati a fare una escursione vicino a Londra.

Ivi dai proprietari del fondo furono serviti con tè, latte, frutta e dolci, ecc. Venti minuti dopo il pasto, cinquantacinque di essi si sentirono in preda a vomiti e diarrea. Condotti all'ospedale poterono essere salvati quasi tutti nel giorno stesso. Alcuni sono ammalati più gravemente, ma si spera nella loro guarigione.

Alcuni ritengono che il latte sia la causa del generale avvelenamento, non per sè, ma per l'acqua con cui era stato mescolato, e che era stata deposta in fiaschi appartenenti a due vecchi custodi della casa di campagna. Si crede che in fondo ai fiaschi vi fossero dei residui dove si erano moltiplicati i batterii velenosi.

I maestri, che sembra non abbiano bevuto acqua e latte, non caddero ammalati.

E così che viene curata l'igiene quando si tratta di figli di poveri operai. Serva ciò di esempio a coloro che continuano a piegare la schiena in ridicoli inchini dinanzi il buon cuore e la generositá della classe borghese.

Francia

I generali che fuggono dinnanzi il nemico risoluto a non voler farsi schiacciare da loro, non si contano più nemmeno in Francia, paese militare per eccellenza. Ed è per questo ch'essi si vendicano forse tutte le volte che trovano delle popolazioni tranquille ed inermi che non possono difendersi al di là del Mediterraneo.

Per fortuna che le loro gesta non rimangono sempre ignorate, ma vengono di tanto in tanto anche a conoscenza del popolo, che altrimenti non potrebbe avere che una ben meschina opinione dell'eroismo e del valore di questi figli di Marte... della Repubblica.

Così il *Matin* pubblica i capi d'accusa di crudeltà che colpiscono i capitani Voulet e Chanoine, dichiarati ribelli per l'uccisione del capitano Klobb mandato nel Soudan per arrestarli.

Il 9 gennaio il capitano Voulet ordinò l'uccisione di 20 donne e dei loro figli, presso il villaggio Say.

Il 13 detto fece appiccare il fuoco a Sansan, città con 10,000 abitanti. All'indomani Chanoine fece uccidere senza processo due ausiliarii perchè non avevano inseguito un indigeno di Karma, bruciando il villaggio stesso. Il 17 pure di gennaio Voulet fece fucilare due prigionieri. E il 24 stesso mese, il capitano Chanoine per vendicarsi di sei spahis perduti in uno scontro, fece 20 prigionieri, di cui 10 furono fucilati.

Non c'è male per la causa della civiltà.

Nella miniera carbonifera Couchard, in Saint Etienne, causa la rottura della corda della gabbia, questa è precipitata al fondo del pozzo della miniera stessa con sedici minatori dentro.

Furono trasportati alla superficie, quasi tutti morti. Tre di essi soltanto respiravano ancora, ma le loro condizioni sono disperate.

Tutti eguali i capitalisti, si in repubblica che in monarchia. Quando si tratta di risparmiare qualche centinaio di franchi, poco importa loro della vita degli operai che lavorano faticosamente in mezzo ai pericoli più gravi per ingrassare le loro pancie borghesi e le loro... casse forti.

La sostituzione di una corda nuova a quella vecchia già marcia, avrebbe bastato a scongiurare questa catastrofe, ma sembra che i signori azionisti della compagnia ritenessero troppo forte una tale spesa a pro della sicurezza dell'operaio.

Manco a dirlo; nessuno si sogna nemmeno di rendere responsabile la Compagnia di questa trascuranza. Gli riderebbero in faccia per giunta!

Transvaal

La minaccia di una prossima guerra coll'Inghilterra fa già sentire i suoi funesti effetti sulla popolazione di questa repubblica sud-africana. Dacchè la crisi è incominciata, ben più di 15,000 persone hanno già abbandonato il paese.

Alla stazione ferroviaria si è avuta in questi giorni una scena pietosa: 180 bambini sono giunti soli da Johannesburg, mandati dai loro genitori, che non avevano i mezzi di partire secoloro.

Poveri genitori! E poveri i bambini sopratutto!

E poi ci sono dei burloni che dicono che la guerra non è una delizia!

Dagli Stati Uniti

Paterson N. J.

Venerdì scorso il nostro compagno Bartolomeo Canova, ritornando dalla conferenza tenuta in quella sera dal nostro compagno Malatesta a Riverside, volendo discendere dal carro ne' pressi di casa sua, cadde così disgraziatamente da riportarne una fortissima commozione cerebrale in seguito alla quale nella stessa notte verso le 6 ore ant. esalò l'ultimo respiro. Lascia la moglie e due bambini.

Domenica ebbero luogo i funerali ai quali concorse gran numero di compagni e sulla sua tomba vennero pronunciati tre discorsi, due dei quali dai nostri compagni ed una dalla Società dei forastieri alla quale l'estinto aveva appartenuto.

La dipartita del nostro caro compagno ci addolora immensamente, essendo egli sempre stato uno dei più attivi e devoti alla causa.

Midway, Kansas.

Il compagno Evening, approfittando del suo soggiorno in Pittsburg, Kansas, si condusse qui il 27 e il 29 Agosto a tenere due conferenze.

Nella prima parlò sulla questione sociale, e nella seconda svolse il tema: "Perché siamo anarchici," raccogliendo numerose approvazioni all'idee esposte.

Nell'ultima conferenza si procedette alla formazione di un gruppo, cui aderirono i compagni italiani e francesi, e che ha preso il nome: "I figli della Libertà."

A corrispondente del Gruppo venne nominato il compagno Domenico Cinorri, Box 22, Midway, Kansas.

Pittsburg, Kansas.

Il compagno Raveggi tenne altre conferenze, di cui due a Frontenac ed una a Chicopee, nelle quali mise in opera tutto il suo studio onde sviluppare in mezzo ai compagni ed ai simpatizzanti la coscienza libertaria e lo spirito d'iniziativa rivoluzionaria.

Il compagno Evening è partito alla volta di Kansas City.

Boston Mass.

I compagni di Boston hanno deciso di ripartire in 3 parti di $13,65 ciascuno il fondo di $40.95 raccolto pei moti rivoluzionari, delle quali una a beneficio dei coatti politici, una per la QUESTIONE SOCIALE e l'altra per *L'Aurora*.

Le schede ed importi relativi sono i seguenti: Scheda 1, collettore F De Carpis $7,35 — Scheda 9, collettore S Lombardi $ 2,75 — Scheda 12, collettore A Brogi, $ 11,75 — Scheda 20, collettore G Rossetti, $3,50 — Scheda 23, collettore U Cerutti $ 6,00 — Scheda 24, collettore A Zenoni $0,25, Totale $40,95.

Il Comitato di Boston ci prega di pubblicare quanto segue:

"Tutte le persone che non hanno messo il loro obolo nelle sopraindicate schede, ma bensì in altre, reclamine verso i loro collettori, poichè noi teniamo a dichiarare di non avere ricevuto altre schede all'infuori delle sopracitate."

SOTTOSCRIZIONE

A FAVORE DEL GIRO DI PROPAGANDA

DI ERRICO MALATESTA

IRON MOUNTAIN, MICH.

Davide Oberto 0,50

CHICOPEE, KANSAS.

S Paganoni 0,50

ERRATA CORRIGE. — Nella relazione pubblicata nell'ultimo numero, alla posta Yohoghani, Pa., devesi leggere: Totale $ 7,00, meno spese di posta $6,85, non $ 6,15, come erroneamente venne stampato.

Amministrazione

SOMME RICEVUTE

Paterson: Pietro San Pietro, G Bove, Gian Bracco Piotin, S Croll, ciascuno 50; B Alberto, F Fusari, L Verolet, ciascuno 0,75; B Sanguinetti, R Rege, ciascuno 1,00; M Tamborini 2,00 — Spring Valley: F Massa 0,50, C Falcetta 0,25 — Brooklyn: V Navarra 1,00 — Seatonville: P Perona, F Colombo, ciascuno 0,50; T Giovannini, S Fassero, ciascuno 0,25; G Bertino 1,00 — Frontenac: A Maniscalchi, I B Caserio ciascuno 0,50 — Pittsburg, Kansas: S Monti 0,50 — Chicopee, Kansas, S. Paganoni 0,50 — Pueblo, : G Mombello 0,50 — Midway: P De Colle, D Gennardi, D Cinorri, ciascuno 0,25 — San Francisco: L Lorenzini 1,00 — Pittsburg, Pa. — J Sella 1,00 — S. Pedro: C Serafini 1,00 Zurigo, Svizzera: G Cattaneo 0,95 — Providence: M Scussel 0,50; Passaic: Varettoni e Spalmacini 1,00 — Westerly: A Bianchi 0,25; Paterson: F Scalvino, Quinto Vercella, ciascuno 0,50.

Sottoscrizione Permanente a favore della "Questione Sociale

PATERSON, N. J.

V Oppedisano 0,40, R Rege, Robino, Tiravanti, ciascuno 0,25; L Fontanella 0,50 — Scheda 12: C Boffa 0,50, B Forno, O Porrino, E Porrino, G Volpatto, J Manin, P Robino, Pietro Re, P Cancino, J Molina, J Costa, ciascuno 0,25; Scheda 13: L Granotti, G Castelli, ciascuno 0,50; P Barbisco 0,25; Scheda 15: F. Aimone 0,50; Secondo Bianco, C Cerino, ciascuno 0,25; G Fontanella 0,10; Scheda 17, F Gallo, B Alberto, A Germanetti, ciascuno 0,25; N N L'preive 0,15; Scheda 23, L Aquadro 0,25, F Scalvino 0,10; Scheda 25, L Minero Re, L Verolet, S Cerino, Montaut, L Bianco, ciascuno 0,25; Marmorino, B Minero, ciascuno 0,15; F Borio, S Tabachin, B Maron, ciascuno 0,10.

Vendita opuscoli: Paterson: Incisioni 1,55, opuscoli 0,70, giornali 0,15. South Wilmington, A Bottino 0,25. Seatonville, P Perona 0,25. Iron Mountain, D Oberto 0,10. Milano, cristo, lire 7, pari a 1,33. Zurigo, Svizzera, G cattaneo, lire 1, pari 0,19. New York; P. Freschi 0,60. Providence, M Scussel 0,50. New York, G Filippone 0,50. calumet, C Tenaglia 1,00. Da Mongrando e Occhieppo, Biellese, lire 6, pari a $1,14. Niantich, M campo.

SPRING VALLEY, ILL.

Vendita cordoni 2,75, Avanzo bicchierata fra compagni 0,50 — Totale 3,25.

SEATONVILLE, ILL.

F. Colombo 0,50; G. Bertino 1,00 — Totale 1,50

PITTSBURG, PA.

J Sella 0,50.

PASSAIC, N. J.

Avanzo bicchierata 0,40.

NEW LONDON, CONN.

G Negrucci, G Rovetti, C Rovetti, G Gentile, G Lombardozzi, N Benvenuti, P Carboni, Selmi Lionello, Un amico, ciascuno 0,50; G Strazzi, A Menghi, F Dondero, L Campo, T Bertolucci, D Robinson, D Levinson, R. Sommariva; A Diamantini, B Turani, M Dondero, A Coduri, A Benvenuti, G Querino, Un americano, Un amico, ciascuno 0,25; A Bertolucci 0,20, M Valieri, G Ramasco, ciascuno 0,30; Vendita Sigari 1,25; A Ricci 0,34; G Porro, G Turani, M Campo, ciascuno, 0,10; U Campo 0,40; Avanzo della festa 3,61. Totale $15,20. — Conformemente al desiderio dei sottoscrittori, abbiamo rimesso la metà di questo importo, cioè $ 7,60 all'*Aurora*.

RESOCONTO DI CASSA

Deficit No. 126	58,92
Tipografo, No. 127	15,00
Tiratura No. 127	8,00
Redazione ed Amministrazione	6,00
Spedizione e corrispondenza	5,90
Diverse	2,14
Totale	$ 95,96
Entrata num. 1 [nuova serie]	52,66
Deficit	43,30

Visto il nuovo indirizzo chè sarà dato al giornale, è necessario che i compagni ci tengano al corrente del movimento operaio nelle varie località, nonchè di tutti i fatti che possono servire alla propaganda.

Opuscoli in vendita presso La Questione Sociale

A. HAMON. **Gli Uomini e le Teorie dell'Anarchia.** Soldi 5.

E. RECLUS. **A mio Fratello Contadino.** 5 cent.

Canti anarchici rivoluzionari soldi 5.

John MOST. **La Peste Religiosa** 5 cent.

P. GORI. **Proximus Tuus.** Soldi 25.

P. GORI. **Primo Maggio.** 25 cents.

C. CAFIERO. **Anarchia e Comunismo.** 5 cents.

Almanacco Illustrato 25 cents.

D. ZAVATTERO. **Che cosa e' l'Anarchia?** — S. FAURE. **Io accuso** 5 cents.

DOTTOR EZIO RUBINI. **Primo Maggio** [frammento] 5 cents.

P. KROPOTKIN. **La Conquista del Pane.** Un volume di 250 pagine 0,75

E. MALATESTA **Fra Contadini** 5 cent.

P. KROPOTKINE. **Al Giovani** — A. M. M. **Alle Fanciulle.** I due opuscoli riuniti in un volumetto di 80 pagine 5 cents.

E. SILVIERI. **Giorgio e Silvio** [Dialogo tra due militari] 5 cents.

RITRATTO DI MICHELE ANGIOLILLO 10 cent.

A scanso di equivoci, teniamo solo disponibili quelli pubblicati.

Le richieste non accompagnate dal relativo importo non saranno considerate.

Tipografia della QUESTIONE SOCIALE.

Setting the Record Straight [Concerning the Declarations of the "Dissidents"][49]

Translated from "Cose a posto [Intorno alle dichiarazioni dei 'dissidenti']," *La Questione Sociale* (Paterson, New Jersey) 5, new series, no. 1 (September 9, 1899)

As readers of LA QUESTIONE SOCIALE are aware, ideological differences between those who until recently edited the newspaper and the group that manages and is responsible for it had reached such an impasse that a parting of the ways was deemed necessary.[50]

The group decided to begin a new series with editors who were in perfect agreement with it; and the old editorial staff stated that they would make a new newspaper.

It was agreed in the meanwhile to create one issue divided between the old and new editorial staff, so that both camps might, independently of one another, set out the reasons for the parting of the ways and the principles that would guide their respective newspapers.

This was done in last week's issue.[51] But imagine our surprise upon seeing in the "declarations of the dissidents," which is to say the part written by the former editors, that the differences over which we primarily parted company, for the most part do not exist and there remain only, or almost only, issues about ways of expressing oneself, which we reject because we find them incorrect and ambiguous, but do not reveal any real disagreement.

We will not insist that the "dissidents" are now expressing ideas that are a far cry from those which (although not without contradictions) they claimed in the newspaper and which caused the separation; since this can be judged by anyone who has recently read LA QUESTIONE SOCIALE. And we would not even talk about it, having every reason to be pleased that the arguments that led up to the rift have not been without repercussions.

However we do not want others, seeing the "dissidents," as they are in opposition to us, express ideas that we have always asserted and championed, to be misled about our ideas; nor do we want certain word games to mislead anyone not used to uncovering the meaning hidden

---

49   The words inside square brackets are part of the original title.
50   With this article begins the debate between Errico Malatesta and Giuseppe Ciancabilla that they would conduct through their respective newspapers, *La Questione Sociale* and *L'Aurora*. It would later erupt into a bitter personal diatribe.
51   See note 32.

beneath obscure phrases; and therefore we believe it necessary to make the following remarks.

The "dissidents" say they belie a movement that is different from ours, and, if we are to judge them by what they are now saying, this would not appear to be true.

They say that "faced with the ignorant, unconscious masses our activity as anarchists can only be to shape anarchist consciousness." And who has ever said or done otherwise?

Is it not obvious that, so that anarchists can band together or organize, it is first and foremost necessary that there are anarchists?

Whenever we come across virgin persons or groups, or opponents of our ideas, do we not start by propagandizing to them, which is to say by trying to shape anarchist consciousness?

Only it would appear that our opponents forget that consciousness, conviction is not a fixed and absolute quantity; they forget that there may be infinite degrees of consciousness and conviction, and that with continuous contact with comrades and through shared work convictions broaden and grow stronger. And they also forget that the organization furnishes the means of propaganda that isolated individuals cannot have available.

But isolation is not what we want! our opponents object. "Whenever,"—they say—"individuals become anarchists and break loose from the unconscious masses, venturing into the fight against the whole of the bourgeois system, by necessity of intuition and practicality they will stretch out their hands on every side in a fraternal chain, from anarchist to anarchist, from comrade to comrade, from group to group, and will unite their efforts in order to defeat the common enemy."

Why, do we not say that, too? Why then do they differ from us? If it is only a question of calling what we call organization a *fraternal chain*, it's really not worth the trouble of making so much noise!

"This has always been done, this is what we do, and what we will always do, without there being any need for organizers to preach that it must arise from organization." No, no; we are not saying that this fraternal chain *must arise* from organization, but we say that it *is* organization. And as regards this always having been done, if our opponents were more familiar with the history of the anarchist movement, they would know that this is only done in times of activity, which unfortunately have not been a regular feature of the movement, precisely because often and at various places the *everyone for themselves* approach has prevailed.

And if it is a good thing that this chain, this organization of forces takes place, then how can it ever be a bad thing to preach it?

But if you preach it, they say, you're going to have "fake, illusory organizations made on purpose"… that is to say they would rather let things happen, naturally, *on a wing and a prayer,* as the saying goes. Whereas we believe that man's greatest gift is his will, and that things that are truly human in character are precisely those that are made on purpose; we believe that *letting nature have her way* necessarily leads to the exploitation of the disorganized masses with no will, to tyranny by a few, who *willingly* organize themselves in order to dominate; and that, in order to bring about an organization that can benefit everyone, people need to *will it* into existence, and to do this they must deploy all of the *skills* that they have gained through observation and experience.

Since humanity started mastering the environment and changing it to suit its own interests, all progress has been a triumph of the will. This is the crux of the matter: that in societies organized along authoritarian lines, in societies most affected by the brute nature from which they have emerged, the will of the few matters; in the societies such that we dream of, which is to say in anarchist societies, everyone's will must matter.

And we indeed want, today for the purposes of propaganda and struggle, tomorrow in order to meet all of the needs of social life, organizations built upon the will and in the interest of all their members.

Our opponents do not believe it is possible to have a party organization without authoritarianism, imposed leaders, suppressed initiatives, etc. If this is not possible in an organization of anarchists, which is to say people who are particularly committed to fight against authoritarianism, how could it ever be possible in a broader society in which immediate benefits are more important than questions of principle? And if there can be no harmonious society (here they agree) other than one "made up of organically functioning associations and collectives, delivering various social services in an orderly fashion," then how can those who believe that an organization without authority is impossible be anarchists?

Our opponents do not even believe that a party organization is a power, "much how army ranks are not real powers, conscious powers, moral powers." Relying on the authority of Max Nordau, they say that "a thousand lambs united in the thought of solidarity can never resist one lion." Forget about Max Nordau, who has uttered many other paradoxes, and let us reason a bit using common sense accessible to all.

An army is not a conscious power with respect to the soldiers who are forced into it, but it very well is one for those who organize and control it; and as for it not being a real power... forsooth! if only it really wasn't. The army, organized by the rulers to defend their interests and keep the people in check, needs authority, and blind obedience; and with all this it is a real power in the hands of those who have organized it. An anarchist organization, based upon the free and conscious will of anarchists, is necessarily refractory to any authority, and constitutes an effective force in the battle against the oppressors.

A thousand lambs united will not be able to resist a lion, because they do not possess, and cannot be given, the "thought of solidarity." But are workers that stupid, that incapable of advancement? And anarchists as well?

If individuals are weak, can a union not provide them with the strength to accomplish that which they are powerless to achieve on their own?! Do we even need to respond to such paradoxes? Does the general, ongoing experience of humanity perhaps not teach us the opposite?

Our opponents say that our organization is not free, even though no one is forced to join it and, once inside, everyone remains at liberty to withdraw from it; and as evidence they mention the organizations of the democratic socialists which afford their members the same conditions of liberty for entry and exit, and yet are authoritarian.

The truth is that the organizations of the democratic socialists are authoritarian because their program is authoritarian. As regards organization itself, no matter how infected it is by authoritarian methods, it still acts as a restraint rather than an incentive to authoritarianism. Indeed, is anyone going to argue that the leading lights of the socialist party would wield less authority over their socialist comrades, if their comrades were unorganized?

The same is true with us. The organization of all is the remedy against domination by a few. In practice, disorganization results in uncontrolled, unaccountable dictatorship, by those of us who can produce a newspaper, deliver lectures, or in some other way hoard the strength of all for the benefit of their own leanings.

*
**

Behind all of this hides a misunderstanding.

Thanks to the authoritarian education that everybody receives in today's society, our opponents are unable to imagine an organization without immediately thinking about a whole hierarchy of bosses and deputy bosses, governing centers, legislative councils, bureaucratic systems, etc.

We on the other hand suggest that those who want the same thing and intend to bring it about using the same methods, should unite, not for the purpose of giving up their will and their initiative, but in order to educate and help each other in the common work, to coordinate into a common cause various initiatives which, in isolation, might be reciprocally neutralized; and to find in the union the means without which the right to free initiative is a simple irony.

We accept, and always have accepted, the principle of autonomy of individuals within groups, and of groups within federations: but we want the common program to be the bond, the only required bond. It is against this idea of a program that our opponents rebel.

But is their rebellion serious?

Forget about their less than witty dig about a "program dictated by one individual." While it seems to us impossible, if there was an individual, blessed with sufficient genius to dictate unaided a new program that wins us over and befits us, we would not deny ourselves its benefits because the initiative had originated from a single individual... and it is odd that we are pushed into saying this by those who are forever talking about individual initiative! The fact is that the anarchist socialist program is the fruit of collective development which, even ignoring its forerunners, lasted several decades, and which no one individual could claim to have authored.

But the issue is this: do our opponents accept or reject the system of ideas that constitute anarchist socialism?

We understand that they want the program to have the maximum breadth, the maximum elasticity possible; but ultimately, even they must acknowledge boundaries, beyond which one cannot go without losing one's right to call oneself an anarchist. Otherwise, in addition to the *we are all socialists* claimed by many reactionaries, one of these days we are going to have to add that *we are all anarchists* from similar reactionaries.

Our opponents seek "the abolition of private property and the socialization of the means of production and exchange"; they want "the de facto abolition of any and every form of State, government, law, authority"; we know that they reject electoral and parliamentary methods and embrace revolutionary methods... so how the hell do they come to us claiming that they have no program! They can more or less diverge from our program, and are within their rights to do so; but claiming that they have no program merely means playing with words.

As they are indeed creating a logomachy (war of words) over the meaning of the word party. *"Party"*—they say—"to us, means clique." They are at liberty to change the meaning of words; but then there is no way of understanding each other.

Party truly has a broader meaning than *organization*. Party means the whole of all those who fight for a given purpose; while a given organization is joined by those who, sharing the same purpose, wish to unite their own forces to struggle in consensus; and therefore within a single party there may be, and there are ordinarily, various organizations.

Our opponents can say whatever they like about not belonging to any party: but as long as they wish for the abolition of any form of government, people will still say they belong to the anarchist party.

Wars against the dictionary are hard to win.

*
**

With the preceding remarks we are far from believing that the issue of organization has been exhausted, and we will surely return to it again.

We simply hope our opponents will set aside debates over the meaning of words, as much as possible, and discuss with us the points on which they actually disagree with our program.

Eight Hours of Work

Translated from "Otto ore di lavoro," *La Questione Sociale*
(Paterson, New Jersey) 5, new series, no. 1 (September 9, 1899)

A comrade from a town in France writes:

"I suggested to several workmates that they subscribe to the paper and everyone gave me the same answer: I don't have time to read.

"And it is a disheartening answer because it is true. Indeed, we work from 6 in the morning until 6.30 in the evening, and many of us have to walk an hour in the morning and an hour in the evening between home and the workshop and vice versa. If someone has a few small chores to do, that leaves just six hours of rest. And what rest! Getting up in the morning we are more tired than we were when we went to bed. Where can we get the time and strength to read, study and reflect upon social problems?

"From this perspective I would perhaps support the eight-hour law; since, economically speaking, it does not improve the conditions of workers, it would at least leave them time to study and delve into the social question. Our rulers understand this, as we do, which is why they are careful not to vote for it, limiting themselves at best to putting on smoke and mirrors for voters."

Allow us to make a few remarks.

We believe that there is no question that working 8 hours for a master is better than working 10, or 12, or 14, or 16 hours. Of course it would not be liberation. Besides the fact that the worker would still continue to be exploited, and remain nothing but a tool in the production mechanism in the hands of the masters, who use the worker as they please for their own profit, the worker would remain vulnerable to wage cuts, lack of work and all the troubles resulting from the battle which, in modern society, every man is forced to fight against everyone else. But, that being so, it is no less true that there are degrees of suffering; and that between a worker, who working 16 hours a day has no time, neither to study nor to wash himself and kiss his children, and one who works 8 hours, there is a real and large difference not only in conditions, but also in opportunity to understand what causes the suffering that afflicts him and to work towards his emancipation.

Does it follow that we should add the 8 hours of work to our program?

No. We are convinced—and all the facts confirm our conviction—that the bourgeoisie will make no concession unless compelled to do so by force, or fear of force, and therefore, since it is necessary to become stronger to squeeze out a little, it would be foolish to not use one's own strength to get everything. After all, when one comes to understand the fundamental injustice of the present organization of society and the remedy which alone can bring well-being, freedom, and peace among men, it is difficult to get excited about reforms that fall short of resolving the problem. We must, therefore, always and everywhere, preach the necessity of a radical transformation of society, and every man's right to complete emancipation from any economic and political oppression.

Yet our program is one thing, but the state of consciousness attained by those masses, without whose involvement our ideals can not be achieved, is quite another.

Today it happens that most workers who rebel against their slave conditions and start to fight back against their masters do not yet understand the justice and feasibility of our program, and limit themselves to asking for some more or less important improvement.

So we must always fly our flag fully unfurled before their eyes, we must always push them to demand greater things; but meanwhile we must encourage and assist them in the battles they want to fight, provided that they are in the right direction, which is to say, that they tend to facilitate future gains and are fought in such a way that workers become used to thinking of their masters and governments as enemies, and to desiring to achieve what they want by themselves.

Many workers wish to not work over 8 hours. Nothing could be more justifiable.

The reform is among those that tend to actually improve the status of workers and facilitate future gains; and we, when we cannot convince them to demand more, we must support them in such a modest claim. But, in supporting them, we must show them the way by which a worker can and must get what he wants, and combat the harmful tendency of waiting for improvements through government action; since *8 hours of work* is one thing, and the 8 hour *law* is quite another.

The comrade, whose letter we quoted, does not seem to have clearly perceived the difference.

Asking the legislative authorities for a law, that requires people to not work and not make others work more than 8 hours, is useless and harmful.

It is useless since the government never concedes anything unless it is convinced that, if something is not conceded, the people will take it for themselves; and when, in order to throw dust in people's eyes or for other special situations, the government makes some law favorable to the people before the people want it and have the strength to demand it, the law is not enforced or it is enforced in such a way as to produce an effect different from the one it appeared to target, and hurts rather than helps workers.

It is harmful, since the workers, waiting for the government to deliver the reform they desire, stop fighting for it directly; and thus either they fail to achieve it, or they achieve it only much later when they are not prepared to force its implementation.

Look at what happened in Colorado. About three months ago the 8-hour law passed by that state's legislature came into force. The masters stated they would comply with the law's requirements, but that they would decrease wages in proportion to the decreased work hours. As a result, the smelters in Denver, Pueblo, Leadville, etc. called a strike.

At first it seemed as if the strike would succeed, as it was spreading to the mines and other industries, and hopes rose of a general strike that would force the capitalists to give in; but the movement came to a halt and the victory remained with the masters.

After two months of struggle the smelters went back to work accepting everything imposed by the companies: and it is not unlikely that, unable to survive with reduced wages, one of these days the workers may call for the law to be repealed or themselves help the masters circumvent it.

It is clear: if eight hours had been won directly by the workers, they would have found themselves strong enough to block wage reductions. Granted by the government, it serves no purpose, or does harm, since the capitalists can always, one way or another, do as they please.[52]

And there is more. The economic and moral conditions of workers are very different from one place to another, from one trade to another. When workers fight directly they can get reforms as they reach the moral and material strength required to impose them. Conversely putting one's faith in the law, given that the law cannot provide for every specific case and must apply to an entire state, or at least an entire trade, the more underdeveloped elements hinder the progress of the rest and are used by the government as justification and power to not concede anything. This is what is happening in England for the 8-hours law in favor of miners, where the fact that a fraction of miners oppose the law is used as an excuse to not pass it.

---

52   Besides meeting opposition from industrialists, the law also ran into difficulty at the institutional level. It was repeatedly found unconstitutional by the Colorado Supreme Court, as it violated the right of workers to sell their own labor as they saw fit. In later years, the eight hours of work would be at the heart of further strikes in Colorado mines, culminating in the Colorado Labor Wars of 1903–1904, during which anti-worker violence would reach some of the highest levels in the history of the United States.

Therefore, when it's not possible to do better, go for the eight hours; but let this be imposed upon capitalists through the direct action of the workers, and not *conceded* by the government.

Beware of Danaans bearing gifts![53]

Discussion
(A Reply to the "Dissidents")

Translated from "Discutendo (Replica ai 'dissidenti')," *La Questione Sociale* (Paterson, New Jersey) 5, new series, no. 2 (September 16, 1899)

Today, Wednesday, we receive the first issue of the newspaper *L'Aurora* which is dated Saturday September 16, and we find inside a "reply" dedicated to us.[54]

The tone of the response in question is rather bitter. We will not imitate our sister publication, because that would only end in harsh words, and we intend instead to reason with the purpose of learning something useful from what our opponents say and supporting that which, nevertheless, we believe to be the truth. We shall only point out that we had spoken of "issues about *ways of expressing oneself*, which we find incorrect and ambiguous" whereas *L'Aurora* says that we have accused them of "incorrect and ambiguous methods." The difference is plain for all to see; and if our opponents misread us so badly, so as to confuse an insult with an opinion, which is a matter for the dictionary to resolve, they must truly be in a troubled state of mind.

And now we come to the discussion.

First of all a few factual issues:

L'Aurora denies that the ideas expressed in the "Declarations of the Dissidents" are different from those previously upheld by the dissidents themselves. Filling the paper with quotations seems useless to us. Our readers, who are the same readers of *L'Aurora*, are familiar with the writings to which we refer and may judge for themselves whether there really is a marked difference between the current of opinion recently expressed by LA QUESTIONE SOCIALE and that now expressed by the "dissidents" and their organ *L'Aurora*. For that matter, all we can do is celebrate an evolution that brings them closer to us.

---

53   These words, now proverbial, come from Virgil (*The Aeneid*, II, 49), who had them spoken by Laocoön to dissuade the Trojans from welcoming the wooden horse left by the Greeks (identified as the "Danaans") into their city.

54   The response was to the article "Setting the Record Straight [Concerning the declarations of the 'Dissidents']," p. 61. *L'Aurora* replied with "Setting the Record Straight (A Response to '*La Questione Sociale*')."

L'Aurora talks about "arguments and behavior that have been able to expose the truly anti-libertarian and authoritarian aspect of the incipient organization." To say this, in Paterson, where all the comrades have first-hand knowledge of the facts, requires genuine courage: courage that will not help hide the truth. We want to do everything possible to avoid issues of a personal nature and so we will not fire back accusations at our opponents. We simply ask them to clarify the facts: it will then become clear that they are leveling charges of anti-libertarianism and authoritarianism against those who did not wish to submit to their authority.

L'Aurora suggests that Malatesta's influence has caused an ideological change among the Paterson comrades. This would not be upsetting to Malatesta, since if he makes propaganda it is precisely in hopes of persuading people; and it should not offend anyone, since those who read and listen and discuss do so in order to broaden their own minds, and, if they become convinced that they were wrong they should think themselves fortunate to have had the opportunity to realize as much.

However the circumstances are different. The comrades from the *Diritto all'Esistenza* group have always held the ideas that La Questione Sociale now supports and had already supported before this most recent period. Recently for reasons better not rehashed, the newspaper came under the control of an editor who was later known to have different opinions from those of the group. The comrades, lacking someone who was able to write, found themselves at a crossroads: either let the paper die, or put up with an editorial team they did not agree with. They preferred the latter course, as a temporary stopgap useful solely to save the life of the paper, and they devoted themselves to finding a way out of such a distorted situation.

The editors of *L'Aurora* are aware of all the conflicts caused by the difference between the ideas of those who used to edit the paper and the ideas held by the group, and we are amazed to see they recall the facts so poorly, and attribute a value to Malatesta he doesn't deserve. Moreover the very fact that Malatesta came to America is proof of what we are saying.

Since Malatesta's ideas are well known, why would the comrades have invited him to come and provided him with the means to do so, unless they shared the same ideas and the desire to see them spread and championed?

But let us discuss ideas, and avoid personal issues.

Two issues are currently under discussion: the organization of the laboring masses and the organization of the anarchists. Since these are issues that will be addressed in their full complexity in the newspaper, we shall limit ourselves in this debate to that which can prevent misrepresentation of our thinking and slander (doubtlessly unintended) of our intentions.

L'Aurora credits Malatesta and us with the idea of seeking first to organize the unconscious masses and then expecting this organization to miraculously develop an anarchist consciousness.

That is not precisely what we are saying. If an unconscious mass did exist, it would not be a human mass and it would be unorganizable. What we say is that society and individual consciousness are tied together by the sort of relationships existing between the chicken and the egg. Which came first, the chicken or the egg?

At the first glimmer of consciousness—which we might almost call physiological—formed (we do not know how, nor does it matter for our argument) during the presocial battle for survival, the first social embryos originated; and then by means of reciprocal action of the social aggregate on the individual and vice versa, society and individual consciousness developed simultaneously. And only within society (and society means organization), only by means of society was man able to arrive at a genuinely human consciousness; just as it was, through society, through the multiple relationships with those who share similar hopes and a struggle for shared interests and ideals, one can arrive at that higher stage of consciousness which we call anarchist consciousness.

How do our opponents think consciousness develops if they think that it can take shape away from the practice of life, simply hearing certain theories be spoken?

What we desire is that every individual, whatever their ambitions, whatever level of consciousness they have reached, band together, organize with those who share common interests and goals, and thus find in union the means to defend and pursue those interests and aspirations, and an opportunity to grow and develop.

But, our opponents say, "an unconscious, unorganized mass, in order to be organized necessarily presupposes an organizer, who will exercise over it a more or less likable, but still authoritarian influence."

And for an unconscious individual to attain consciousness, for somebody not familiar with our ideas to learn them, does that not therefore require somebody to conduct propaganda work, and thus consequently wield influence over them?

If there is a danger of authority, it is greater in the second case, when the target of the propaganda owes all his ideas to a propagandist, rather than the first case, when the individual lives in an ongoing exchange of ideas with a community and thus forms an increasingly enlightened consciousness without becoming indebted to any particular individual.

But is this fear of the influence that one individual may wield over others justified and reasonable? Is not perhaps the influence that men wield over one another, rather, the source, and the necessary condition of society and progress? When we speak and write are we not perhaps seeking to exercise our own influence? Isn't our battle with the other parties a battle for influence, an ongoing effort to combat influences that we see as harmful and to make the ones we regard as good succeed?

When we fight against authority we certainly do not intend to abolish the moral action that men exert over one another: that would be impossible, and even if it were possible it would mean returning men to an animal state. The authority that we want to destroy is imposition, not persuasion.

*
**

And we come to the organization of anarchists.

As *L'Aurora* correctly says, within the anarchist party or movement, we form a special organization, a special party, if you prefer to call it that, made up of those who not only think the same way and share the same goals, but who also believe in the usefulness of banding together and working in unity.

Will our organization be "the anarchist party"? That depends on what others will be and will do. If those anarchists, who do not embrace our methods or for some reason do not want to unite with us, fail to make the public aware of their existence—either for lack of numbers or for lack of organization—the public will say that we are the anarchist party; if the opposite should come to pass we will only be and appear as a given element of the party, a given current of the anarchist movement.

Are we saying that outside of our party, outside of our program there is no liberation?

Who ever imagined such a thing? We merely spell out the methods that we deem best and follow them. If others indicate and practice different methods, we will accept or reject those, depending on whether or not we deem them good. Results will later validate or invalidate our opinions.

L'Aurora accepts the part of our program that concerns our goals; but it rejects our tactics, or rather it does not want anarchists to declare their methods of struggle, so as to be able to recognize and unite with those adopting the same methods.

L'Aurora is entirely free to open its arms to all and get along, if it can, with all who call themselves anarchists.

As for us, while we would like everyone to spell out their currents of opinion and put their ideas to the test, we believe that the confusion would be very damaging to both the development of ideas and the action these ideas must exert in life. Everybody is free—but united only when they agree with each other and then only on those issues upon which they agree.

How could we, for example, join and not fight against those anarchists—and there could be some—who accept parliamentary tactics?

How could we present ourselves as comrades in a workers' association with those anarchists who instead of getting involved to fight alongside the workers and attempt to broaden the fight and steer it in the direction of total abolition of capitalism and government, get involved with the purpose of hurting the association and think they are doing the right thing by breaking strikes and going to the extreme length—and this has happened—of being paid by the masters in order to preach that workers' resistance is a useless and damaging activity?

When the revolution arrives, in Italy for example, there may be anarchists who, for fear of a return to the monarchy, believe it would be expedient to help the republic consolidate itself. Could we agree with them, we who believe that if the republic does consolidate itself it will be the same as the monarchy?

In short, it may be the case that we are wrong, and that those who embrace methods others than ours are right. But it is clearly impossible that everyone is correct.

Saying that all means are valid is among the greatest mistakes ever spoken.

*
**

And now let us look at why our organization would be authoritarian.

L'Aurora alleges that we admitted that organization in and of itself is infected by authoritarian methods. Our opponents should reread what we wrote and they will see that we were talking about the organization of the democratic socialists and not our own. What the hell!

We said that organization is a guarantee against the dominance of individuals, and that even among the democratic socialist organization, despite the authoritarian practices by which it is infected, serves more as a restraint than an aid to authoritarianism. Indeed, when in Italy the chapters of the International were broken up largely because of the work of Costa, who found those chapters a hindrance to his doing as he pleased, he wielded an authority, a dictatorship over his disorganized comrades that was certainly greater than that now exercised by all the socialist deputies taken together.

But let us talk about our own organization.

Our organization, we argue, is absolutely not authoritarian, because nobody has the right to impose their will on anyone else, and nobody is forced to follow decisions that they have not accepted.

We have a shared program, and this represents not a requirement imposed upon others, but what each of us believes, the very purpose why we have banded together.

We published our program, they object, without first discussing it with every comrade in the United States. If material difficulties did not prevent us from doing so, we would gladly discuss it with comrades even all over the world; but that is not a necessity. Ours is not a new program, and for a long time has been the belief of part (we are not about to argue whether we are a few or nearly all) of the anarchists. We are republishing it, and think we are interpreting the wishes of the immense majority of Italian comrades living in this country. Moreover nobody is under any obligation to accept it; everyone however will think that it is fair that we make propaganda—exercising our influence—in favor of the views in which we believe.

But we, they continue to object, we delegate roles. And is it possible, we respond, to live without doing so? And what would be the utility of the association without division of labor and delegation of roles? If our opponents have money that belongs to the group would they not have a treasurer? Don't they have somebody in charge of editing their newspaper? If they have a letter to write, are they not going to commission one person to write it?

But we accept the will of the majority in group resolutions!

Let us be clear. For us the majority has no rights over the minority; but that does not impede, when we are not all unanimous and this concerns opinions over which nobody wishes to sacrifice the existence of the group, we voluntarily, by tacit agreement, let the majority decide.

For example take the selection of a meeting date: would it make sense to disband the group because the same date does not suit everyone? Or does the majority need to defer to the minority?

Our opponents speak willingly about anarchist education. They have never considered that not only must an anarchist learn to do as they desire, but also to do so in a way that does no harm to others; they must seek the full expression of their own personality, but must also have that spirit of flexibility, without which any difference of opinion would create an unresolvable conflict, making a society without authority impossible.

To conclude. Our opponents do not accept our ideas: indeed they fight against us. But they do not say they find *all* tactics acceptable, since they start with rejecting ours.

The Twentieth of September Celebration

Translated from "La festa del XX settembre," *La Questione Sociale* (Paterson, New Jersey) 5, new series, no. 2 (September 16, 1899)

Despite the propaganda made by socialists and anarchists against these spectacles that dishonor and ridicule the Italians in this country, this year there will once again be some who, to celebrate the Twentieth of September, will shamelessly show themselves off wearing the uniform of Italian soldiers.[55]

But this does not mean that our propaganda has had no impact: many have understood what a foolish and undignified thing they are doing; and if out of old habit and to avoid separating from their friends they still do it, they do so reluctantly and try not to be seen. Some go along with it, they have said so themselves, because they have already bought the uniform and do not want to have spent money for nothing, like the miser who, having bought himself a laxative, and no longer having any need of it, drinks it anyway... to let nothing go to waste! At a public gathering—and not one of his friends contradicted him—one of them told us that they had no intention of paying any sort of tribute to the government of Italy and that they dressed up as officers of the Italian army the same way as they might dress up as clowns!

Let us hope that this is the last time we see such masks.

Indeed, what is this holiday all about?

Celebrating the Twentieth of September is understood as an opportunity to declare one's opposition to the government of priests... provided you do not forget that the Italian government entered Rome by force, spurred on by the threat of revolution; that it left the priests as much strength and power as it could, which the priests needed; and that through its policies it managed to make people long for the Pope's government.

But why then dress up as the King's soldiers?

Those who make great show of putting on a uniform, which still drips with the blood of Italy's proletarians, have been forced to flee from Italy by poverty that the government helps to generate; for the most part they come from towns where soldiers have used rifles against peasants calling for a decrease in taxes; many of them are deserters or draft-dodgers; none of them would go to Italy if the King were to call upon them to defend his cause; in reality none of them are friends of

---

55   September 20, 1870 was the date of the breach of Porta Pia and the consequent annexation of Rome and what was left of the Papal States to the Kingdom of Italy. Malatesta had also referred to this holiday in his lectures (See "Malatesta Lectures," p. 78). On the occasion of this anniversary anarchists and socialists held a joint demonstration at the Proletario Hall in Paterson, at which Malatesta and Esteve spoke on behalf of the former and Rondani and Cianfarra on behalf of the latter. Brief reports of the demonstration appeared in *La Questione Sociale* and *Il Progresso Italo-Americano* of September 23 and in *Il Proletario* of September 30. This last newspaper, in its September 23 issue, also referred to a similar lecture given by Malatesta and Rondani in Newark (New Jersey).

the government... then why this apparent reverence for the government that they flee and hate?

We believe the reason is the following. These Italians feel unloved, left out by workers in other countries, and think they gain importance and respect by commemorating the military might of their country of origin.[56] In reality they succeed only in turning themselves into a spectacle... and reminding any who might have forgotten about the beatings the Italian army has suffered every time it has entered the field against armed soldiers rather than defenseless workers.

May our fellow countrymen reflect upon the reasons why they are generally looked down upon, and may them realize that it is because they show so little solidarity with other workers and readily accept lower wages.

May they unite with workers of every nationality, may they show solidarity with them in the fight against the masters, and they will get the sympathy and respect, to which they are entitled as men and as workers.

Regarding Anarchists Who Vote

Translated from "A proposito degli anarchici che votano," *La Questione Sociale* (Paterson, New Jersey) 5, new series, no. 2 (September 16, 1899)

Here and there around Italy, in recent times, there have been comrades who have gone to vote.

The democratic socialists eagerly rejoice at this embrace of their tactics, and as is their habit of pronouncing us dead and buried every time persecution prevents us from conducting major public activity, cite this fact as evidence that the abstentionists are performing an act of contrition and joining the electoral flock.

Moreover, many of our comrades, naturally guided by contrary reasons, credit the matter with excessive importance, and deplore it as a betrayal of our entire program.

We loudly criticize the act; but we are not very upset by it, because we know from long experience that, generally speaking, this is a matter of passing weakness, prompted more than anything else by a great desire

---

56   Similar ideas had been aired in the Paterson lecture against the Twentieth of September. *La Questione Sociale* mentions that "all agreed to stigmatize the patriotic racket kicked up by the Italian jingoistic bourgeoisie and assisted by the thoughtlessness of that part of the Italian population that naively—unfortunately all too naively—thinks it can command the respect of Americans by flaunting the liberticidal uniforms of the Italian soldier."

to do something and the inability to discover, in today's difficult circumstances, another more effective way that is more consistent with our aim, ·to fight against the government. We know that these comrades, although they have fallen into contradictions by going to vote and thus appear to support parliamentarianism, remain at heart what they have always been and soon, once the intoxication of the moment has passed, will return to their old selves and fight the good fight alongside us.

What is happening today is not a new phenomenon. Unfortunately, in every period of the movement, there have been anarchists who, though broadly acknowledging the contradiction between our aims and the parliamentary approach, in practice have then gone out and voted; either on account of sympathy for personal friends, or because they have been dragged into the machinery of local campaigns, or for fear that their abstention would benefit the government-endorsed candidate and thus they would find themselves exposed to criticism and suspicions, or perhaps for worse reasons.

But what does this prove besides the fact that anarchists are also subject to all kinds of human weaknesses?

Since when have individual inconsistencies been proof that a party is wrong in remaining loyal to its program?

Even worse things happen in times of great persecution. The government blocks ordinary means of propaganda and agitation from us and many anarchists, having no other means of action suited to the circumstances, lacking anything better, say that they oppose the government by going out to vote—only to revert to previous methods once the situation becomes normal again. Then there are protest elections, and in that case the noblest sentiments of generosity, solidarity with the persecuted, hatred of persecution, not guided by a sufficiently clear concept of the duties our ideal requires from us, drive many toward the ballot box who, in different circumstances, would be proud opponents of anything suggestive of parliamentarianism.

So there is no reason for the parliamentary socialists to open their hearts to the hope of seeing us all convert, as we have no reason to fear the destruction of our party.

This is not to say that our comrades should not actively combat this kind of weaknesses and look for ways to prevent it.

Parliamentarianism is the big danger of tomorrow, and we must do what we can to prevent the fallacy from taking root that a *good parliament* might be possible, which would be just as harmful as the theory that there might be such a thing as a *good king*.

It will be the parliament elected by the people that will strangle the next revolution in its swaddling clothes. We will be the ones who, by opposing the parliament and seeking to obstruct appointments, will ensure that the revolution really is a serious undertaking that leads to the emancipation of workers.

We will revisit this important topic in detail.

Malatesta Lectures

Translated from "Conferenze Malatesta," *La Questione Sociale* (Paterson, New Jersey) 5, new series, no. 2 (September 16, 1899)

Many comrades ask us to publish reports of Malatesta's lectures.

We are sorry we cannot accommodate them, but the undertaking is impossible.

If we were to provide a short summary, it would serve no purpose; and if we were to attempt in-depth reports, there would not be enough space.

Our comrade does not waste his time; so far he has delivered a series of lectures on the following topics:

The anarchists' response to the current situation in Europe;
Parliamentarianism;
The Twentieth of September Celebration;
Anarchists and what they want;
The Social Question;
The Family;
Anarchists and Workers' Unions;

In Passaic, a lecture on the subject "The Needs of the working class" was unable to proceed as Malatesta was unavailable, and his place was taken by comrade Esteve.

All of these lectures left a deep impression on the minds of those present.

Malatesta will be giving the following lectures soon:

Friday, September 15 in Newark
Saturday, September 16 in Orange Valley
Sunday, September 17 in West Hoboken[57]
Monday September 18 in Brooklyn

On September 23 comrade Malatesta will begin his propaganda tour in

---

57   West Hoboken, in New Jersey, corresponds to today's Union City.

the United States and will leave directly for Barre, and later will return by way of Boston, to New York.

From September 22 onwards, comrades living in the intermediate areas of West Quincy, Providence, New Haven, New London, Bridgeport, Danbury, and others along the route are asked to write to the following address: Errico Malatesta, 47 Granite Street, Barre, Vt.

Anarchist-Socialist Federation

Translated from "Federazione Socialista-Anarchica," *La Questione Sociale* (Paterson, New Jersey) 5, new series, no. 3 (September 23, 1899)

The opponents of organization have a habit of reproaching us for the fact that after all the time we have been talking about organization of anarchists, we have never managed to build the wide-ranging, enduring, and continually developing organization we desire.

As an argument against organization this means nothing. We have not yet managed to organize ourselves as we would like, just as we have not thus far managed to make the revolution, without this proving that we are wrong to want to get organized and make the revolution. The organization of us anarchists, and the anarchist organization of the masses, which would be free from authoritarianism, is not something that can be achieved in a day or in a year: it is the ongoing purpose of our work, and when we succeed it can be said that we have won. Not having won thus far is not enough to persuade us that we should stop fighting to win! Besides, what matters more than an effective, consistent organization, the likes of which faces tremendous difficulties given today's conditions—scarcity of resources, continual changes in residency, often a lack within groups of those skilled and able to sustain sufficiently active correspondence, and above all government persecution, which makes writing and keeping addresses dangerous and which, by regularly breaking up our groups and conducting mass arrests, periodically undoes the work already performed—what matters more, again, is the spirit of organization, that is the belief in the usefulness and necessity of seeking the cooperation of others in all things, and the readiness to join other comrades and work together, as soon as the opportunity arises.

When this spirit exists, an organization can be broken up a thousand times, due to internal difficulties or external violence; but the work performed during the time of its existence is never lost, and soon it can resume stronger than before.

This however does not justify the inactivity of so many comrades, who favor organization but remain isolated or almost isolated, and do

Source: Archivio Centrale dello Stato, Rome

not engage in any form of ongoing methodical activity in coordination with others. They lack the spirit of organization that we just mentioned; they lack the depth of conviction that brings about the will, the urge to act upon one's own ideas, and they lack the practice that preserves and develops one's faculties.

Therefore there is a need to deepen our convictions through study and reflection, and to act in accordance with these convictions.

The situation here in the United States, though bad, is exceptionally favorable for us as compared to continental Europe: there are more resources than elsewhere, and there is the possibility of a kind of work that keeps developing, perhaps slowly, but without too much danger of brutal intervention by the government. We need to take advantage of the circumstances to build a force that, sooner or later, in one way or another, can help our cause when the occasion arises, especially in Italy, which is the country we come from, whose language we speak and where consequently we can exercise our influence with greater efficiency.

Below we publish a *statement of principles* and a *social pact* that some years ago, by the initiative of the San Francisco comrades, served as the basis for an attempted Federation between the Italian anarchists of North America.[58] To the best of our knowledge, many groups supported the Pact, but then, we believe, because they did not create an agency especially responsible for maintaining relations between the different groups, correspondence ceased and the Federation died before it could be fully formed.

It is time to resume this attempt with a firm determination to succeed.

We therefore propose that any willing group take the initiative and appoint a *Provisional Correspondence Committee,* which will collect support from groups (and comrades not yet in a group) of the United States. The document we publish below might serve as a basis for affiliation, as it rather adequately presents anarchist-socialist principles and the method by which anarchists group together. Once a given number of members has been reached, a congress, or something of the sort, may establish the definitive format of the Pact and replace the temporary committee chosen by just one group with a committee appointed by all.

Thus we wait for someone to take this initiative. In the meantime, here is the document:

[*Under the title "Anarchist-Socialist Federation of Italian Workers in North America" follows an 11-item "Statement of Principles" and a 13-item "Social Pact" of the "Italian Workers' Anarchist Socialist Alliance," which was founded in San Francisco on the basis of the aforementioned statement of principles and*

---

58   The initiative had been taken in the first months of 1896, during Pietro Gori's long coast-to-coast propaganda tour.

that, according to the first item of the Pact, "adheres to the solidarity pact of the Anarchist-Socialist Federation of North America, which is inspired by these same principles."]

[Untitled]

Translated from *La Questione Sociale*
(Paterson, New Jersey) 5, new series, no. 3 (September 23, 1899)

New York's *Il Proletario* boasts of being "the *only* Italian socialist newspaper in the United States."

If they said this on the fourth page, among the more or less charlatan-like news it deems fit to print, we should think no more about it. But since the claim is made in the central part of the newspaper, where there should be a strict requirement that nothing untrue be published, we ask our kind sister paper to explain to us why, according to it, we are not socialists.[59]

If they do not respond... we will not say anything, but we will certainly think poorly of them.

On Behalf of Cesare Batacchi

Translated from "Per Cesare Batacchi," *La Questione Sociale*
(Paterson, New Jersey) 5, new series, no. 3 (September 23, 1899)

After twenty years—twenty years spent in a penitentiary by honest workers, guilty only of professing anarchist socialist principles and belonging to the International—public opinion is finally awakening to the fact, which has been clear to anyone who has ever looked at the subject, that those who were convicted for tossing a bomb into the middle of the parade in Florence in 1878 were the victims of an enormous judicial disgrace.

Of those convicted only Cesare Batacchi remains in the penitentiary, and under the terms of his sentence he must stay there for the remainder of his life.

It is necessary to rescue him, but to do so will require strong and persistent action to force the government to do justice. It would be a deadly

---

59   The fourth page of *Il Proletario* was usually given over entirely to advertising. The phrase in question was framed by a small box, published regularly on the front page, which read: "Workers! Read *Il Proletario*, the only Italian socialist newspaper in the United States."

mistake to think it's enough to draw the attention of the authorities to this appalling abomination. Even prior to sentencing the authorities were aware that the arrested men were innocent; they had proof thereafter that the witnesses for the prosecution were false, and they never wanted to review the case.

If we want to obtain this act of justice, as any other, we must impose it.

For the comrades in Italy, this is an opportunity to show their courage.

Remember Batacchi is a comrade of ours and is in a penitentiary for having followed our ideas.

Them too!

Translated from "Anche essi!" *La Questione Sociale*
(Paterson, New Jersey) 5, new series, no. 3 (September 23, 1899)

There had remained one last remnant of the old republicanism in Italy. They were hardly modern folk: uncompromising in their defense of the sacred institution of property, they retained all the wrath that inspired the Mazzinian attacks against the International, they had no understanding of contemporary problems, and promised us a republic that, apart from words always full of promises and most likely good intentions, would have been the undisputed kingdom of the bourgeoisie. But they had something that made them likable: they were obstinate enemies of the monarchy and wanted no contact with it, vesting all their hopes in revolution. They were the only republicans who remained abstentionists and who had no aspirations to serve as deputies in the monarchy's parliament.

Now it seems that they too, retracting old and recent excommunications, are following the way of the others.

According to the republican newspaper *L'Italia*, which is pleased by the development, "in the upcoming electoral contest the last stubborn supporters of abstentionism, including some of the most uncompromising, will conform to the universally accepted rule of conduct and perhaps will give their name to the struggle."

Did you understand that? now running in the electoral race with the hope of becoming a deputy, with all the major and minor perks of the job, is described as giving one's name to the struggle!

Another time these same people gave their skins to the struggle with the prospect of being killed or ending up in prison.

We liked them better the way they were before.

SECTION III
Touring New England

[Untitled]

Translated from *La Questione Sociale*
(Paterson, New Jersey) 5, new series, no. 4 (September 30, 1899)

We have received and publish:

New York, September 23, 1899

Dear friends,

I hear there is someone who, speaking about my lectures, describes me as saying things... different from what I actually think and say.

I really cannot understand why some people—those same people who feign fear of predominant personal influences—are so preoccupied with me personally. The value of ideas resides in their inherent truth or falsity, and they should be defended or opposed for their own merits, without so much concern for the person who professes such ideas.

In any case, since they are so preoccupied with me, allow me to state that I cannot be considered responsible for ideas that my opponents attribute to me.

Anyone wishing to know for sure what my thinking is need only come and listen to me and engage me in discussion; or read LA QUESTIONE SOCIALE (new series) with which I am in perfect agreement.

Forgive me for being forced to talk about myself.

Sincerely yours
ERRICO MALATESTA.

Oddino Morgari's "True Anarchist"

Translated from "'Il vero anarchico' di Oddino Morgari," *La Questione Sociale*
(Paterson, New Jersey) 5, new series, no. 4 (September 30, 1899)

Oddino Morgari, a socialist deputy in the Italian parliament, is a friendly and good man: no one who knows him will question his good faith, his passionate desire to do good. But for anybody wanting to know and understand the truth, it is dangerous to rely upon the descriptions of people and things that he publishes in *Avanti!*

He is an artist: he is deeply impressed by the outward appearance of things, by sharp contrasts, by the exceptional—and he seeks and masterfully manages to convey to his readers the impressions he has acquired. As for getting to the bottom of things, dissecting them, and looking at them from every angle... that is too prosaic for him. And good Oddino is indeed sincerely convinced that he is the most practical and least *poetic* fellow in the world!

For instance: some time ago he paid a visit to the *coatti* on Lampedusa, he was impressed by the fact that the lack of rain renders the island infertile and for this reason land ownership is nearly more a burden than a blessing… and he promptly deduced from this that poverty depends on the scarcity of products, and that the social question is a problem of production.[60] Had he reflected further and had he not so readily given in to the pleasure of saying something new (which then turns out to be the old lie with which the bourgeoisie's doctors have tried to justify the current state of affairs) he would have realized that on Lampedusa as elsewhere poverty today is produced by the economic-political organization of society, and not by "thankless nature," which man has by now tamed sufficiently to bring forth bread… and dripping for all. He would have understood that if it were not for the capitalist system attracting capital and labor to where the greatest personal profit lies for the masters regardless of the needs of the population, if it were not for the government's fiscal system and if it were not for the state of ignorance in which those islanders find themselves on account of their social circumstances, Lampedusa would have been made fertile by means of artesian wells and the introduction of crops suited to its soil and climate, as has happened on much more sterile rocks when the capitalists or government have so desired;—and had this proved impossible the islanders would gladly have abandoned the place and gone off to work in places where their labor provided products. He would have understood that, even without land, the Lampedusians could have lived bountifully from the products of fishing (sponges and sardines) had the local and foreign capitalists not been able to profit from the fact that the fishermen have neither the tools for work, nor the capital to feed themselves until the fish have been caught and sold, to exploit them unscrupulously;—and he would even have come to the old socialist conclusion, that the social problem is largely a problem of wealth distribution, since the scarcity of products depends upon the hoarding of land and capital, rather than upon man's inability or nature's infertility.[61]

Similarly Morgari deceived himself when he tried to deal with the anarchists and anarchy.

---

60   Morgari had discussed Lampedusa's economy in the series of articles we have in part reprinted at the beginning of this volume and especially in "A proposito di piogge" (Regarding the rains), in *Avanti!* of March 3, 1899. The paper's own editors had added on a note of dissension to the end of the piece, to which Morgari responded on March 5 with his article "Sempre a proposito di piogge" (Again regarding the rains).

61   Malatesta would return to and expand upon this matter in the article "Production and Distribution" (see Volume V of these *Complete Works*).

He saw some anarchists, and became interested in their personal traits; he learned about their adventurous lives, he observed the kindness of one, the coarse energy of another and he felt and expressed the sympathy that a sincere and good person never fails to feel towards good and sincere folk. But he failed to understand, and maybe never even tried to find out, what anarchy is, what anarchists want.

Listen to him and judge for yourselves:

"Gavilli does not deny being an authoritarian; he would use violence against his own comrades if it would advance the purposes of humanity.[62]

"With what right? Don't anarchist principles advocate above all else absolute personal freedom, a complete absence of authority?

"But the *true* anarchist *feels* more than he thinks. He is the poet of the social question. He gleans his ideas more from his temperament than from the facts. If logic does not agree with it, too bad for logic.

"He is a strong fellow who *needs* freedom and upon that need he builds a theory that extends to the weak, without thinking that the weak would instead need to be protected against the freedom of the strong by means of the law.

"With regard to food and drink, and thus production (which requires a highly complex technical and practical social organization, subordinating the whims and interests of individuals to the rational interests of the mass) the anarchist cares as much about this question as he did about the first pair of shoes he wore as a child. The subject is too excessively pedestrian for his flights of fancy and he breezes past the issue by asserting that we already produce three times what is necessary for all, therefore the problem is simply a matter of breaking the bonds of ownership and giving people the freedom to enjoy the bounty.

"One cannot persuade the *true* anarchist; you need to accept him as he is, impassioned and violent, sometimes mild-mannered, sometimes wild, always naive, highly ambitious, but ready to make sacrifices, waiting for the years to pass and the experience of life and matters to pull his feet down to this gray reality, as is unfailingly the case when he is intelligent. In which case he matches or indeed surpasses us.

"... thus Gavilli saw fiery sentiment give way to experience and the practical sense within him and the need to be useful predominate and lead him to what is usually described as possibilist tactics...

"—I heard your lecture (he said to me squeezing my arm in a friendly way) and, frankly, 'there is nothing more to say.' Once upon a time

---

62   The reference is to Giovanni Gavilli, an anarchist who had been in *domicilio coatto* on Pantelleria and whom Morgari had met during his visit to the islands of *coatti*. The Morgari article in question was "Un'isola e un uomo" (An island and a man), in *Avanti!* of September 6, 1899. That was followed up by another two articles by Morgari about Gavilli, on August 27 and 29.

I used to hate you. Now I have even found myself encouraging people to register as voters. It is all good, it all helps. Now I see that you are destined to win and that the anarchist society we dreamed of must be preceded by a period of 'authoritarian' socialism. If I was not certain that legal routes will be cut off, I'll be blunt, I would side with you, but I have that certainty and remain an anarchist."

*
**

We are leaving to Morgari the full responsibility for what he says of Gavilli. And we declare that the idea Morgari has of anarchists is simply burlesque; and if Gavilli had truly and deliberately uttered the words that Morgari has him say, and these were not instead hurried conclusions gleaned from a few words spoken in a moment of frustration, Gavilli would not be an anarchist, neither "true" nor "fake."[63]

"Fake" anarchists are scoundrels and spies who may enter our ranks, like in any other subversive party; but, no matter how honest and sincere they may be, no one can be an anarchist who is *authoritarian* and who *would use violence against his own comrades if it would advance the purposes of humanity*, just as someone is not an anarchist who *remains an anarchist just because he is certain that the government will cut off legal routes.*

There are those who, misled by certain contingencies of the present struggle, have believed they could satisfy their violent instincts and their desire to command by joining our ranks and using our means, but they contradict anarchist principles and would have a hard time explaining why they claim to be supporters of anarchy; they are not the ones who, made wise by the years, change over to government socialists... if they don't become something even worse.

The anarchist leaves the pretension of saving people by force to the Torquemadas and Robespierres of every religion and party. He does not claim the right to use force to impose his own will, even for the purposes of doing good; and he believes that violence can very well be used to oppress and degrade, but is powerless to elevate and emancipate; and he accepts and uses material force only to defend himself and others from the material force that the government and the capitalists use to keep the people subdued.

And what are we to think of an anarchist who states he is only an anarchist because the government precludes legal routes, and that he would otherwise go to vote and expect parliament to implement his ideals?

Anarchists are revolutionaries, they want to overthrow the current regime through insurrection, because they are convinced there is no other way to succeed; but they are anarchists independently of this need to resort

---

63   Gavilli himself would reply to Morgari in an open letter published in the single issue *I Morti* on November 2, 1899.

to violent means. They are anarchists because they do not want government, they do not want parliament, nor any sort of legislative power; and if parliament enjoyed full powers and there was no danger of violence from the king's ministers, they would be anti-parliamentarians all the same. Otherwise, what would distinguish them from abstentionist republicans?

"The anarchist society will be preceded by a period of authoritarian socialism." Perhaps; but an anarchist can not desire that, nor work to bring it about. Authoritarian socialism would not help prepare people for anarchy; but it would be a phase in the struggle between the principle of freedom and the principle of authority, or, in practical terms, between those who want to be free and those who cannot seem to decide to be everyone's equals and want at all costs to stand over the rest and give orders.

According to anarchists, the people will grow accustomed to anarchy not through authoritarian socialism, but by fighting against that as much as against any other incarnation of authority.

That the "true anarchist" is not concerned about issues of food and drink, which is to say production, and finds such matters "too pedestrian for his flights of fancy" is another... poetic license taken by Morgari. Quite the opposite, among the many reasons we reject authoritarian and dictatorial methods, advocated by certain revolutionaries, extremely fundamental is the belief that the issue of production is of vital importance and that it cannot be resolved through authoritarian means, but must be resolved by means of the direct efforts of freely associated producers themselves. And besides, one of our best-known writers, Kropotkin, has made a specialty of the technical study of the issue of production, especially agricultural production.[64]

True, some anarchists argued that we produce a lot more than is necessary for all, and this was a serious mistake; but even that is not enough to justify the fantastic notion that Morgari has of the "true anarchist."[65] That error is, in terms of its consequences, in all cases less serious and less dangerous than the error peddled by Morgari that socialism should target increased production over greater equality in distribution.

Let Morgari be persuaded: the anarchist is a person no different from the rest; he is merely someone who subscribes to certain specific ideas. Let him find out about those ideas, which go by the name of anarchist, and it will be the case of judging whether someone thinks and acts in accordance with those ideas, and thus whether or not he is an anarchist.

---

64 *Fields, Factories and Workshops*, one of Kropotkin's most important works on the subject, had been published the previous year.

65 Malatesta refers to the theories set out in the pamphlets *Les Produits de la Terre* and *Les Produits de l'Industrie*, published in Geneva between 1885 and 1887. He took issue with these theories, which had become popular among anarchists, in the article "The Products of Soil and Industry" in December 1891.

Buffoonery

Translated from "Buffonate," *La Questione Sociale*
(Paterson, New Jersey) 5, new series, no. 4 (September 30, 1899)

A little while ago the city of Chicago invited President McKinley to lay the first stone of a public building.

When the workers found out about the invitation extended to McKinley, they protested and announced that they would go on strike if the first stone was not cut and put in place by a member of the trade union.

It was pointed out to them that McKinley had been invited in his role as President of the Republic, and should not be mistaken for a wage-earner there to compete with the organized workers. But the workers held their ground... and to avoid conflict McKinley was given a union card as an honorary member of one of the Chicago bricklayers' union!

We feel embarrassed for the workers who went along with such crude comedies; and we look for and hasten the day when the workers will understand that the republic's presidents are, just like the kings, the defenders of the capitalists.

And we marvel that one Dr. P. Briganti, who must be a socialist, as he writes in *Il Proletario*, the "only" Italian socialist newspaper in the United States, has gone into raptures over the clumsy mystification of McKinley as a member of a labor union, and says that the applause the workers directed towards McKinley will be "a demonstration by free people aware of themselves and of the dignity of their own class, a demonstration made to a man who standing at the apex of the honors and power that a republic can grant a citizen, is not above mingling with the working man."[66]

Poor socialism, to have fallen into such hands!

The Principle of Organization

Translated from "Il principio d'organizzazione," *La Questione Sociale*
(Paterson, New Jersey) 5, new series, no. 5 (October 7, 1899)

There are anarchists who, while admitting that men must organize in defense of their ideas and interests, always see in organization an authority or danger of an authority; and so they agree to it reluctantly, forced by the obvious fact that the individual person is powerless when it comes

---

66   P. Briganti, "L'eloquenza dei confronti: A Chicago e a Torino" (Telling comparisons: in Chicago and in Turin), *Il Proletario* (New York) 4, no. 23 (September 23, 1899).

to acting effectively and defending themselves alone. They attribute this powerlessness to the present circumstances of society, to the lack of consciousness and initiative in the individual; and they hope that a day will come when each will be willing and able to take care of themselves and there will no longer be any need for organization.

We believe instead that organization is not a passing need, not a matter of strategy and opportunity, but is rather a need inherent to human society, and should be regarded by us as a matter of principle. And we believe that, far from there being any contradiction between the idea of anarchy and the idea of organization, anarchy cannot exist and is unthinkable as anything other than the free organization of all common interests, by the interested parties themselves.

And in fact, what is man in isolation? Can he survive? Can he even come into existence, if by man we mean something superior to a brute?

Do we need to prove that it is only through contact and cooperation with other men that humanity has managed to rise above animality and little by little reach the level of development at which it is now found? That only by profiting from the labor and ideas of everyone, the individual human can meet his material and moral needs and proceed along the path of progress?

"But we (they object to us) in rejecting organization do not mean to reject agreement, association. Organization is necessarily authoritarian, since organization means regular and uniform operation of organs for a given purpose. If those organs wish to operate according to their inclinations they must renounce organization."

And we reply: What on earth could an unorganized association be, if not co-existence, a material joining of units without defined relationships, without organic links? And what would be the point of association if it does not mean coordinating efforts and cooperating towards a common goal? The pure and simple sum of separate units assumes in and of itself rules, since the efforts only add together on condition that they act simultaneously and in the same direction.

A sufficiently developed society is not possible without some division of labor; which means, without each individual shouldering a certain portion of the social work and becoming an organ within the organism. If we need houses we need bricklayers and ten other kinds of workers; and if these people genuinely want to work and build houses, they need to come to agreement and submit to the necessary rules.

The difference between society today and what we call anarchist society is that today work is organized at the behest of a privileged class, without the will of the workers and against their interests; while, in our opinion, it should be organized by the workers themselves, guided by their own interests.

And authority exists when those who work, produce, and act in any way cannot come to an agreement with others and regulate their own activities in harmony with their own interests and their own likings, and must obey rules imposed by others for interests other than their own. And such authority, along with the exploitation that results from it, comes not just from material violence, but also (and in advanced societies we may say primarily) from the fact that people, not being able or inclined to organize in order to achieve the purposes of society, find themselves forced to submit and appeal to the organization that a few (the government and the capitalists) have created instead of them... and to their detriment.

Divide and rule is an old and yet still true maxim of government.

There are two styles of organization that correspond to two different concepts of human society, to two opposing ideals.

Everyone knows and, openly or silently, acknowledges that man needs man, and that society is the result of this need and the need to satisfy it. But some, elevating the current situation to a standard and resorting, in order to justify it, to a crude analogy, argue that the purpose behind association and cooperation between people is to contribute to the well-being and perfection of "society" and that the good of individuals has to be sacrificed for the sake of the "collective good," just as in a fully developed animal organism the work of the cells and the various organs is done for the benefit of the whole organism, which alone has consciousness and is properly capable of pleasure or suffering. And since in human society every individual possesses consciousness, whilst no collective consciousness exists, the "collective good," of which the aforementioned theorists talk about, means, in practice, the good of those who give the commands.

Others however think that the purpose of society should be the well-being and development of every one of its members, hence they should all have equal rights and equal means, and nobody should be able to force another to do something against his own will.

The first concept corresponds to the authoritarian organization, the ideal of which is to concentrate power in the hands of some, and to reduce the others, the large masses, to flawless tools of production, blindly obedient to the orders of the few.

A choice must be made between these two types of organization. Free association with others on the basis of equality and solidarity; or let the masters and government and bosses assign you a place in an organization made without you and against you, and let them control and exploit you as they please. There is no other way out, unless you wish—and can— be a master and commander, and do unto others as you would not have them do unto you.

Living in isolation, or connected with others only mechanically, is not possible. *The organ that in order to function according to its own inclinations rejects organization,* would cease to perform any organic function—and would die.

Revolutionary Alliance

Translated from "Alleanza rivoluzionaria," *La Questione Sociale* (Paterson, New Jersey) 5, new series, no. 5 (October 7, 1899)

Our readers are aware from the pamphlet *Against the Monarchy*, a substantial part of which we have reprinted, that in Italy there has been a proposal for an alliance between the various anti-monarchy parties in order to rise up against the monarchy and overthrow it.[67]

Based on direct information, we can confirm that the proposal has been favorably received by action-oriented elements of various parties, and it is hoped that practical results will be achieved.

Being convinced that it is our duty to always fight against every kind of government, being convinced that in order to advance toward the realization of our ideals we must smash the militaristic yoke that oppresses Italy today, we are ready to cooperate, with anyone who is genuinely willing, in the fight against the monarchy. Not that this is something new for us. Enemies of the institution of government, no matter what form it may take, and therefore of monarchy, which is the most reactionary form of government; adversaries as a matter of principle to parliamentary methods of struggle and persuaded of the impotence of unarmed struggle against the violent methods that governments use, our party's entire history has been one ongoing impulse towards insurrection—insurrection against the monarchy that is the first obstacle which, in Italy, has always blocked our path forward. And we have always invited and incited the other anti-monarchist parties to join with us in that insurrection... and we have always found them unwilling.

Will the alliance have better success this time, when the proposal is not from us, but instead comes from elements of other parties, driven to this by the obvious necessity of the situation?

---

67   Besides being anonymous, the pamphlet had been written in such a way as to not disclose the writer's political inclinations, perhaps to avoid preconceived hostility or to place the proposal's intended audience on an absolutely equal footing. In this article, too, Malatesta discusses the project for a revolutionary alliance as if it were coming from a third party. For the reprinting of the piece in *La Questione Sociale*, see note 17.

We hope so; although the electoral enthusiasm of socialists and republicans makes us doubt their desire to rise up. It seems to us that people who are really determined to let gunfire end it all should not be raising hopes among the people of obtaining, under the monarchy, universal suffrage and being able, under the monarchy, to use suffrage as an instrument of emancipation.

In any event our primary concern is with organizing our party and readying ourselves for action. If others are willing to act with us, so much the better; if instead they want to leave us as the only revolutionary party in Italy, the only party that is practically anti-monarchist, we shall act on our own, and attract to our side those among the socialists and republicans who do not believe in the possibility of the monarchy being toppled through the ballot.

But let us understand one another.

Ready to rise up against the monarchy alongside anybody who is ready to rise up, we remain anarchist socialists as always, and we have no intention of removing even a single corner from our flag.

We want to work with anybody in toppling the monarchy, but we have no intention of restoring the bourgeoisie's good name and awarding it a period of unchallenged domination under the protection of a republican government.

We are anti-monarchist, but we are also anti-republican.

And in fighting against the monarchy alongside the socialists and republicans, we are absolutely not working to help them establish the republic. Quite the opposite.

Are We Socialists?

Translated from "Siamo socialisti?" *La Questione Sociale*
(Paterson, New Jersey) 5, new series, no. 5 (October 7, 1899)

Il Proletario is not happy that we asked it why it calls itself "the *only* Italian socialist newspaper in the United States"—and we can understand why.

From the confused manner in which it responds we can tell that our question caused some embarrassment.[68]

While recognizing that such distinctions, meaning the dividing lines between the various schools of socialism, *are necessary,* our brothers from *Il Proletario* declare that *they do not use such a wealth of words, and, very modestly, simply call themselves socialists.*

---

68   The response is contained in an untitled short note in *Il Proletario* of September 30, 1899, p. 2.

This is lacking in logic. *Il Proletario* is entitled to call itself *socialist,* without further qualification, but it cannot describe itself as the *only socialist newspaper,* if it acknowledges that there are other schools of socialism and other newspapers that defend these schools.

But does *Il Proletario* genuinely acknowledge the existence of other schools of socialism different from its own?

It would seem not, judging by a passage of its response, prior to the words we have reproduced in italics. From this passage, despite a grammatical construction which, we hope, can be attributed to its typographer, we are able to understand that the editors at *Il Proletario* spent *a happy quarter of an hour on the protest from the anarchist... socialists,* much as they would on a similar *protest from the Catholic... socialists.*

This means that *Il Proletario* thinks neither the anarchists nor the Catholics, or religious people in general, are really socialists. But if they were to ask us why, we would feel morally obliged to tell them, and might even regard their question as a stroke of good luck, because it would furnish an opportunity to spread our ideas and combat what looks to us like a mistake or a deception.

If *Il Proletario* thinks that we are not socialists, it should tell us the reasons why.

Loopholes will not do; either they provide us with an explicit and reasoned response, or let us conclude that they are not very considerate in illuminating their readers.

[Untitled]

Translated from *La Questione Sociale*
(Paterson, New Jersey) 5, new series, no. 5 (October 7, 1899)

Replying to what we said in our no. 2 issue, *L'Aurora* relates and gives a version of the events preceding the *parting of the ways* that differs from our own.[69]

We see no point in responding, since the comrades from Paterson and surrounding areas have direct knowledge of how things stand, and more distant comrades would find it hard to judge the claims of both sides and reach an informed conclusion as to where the truth lies.

This being a discussion that does not help our propaganda, and which has already shown a clear tendency to descend into gossip and

---

69   "Cose a posto (Replica alla 'Questione Sociale')" (Setting the record straight: A response to "La Questione Sociale"), *L'Aurora* (Paterson) 1, no. 2 (September 30, 1899). The article to which *L'Aurora* was responding is "Discussion (A Reply to the 'Dissidents')," p. 69.

insolence damaging to our propagandà, we are opting to leave it at that, and to continue along our path—in the hope that "L'Aurora" can, in its own way, do the most good possible for the common cause.

Universal Suffrage

Translated from "Il suffragio universale," *La Questione Sociale* (Paterson, New Jersey) 5, new series, no. 6 (October 14, 1899)

For many years the supporters of democracy (which means *government of the people*) have argued that universal suffrage is the legitimate source of law and the cure for all of society's problems.

When everybody has the right to vote, they say, the people will send their friends to power and see their will triumph. If the institutions founded by those elected by the popular vote are not perfect, if they should betray the interests of their mandates, the voters will simply need to lay the blame upon themselves, and vote better the next time.

Furthermore, the most radical add, for greater security one can establish the revocability of the mandate and the referendum, meaning that voters are always free to remove their elected representative and nominate another, and that the laws passed by deputies are not valid until they have been approved by the people in a direct vote.

But universal suffrage was in force at various times in almost every civilized country, even in the form of the plebiscite, which is direct voting by all on a given issue; it was practiced as an achievement of the insurgent people, or as a concession from victors who saw it useful to fortify their domination with the appearance of popular consensus—and was always used to sanction any sort of usurpation, always complying with the desires of whomever held power and from a position of power consulted it. Universal suffrage has long been the norm in many countries; in some the referendum also exists—and the people remain enslaved, and the bourgeois, the ones who possess and exploit social wealth to the detriment of the workers, are no more inconvenienced than before.

Fallen into disgrace, the pure and simple democrats have joined forces with the self-described democratic socialists; and they also claim to do good for all by means of a people's government emerging from universal suffrage. And they act everywhere to gain this suffrage, and strive to attract the workers, telling them the world's grossest and stupidest illusion: once you vote, you will be the ones in charge.

And universal suffrage is not going to be, just because it is invoked by the socialists, any more beneficial than it was when the democrats heralded it.

How come universal suffrage was never used in the past to emancipate the people? and why will it not do so in the future?

There should be no need to remind the socialists of the impact that material conditions have upon the minds of men, nor how those in possession of wealth always manage to win and dominate, nor how the workers cannot achieve political emancipation when their economic subjugation persists. For socialists—those who have not stopped being such—universal suffrage could at best help organize the future society: but it must always be preceded by revolutionary expropriation and by making available to all the means of production and all existing wealth. It could, for authoritarian socialists, be the source of law in a society founded upon equality of conditions; but it could never be a means of escaping current conditions, never an instrument of emancipation.

Instead the so-called socialists demand suffrage today as the supreme means of achieving economic equality and realizing socialism. And if in some countries they speak of revolution, and maybe they will incite or support it, this is only to gain universal suffrage; making the republic, and perhaps supporting the monarchy where the monarch, while hanging on to the throne and the attached civil list,[70] is willing to yield full sovereignty to universal suffrage. Meaning that they, for all the socialism, would accept the political conditions that exist in France, in Switzerland, and in the Americas, and that for years and centuries have failed to bring about socialism or even to slow capitalist accumulation... much less prevent massacres of recalcitrant workers.

But let us assume that there are the necessary conditions for everyone to be able to vote freely, and know how to vote well; let us suppose that the social revolution has actually been completed, that everyone now enjoys independent economic conditions, and that the new conditions have already brought forth an intelligent and educated public. Universal suffrage, meaning a government elected by universal suffrage, would be just as impotent, due to elements inherent to its nature, in representing the interests of all and satisfying them.

First of all, the government "elected by the people" is actually elected only by those who win the electoral contest; the others, who may be a massive minority or indeed a majority, are left without representation. It would therefore be a regime in which the lawful majority (which is then

---

70   The Civil List institution was an annual assignment of money to the monarch to provide them with the means necessary to maintain the decorum that suited them.

the actual majority only in the best of worlds) has the right to command the minority.

This would already be a very bad thing, since the minority may well be as right as the majority or even more, and in all cases the rights of each individual are equally sacred, whether they find themselves in the major-ity, in the minority or indeed on their own. But the reality is even worse.

The elected law-makers may have been appointed by the majority of voters; but the law is made only by a majority of these, and therefore it is most often the case that those approving a law represent only a number of voters that is a minority by comparison to the whole electorate.

So with the system of universal suffrage, as with any other system of representative government, very often, even where elected represen-tatives truly carry out the wishes of the electorate, it is the minority that rules the majority. And if domination by the majority is unfair and tyrannical, domination by the minority is even less fair and more dan-gerous, all the more so since through the alchemy of politics the most enlightened, most progressive, and kindliest minority is not that which remains in power. Quite the contrary!

But there are other more significant considerations that account for the fallacy, not only of this system of representation, but also of the referen-dum, direct legislation, and any other system not founded upon the free will of each person, freely agreeing with the others.

They speak of people and people's interests; but the people are not a singular body with singular interests. It is simply a collective noun, which indicates a group composed of many individuals and many com-munities, each of which has different ideas, passions, and interests, that are different from and often contrary to each other.

How could a government, a parliament, ever represent and satisfy opposing interests? How could an electorate, which can offer but one solution to each question, satisfy all the individuals who comprise it and who are affected by an issue in different ways?

In a parliament, as in a country, each interest finds itself in the minority compared with the sum of the other interests, and if it is the collective that must decide on particular interests, each interest will find itself abandoned to the discretion of those who have no such interest, or are unaware of it, or do not care, or have different and opposing interests.

On a given issue, for example, Sicily, Piedmont, and every other region in Italy have different interests. If the Italian people as a whole must decide for everyone, each region will necessarily be subjected to the will of the other regions taken together; and each will be oppressed, while it competes to oppress the others. Thus the interests of miners, for example, will be determined by the mass of the population among whom they are a small minority... and so on for every trade, for every locality, for every opinion.

There are certainly general interests, shared by several communities, entire nations, and even the whole of humanity and that consequently require the participation and agreement of all the interested parties; and, once the antagonism generated by private ownership has been destroyed, those broader and shared interests will continue to grow and expand.

But who determines which interests are exclusive to an individual or a group, and which are more or less general interests?

If there is a government, representative or not, it must necessarily decide for itself on several jurisdictions and determine which interests fall under the exclusive responsibility of the individual, which are the concern of broader and broader groups, and which should be regulated by the central government; because otherwise, each would deny the government's jurisdiction on these issues where the government-made law does not suit them—and the government could no longer govern.

And since any government, any established body, naturally has the tendency to always widen its sphere of action, it always comes to want to be involved with everything, with the excuse that everything is of a general interest; and so every liberty is stifled, and each person's interests are sacrificed to the interests—political or otherwise—of those who are in power.

The only way to determine which interests are collective and which community should make decisions regarding them, the only means of destroying antagonisms, of harmonizing opposing interests and reconciling freedom of the individual with the freedom of everyone else, is voluntary agreement between those who feel the usefulness and necessity of the agreement.

Only by moving from the individual to the group, and from the group to broader communities can we arrive at a social organization in which, while each person's wishes and autonomy are respected, there is the benefit of maximum social cooperation, and the way is always open to further improvements, and all future progress.

One final observation.

In any political body today there are huge differences in material circumstances and intellectual and moral development between one region and the next, between one city and the next, one trade and the next, one party and the next; as well as between city and countryside, etc.—and the most wretched, most backward, most reactionary parts are always the great majority.

This is a matter of fact, that can be verified in every country in the world. Everywhere, because of the State which forces the most widely divergent and contrary elements to stay together, because of the law, which all are forced to obey, everywhere it is the most backward regions that give their respective governments the strength to hold the more advanced in obedience, and thus prevent them from organizing themselves in a way that corresponds to their aspirations and their degree of material and moral development; it is the rural areas that restrain the cities; it is those brutalized by poverty, the illiterate, the subjugated, the superstitious who are tools in the hands of the rulers to oppress the intelligent, the open-minded, the rebels.

Now, with universal suffrage the law-makers come from the majority; then it is the majority among the legislators, which is to say, the most archaic among them, which make the laws. The result therefore is that the law is made not only by the minority, but by the most backward minority.

Add to this the illusion that the most progressive minorities are forever hopeful of being able to peacefully secure a majority and allow themselves to be paralyzed by legalities, and it will be clear how, far from being a tool for emancipation and progress, universal suffrage is instead the most effective means of preserving and consolidating oppression... when it is not a means of going backwards.

For example, let universal suffrage be bestowed upon Italy, and instead of making progress, you will have established, worse than it is today, the rule of the priests and of the large rural landowners.

But does that mean we want rule by the minority? do we want what is called enlightened despotism?

Certainly not: first of all because we do not accept that anyone has the right to impose their will on others not even to do good, nor do we believe in doing good by force; secondly, because every person believes they themselves are right and there would be no supreme court to decide who truly is right; and finally because, when it comes to commanding through force and dominating, it is not the best ones who have the suitable qualities for successfully doing so, but rather the deceivers and the swordsmen.

We believe that the only way of emancipating oneself and making progress is for everybody to have the freedom and means to spread and IMPLEMENT their own ideas—and this is Anarchy. Then the more advanced minorities will persuade and drag along the more backward through the force of their reason and example. Besides, this is always how humanity has made progress, thanks to what little freedom governments have been unable to suppress.

*
**

But, they often respond: If universal suffrage does not really serve the good of the people, how come governments never concede it freely, and have instead opposed it for as long as they can?

This can be partly explained by ignorance, fear, and conservative blindness that are characteristic of the ruling classes, but above all by the true fact that with the arrival of universal suffrage there is a shift in interests and a change in government personnel, which is feared by those in office and who have more to lose than to gain from change.

But a change in rulers does not mean that the governed are in a better position.

*
**

The only one way that gaining universal suffrage could be useful is to practically show its fallacy to those who expect positive effects from it. It would be yet another illusion, another error out of the way; and most of the time people only arrive at the truth after they explore all the possible mistakes.

But even this single benefit cannot be achieved unless someone vigorously fights against this falsehood which is among the worst of the lies used to deceive the people.

The "Resistance" of the Republicans

Translated from "La 'resistenza' dei repubblicani," *La Questione Sociale* (Paterson, New Jersey) 5, new series, no. 6 (October 14, 1899)

The republicans assembled in congress are "unanimous in stating that in the face of the government's provocations, the violations of public law which it has perpetrated and its manifest inability to govern with freedom, it is indispensable that we give the Party's action the character of relentless and permanent *resistance* by any means with the purpose of guaranteeing the country peace, freedom, and economic prosperity."

And the Party's organ, *L'Italia* comments as follows: "No rhetorical outbursts, none of the old conspiratorial formulas, in the classic sense of the word, but rather the clear vision that revolutions are not scheduled by congresses, nor are they resolved by deadlines, but rather the practical, precise, modern concept of *proportional resistance adapted to the adversaries' resources and spheres of action.*" (Our italics).

Very good! but what did they then decide to do?

Here it is: in the forthcoming political elections support etc., etc. In short vote, vote, vote... and go into raptures and believe that the monarchy is beaten if somebody shouts a little loudly in parliament and shows that in the end, from time to time, it may come to pass that a deputy is not a complete eunuch.

And this is called proportional use of their means to match the means of the adversary, at the very moment when that adversary, the government, has no means other than handcuffs and gunfire!

In Milan the commoners in revolt replied to the soldiers' gunfire by throwing harmless tiles from the rooftops, and were of course massacred without doing any damage to the enemy. One could think that they would have had more success if, aware of the needs of the struggle, they had equipped themselves with bombs and had hurled those upon the soldiers instead of tiles. But oh no! that person would not be a "modern" man: they would be a rabble-rouser, a forty-eighter. What they needed to do was cast their votes!

If we were in Bava-Beccaris's and Pelloux's shoes we would send the republican congressmen our calling cards... as a way of congratulating and thanking them.[71]

Even we know that in *public* congresses nobody makes agreements for making the revolution. But, if a congress is held, it is to express at least the opinion of the congressmen, and to seek to give the movement the direction which is in their wishes and the wishes of those who sent them to congress.

The revolutions of the republicans gathered at congress in the Ticino canton show that they are very platonic republicans. And if they really represent the general trend of the republican party, it means that the republic, if it ever comes to pass, will be made by the monarchists who, when we have them by the throat, will strive to salvage as much as possible of the current institutions and stop the revolution by proclaiming the republic.

Not before.

Delegation and Delegation

Translated from "Delegazione e delegazione," *La Questione Sociale* (Paterson, New Jersey) 5, new series, no. 6 (October 14, 1899)

In a letter defending electoral tactics and parliamentarianism published in Rome's *L'Italia,* and which we know of only from the extracts reprinted in *Il Proletario*, Saverio Merlino includes the following passage which is intended as a rebuttal of anarchist ideas.

"I am unable to understand how the tiniest association or community

---

71   Fiorenzo Bava-Beccaris had led the repression of the Milan riots in May 1898 (see note 19); Luigi Pelloux was the current prime minister.

can exist without the individuals comprising it delegating duties to one or more of their number."[72]

Nor can we. But Merlino, who was not ranked last among the propagandists of anarchism, should not, just for polemical convenience, alter the fundamentals of anarchist ideas… not even if by chance the comrade with whom he is arguing has expressed himself poorly.[73]

We understand that Merlino has changed his mind; but we cannot understand how he could have forgotten the ideas that he championed up until a short time ago and that are spelled out in many of his writings.

Merlino should not ignore that delegation of duties is one thing, while giving a few people the right to make the laws for everybody else is quite another.

Parliament is a legislative body, and the anarchists are against it because they do not want people to be compelled to submit to the will of others. This does not mean that people should not come to mutual agreement and divide up the work useful to everyone according to everyone's abilities.

Merlino ought to know this.

The Anarchists and Workers' Societies

Translated from "Gli anarchici e le società operaje," *La Questione Sociale* (Paterson, New Jersey) 5, new series, no. 6 (October 14, 1899)

Our friend Carlo Gussoni of Paterson writes us:

I hope you will answer the following question:

What would be the attitude of organizationist anarchist socialists on the issue of workers' craft and trade Unions?

I am asking because I have noticed that in cases where these Unions must exercise their influence on the masters, many of the organizationist anarchist socialists, although members of these Unions, are not present at the meetings in which questions most vital to the existence and purpose of the Unions are raised.

---

72   "Verso il partito socialista" (Towards the socialist party), *Il Proletario* (New York) 4, no. 25 (October 7, 1899).

73   Francesco Saverio Merlino was, up until 1894, one of Italian anarchism's leading figures. In 1897 he engaged Malatesta in a lengthy debate on parliamentarianism (see Volume III of these *Complete Works*), during the course of which he officially declared his separation from anarchism.

Here is our reply:

Anarchists who join labor Unions, and then take no active part in their lives, do a lot of harm; and it is up to the most active and most consistent to encourage the others and make them match their conduct with their ideas.

Workers' societies do not help emancipate the workers, since their slavery depends on causes that cannot be destroyed unless the whole social system is transformed by revolution; and often they are of no service even with it comes to securing material improvements, even small and transitory ones, since broader economic factors, which the labor union is most of the time powerless to counteract, determine wage rates. But they can still help to educate, to morally uplift the working classes and to prepare and train them for the struggle.

However, to achieve this, it is necessary that the most advanced, most conscious elements contribute their ideas, their initiative, their combativeness. And wherever anarchists have done so—and we admit that to date they have generally done so rarely and erratically—wherever they have done so, they have achieved splendid results, thereby proving that anarchist ideas and spirit can very easily penetrate the masses, as long as the propaganda is brought to them and in ways accessible to their intelligence.

The big disadvantage of workers' societies is that the vast majority of members do not take any part in their social life, beyond the appointment of leaders, and payment. Thus they are a small-scale reproduction of the system of government that afflicts us in wider political society. Everybody pays, and then allows themselves to be guided, exploited, betrayed… in addition with the illusion that they are the ones in charge, because they are the ones who vote.

Therefore the first task of anarchists within workers' societies is to rip the members out of their passivity, excite their initiative, and see to it that they live and battle with the active endeavors of all, and thereby come to understand the uselessness and harm done by presidents and committees with authoritarian assignments and lavish stipends, and eliminate them. But how can anarchists ever induce others to play an active part in the business of their unions, if they are the first to lose interest, and do not even go to meetings?

Authority is not destroyed by talk, but by actions. When it is armed with rifles the fight requires gunfire; however when it is based on the acquiescence and apathy of those who are subjected to it, it is necessary— and there is no other method—to provoke a rebellion of consciousness and activity among all.

Organizing, and then not caring about the organization, is the same as doing nothing. Others will act on behalf of the inactive, and will use their union dues to impose their own ideas, often their own interests, just as if people were not organized.

And this happens, and must happen, not only within the labor unions, but everywhere, including inside anarchists' own organizations.

Let this be taken to heart by those anarchists, who act as if they believe that the benefits of organization depend upon an almost miraculous virtue of the word, and that it is enough to register in a circle and pay some dues, for everything to go well.

For New York's *Il Proletario*

Translated from "Per il Proletario di New York," *La Questione Sociale* (Paterson, New Jersey) 5, new series, no. 6 (October 14, 1899)

Il Proletario is a propaganda organ, and as such it should eagerly seize the opportunity to argue in defense of its ideas.

Instead it struggles to slip through the hands like an eel, almost as if it were afraid of debate.

We asked it whether it considered us socialists or not—and why.[74]

It gave us an obscure reply, but it was clear enough for us to understand that, as far as it is concerned, the *anarchist socialists* are every bit as socialist as the *Catholic socialists*, meaning not at all. But it failed to say why.

We persisted with the question,[75] and now it responds that it seems we are becoming socialists and once we have developed our thinking more fully along essentially socialist lines, then "it will be delighted to announce that the Italian socialist press has been enriched with a new organ."[76]

We know this old tactic.

Not so long ago, when the entire anarchist press was violently suppressed, and every anarchist capable of writing was either a prisoner or a fugitive, the democratic socialists in Italy, in a rather shameful competition with their comrades in Germany and other countries, used to say that anarchism and socialism were two absolutely opposing ideas, and that anarchists were bourgeois, or lunatics, or spies.

These days they dare not go that far, and they say... that we are becoming socialists.

The truth is that we are socialists—and more authentic ones than they are—and have been since the beginning of our movement, which is to say, for ten years before there was any talk of democratic socialism in Italy.

---

74   See the brief, untitled note from September 23, p. 82.
75   "Are We Socialists?" p. 96.
76   This was an untitled short note on p. 2 of the October 7 issue of *Il Proletario*.

But if *Il Proletario* thinks that we want it to certify us as good socialists, it is mistaken.

We merely want it to tell us if those who seek to abolish private property and government are socialists, or whether instead socialists, as some of its supporters have already argued, are only those who seek the conquest of public authority by the proletariat—and then debate the issue with us.

⁎

Il Proletario, referring to what we said about Dr. Briganti's article, charges us with "blatant bad faith," because, it alleges, Dr. Briganti only wanted to stress that "in America the president *sees nothing wrong with mingling with the working man*, whereas back home the head of State does not stoop to acknowledge the working man as an equal."[77]

On which point we are in perfect agreement.

We are waiting, one of these days, for Dr. Briganti and *Il Proletario* to sing the praises of Victor Emmanuel, who in Naples asked passers-by in the street for a light for his cigar, or the King of Portugal, who once dropped in on a Turin workers' society and addressed them as comrades because "he too labored... at his people's happiness," or King Humbert, who *cordially* shook hands with the enslaved workers who addressed him!

As for "blatant bad faith," we are not going to respond to that, because we would not want *Il Proletario* to take the pretext of our vivaciousness to state that it has been insulted and thereby escape the discussion of ideas in which we invited it to participate.

Dreyfus's Conviction [by Charles-Albert]

Translated from "La condanna di Dreyfus," *La Questione Sociale* (Paterson, New Jersey) 5, new series, no. 6 (October 14, 1899)

[*In this article, taken from* Les Temps Nouveaux,[78] *Charles-Albert condemns the "despicable half-solution employed in Rennes," and foreshadows that "this camouflaged acquittal, which seems so designed to placate, is an order or a wish handed down from above."*][79]

---

77   "Corrispondenze. Da Paterson," again in the October 7 issue of *Il Proletario*.
78   "Le verdict," September 16–22, 1899.
79   In the second military trial held in Rennes following the re-opening of the case, Alfred Dreyfus was convicted of treason with extenuating circumstances, notwithstanding the fact that the charges had been shown to be baseless. Dreyfus agreed to apply for clemency, which was granted to him by the president of the Republic, Émile Loubet.

After the conviction the government has pardoned Dreyfus, in order to be done with the *affair* and cover up the shame of the military chiefs of staff and the military judges.

Thus ends the hope of seeing the head of the reaction crushed, a hope that induced socialists and even anarchists to speak up in defense of the republican government and applaud Loubet and back Waldeck and Galliffet.[80]

They will now be convinced that a government can never champion freedom and will never oppose the chiefs of the army, who are its protectors... and often its commanders.

Our Correspondence. From Barre, Vermont. Malatesta Lectures [by S. Pallavicini]

Translated from "Nostre Corrispondenze. Da Barre, Vermont. Conferenze Malatesta," *La Questione Sociale* (Paterson, New Jersey) 5, new series, no. 7 (October 21, 1899)

The last of the five lectures given by comrade Malatesta—organized by the Barre anarchists—was held on this Thursday the 5th.[81] Dr. Dino Rondani was unable to attend the last two because he had to urgently return to New York.

There was a very wide-ranging debate between Malatesta and Rondani on two topics: "Parliamentarianism, Evolution, and Revolution" and "Fatherland, Family, and Religion." In elaborating his thinking on the subject of Parliamentarianism,

---

80   In a France deeply divided by the Dreyfus affair, President Loubet, who favored a review of the trial, came under furious attacks, including physical assault, to which Dreyfusards responded with demonstrations of solidarity. In this climate of crisis which raised fears of a nationalist coup d'état, Loubet asked Pierre Waldeck-Rousseau in June 1899 to form a new government of "republican defense," whose members ranged from minister of war Gaston de Galliffet, the notorious "butcher of the Commune," to Alexandre Millerand, minister of trade and industry, the first socialist in a government under the Third Republic. On these matters, see also the article "The Socialist Split in France," p. 111.

81   The September 30 issue of *La Questione Sociale* carried this summary of Malatesta's schedule of lectures in Barre:

  ...On Tuesday September 26 he spoke on the topic "The Social Question and what anarchists want"; on Thursday September 28, on the topic "Parliamentarianism, Evolution, and Revolution."

   Saturday September 30, he will address the topic: "Fatherland, Religion, Family."

   Tuesday, October 3 he will speak about "Workers' organizations and the anarchist movement."

   Thursday October 5 on the topic "How and when anarchy will triumph."

Malatesta pointed out that socialists who think along the lines of Rondani have lately declared themselves supporters of a tactic destined to set their party back many steps, since that tactic tends to ensure that socialists in Italy have to co-operate with revolutionary action in establishing a republic, then leaving the "new government" the task of legislating for the people's economic good and for the social and political freedoms they will want and will demand through their representatives "freely elected by universal suffrage." In Rondani's opinion, anarchists too should take part in the upcoming demolition of the Italian monar-chy and—like the socialists of 1900—"loyally" contribute to raise the republican bourgeoisie to power and consolidate their rule, so as, they say, to radically destroy the Savoy tree which bears fruit today—to a greater or lesser extent tasted by the people—that have the names of Camorra, Reaction, Tyranny.

On this subject, Malatesta said that the anarchists will certainly take part in the upcoming revolution in Italy and that they will do their best to cooperate in destroying the monarchy, but will not, however, act as Rondani predicts when a new power takes the place of the one abolished. The anarchists—said Malates-ta—are tenacious enemies of any and every authority: if tomorrow they copartic-ipate in a revolution in Italy, they will be doing so with the firm aim of preventing, as far as possible, the long-term establishment of the "bourgeois" republic for which Rondani has such high hopes: by fighting it in this manner, the new power will unfailingly be too weak to indulge itself in the luxury of suppressing and restricting the liberties that the people will have won. Anarchists expect little from the monarchy, but even less from a republic based on popular referendums and universal suffrage.

The causes of social misery can be traced to the authorities that sanction property and protect it with rifles and cannons: we must therefore destroy the hundred-headed beast that goes by the name of government if we wish to be sure that—in the future—humanity will be truly emancipated from political and economic domination.

And here allow me to observe that *Il Proletario*, in its latest issue's brief report of what was said by the two adversaries on this point, does state that "Malatesta admits that a concerted effort may be necessary in order to tear down the hurdle to all progress, the Monarchy," but completely forgets to mention the *highly convincing* arguments that our comrade made against the responses from its editor-in-chief. And yet the discussion of the issue was quite lively and prolonged![82]

. . .

On Religion, our friend Rondani repeats the same arguments you were al-ready told about in a prior article of mine,[83] despite Malatesta having argued at length for the absolute necessity of fighting against this root cause of the subju-gation and moral humiliation of the working masses which survives for reasons

82   See "Correspondence. Barre, Vermont," p. 258.
83   S. P., "Dagli Stati Uniti. Barre Vt. Conferenze Rondani," *La Questione Sociale* 5, no. 125 (August 19, 1899).

that even Rondani *admits,* resulting from that institution that supports the tyrannies of government and the bourgeoisie and has always absolved the kings, the ministers and the generals who order and carry out the bloody crackdowns on the people that history has recorded.

On the subject of the economy, the family, and the fatherland, as well as workers' organizations, the democratic socialists and libertarian socialists found themselves nearly in agreement ...

The Socialist Split in France

Translated from "La scissione socialista in Francia," *La Questione Sociale* (Paterson, New Jersey) 5, new series, no. 8 (October 28, 1899)

Object lesson.

The democratic socialists have a habit of saying that the electoral struggle educates the people in socialism, and that the socialists' entry into parliament prepares the way for the triumph of the proletariat.

Let them meditate on what is happening in France.

With the excuse that the republic was in danger and that all progressive forces needed to unite to resist the clerical and legitimist reaction and bring the Dreyfus Affair to a just conclusion, one of the most important socialist members of parliament, Millerand, thought it wise to accept a position in a bourgeois cabinet, headed by the arch-bourgeois Waldeck-Rousseau and featuring Galliffet, the notorious butcher of Parisians.[84]

This event did not go without protest.

On behalf of various socialist groupings, Guesde, Vaillant, Lafargue, Deville, and several others published a manifesto, whose criticisms of the policy of compromise and the whole tactic adopted by the socialists in recent years, could have been signed by anarchists.[85]

"We must (the manifesto states) put an end to a so-called socialist policy, made up of compromises and deviations, which for far too long

---

84 See note 80.
85 In January 1899 the various French socialist forces had formed a "socialist committee of accord," but the Millerand affair rekindled their divisions. The manifesto that Malatesta is talking about, addressed "To working class and socialist France" dated from July 1899. Jules Guesde and Paul Lafargue were among the signatories belonging to the French Workers' Party, of Marxist inspiration, and Édouard Vaillant among those from the Blanquist-inspired Socialist Revolutionary Party. The manifesto was also endorsed by members of the Revolutionary Communist Alliance. Gabriel Deville, another historical figure in French socialism, was not among the signatories. For a profile of the socialist forces involved, see "*Socialist* Congress?" p. 189.

has replaced the class and consequently revolutionary politics of the militant proletariat and socialist party...

"The socialist party, a class party, cannot be or become a ministerial party, under penalty of suicide. It should not share power with the bourgeoisie in whose hands the State can only be an instrument of social conservatism and oppression. Its mission is to seize power from them and use it as a tool for liberation, for social revolution...

"The contradiction between these two policies ('the reformist tactic and the revolutionary tactic') unfailingly had to arise one day or another. And the entry of a socialist into a Waldeck-Rousseau cabinet, arm in arm with the executioner of the Communards, has brought it to light so seriously and scandalously as to rule out any further agreement between those who have compromised socialism's honor and interests and those whose mission it is to defend them."[86]

All of this is great; but the signatories of the manifesto are not the ones entitled to say so, since they are the very ones who sent French socialism down the slippery path of parliamentary and reformist politics and who, long before Millerand, compromised socialism's honor and interests with all manner of deals and lies. Well before Millerand was admitted into the socialist party with all his baggage as a bourgeois democratic politician, the French socialist organizations, following the example of the German party, had left their socialist principles in second place in order to dabble in petty, unfeasible, and insignificant reforms, setting aside socialism and revolution, as Kropotkin puts it, for holidays and solemn occasions.

Have not socialist members of parliament already backed repeatedly bourgeois cabinets, like those of Bourgeois and Brisson, that contained not even one of their number? Did they not refuse to vote to repeal the "wicked laws"—something worse than Pelloux's "political measures"—for fear of compromising the Bourgeois cabinet?[87]

Guesde and his people referred to the anarchists as "imbeciles, lunatics or spies" because they said many things that they themselves are now saying in their protest against Millerand.

---

86   In the original French text this paragraph and the preceding one appear reversed in order.

87   The Radical Léon Bourgeois governed France from November 1895 until April 1896, with decisive support from the socialists; Henri Brisson was prime minister for about four months in 1898; repressive measures known as the "wicked laws" (lois scélérates) were introduced between 1893 and 1894 following the anarchist Auguste Vaillant's attack at the Chamber of Deputies, followed in June 1894 by the killing of President Sadi Carnot by another anarchist, Sante Caserio (see also "The 'Wicked Laws' in France," p. 163); the "political measures" proposed by the Pelloux government in 1899 aimed to restrict freedom of the press, association, assembly and strike (on the ensuing parliamentary battles see "Minority Rights and the Ballot Box Trial," p. 139).

Guesde was happy and enthusiastic about the election of Lafargue, which was successful due to a coalition of socialists and Catholics.

Guesde, Vaillant, and others have repeatedly lent the support of their names to impostors from the ranks of the petty bourgeoisie and have also defended them against the workers.

To secure a seat as a member of parliament, Guesde trampled over everything he had adored, and even went so far as to post vile patriotic fliers in his name, printed on tricolor paper.

At the 1896 London congress, to bring in Millerand, who claimed he was fully entitled to take part in the congress only because he was a member of parliament, Guesde insulted the representatives of France's organized workers.[88]

Guesde, Deville, and the whole lot of them strove for years to diminish socialism and have the petty bourgeoisie accept it as a harmless thing that respected vested interests and consisted entirely of little democratic reforms.

And now that Millerand, more logical or more cunning than them, has drawn the consequences of a long-followed policy and seized power at the first favorable opportunity, what are they complaining about?

Aside from reasons of ambition and personal rivalries that may have influenced the split, we can readily understand how Guesde, former Bakuninist, former anarchist, and Vaillant, former member of the Commune and friend of Blanqui, may have rebelled against the logical consequences of their premises, when those consequences reached the point of bringing together a socialist with Waldeck-Rousseau and Galliffet in the same ministry.

But the young, who are free of the influence wielded by revolution memories, even unconsciously, over the minds of those who were once serious socialists and revolutionaries, the young who have never known any other socialism but the fake socialism preached today by the democratic socialists, are for logic, and back Millerand against those who today come to make a late appeal to principles long since betrayed and forgotten.

Jaurès says: "... if there is a compromise it dates from the day when the socialist party agreed to an immediate action program, a program of reforms and compromises. They require the legal protection of workers' associations, the establishment of a ministry of labor, retirement

---

88   At the London Congress (see note 27), in contrast with the close, painstaking scrutiny of the anarchists' mandates, Millerand asserted his right to take part with no mandate at all, simply because he represented the socialists in parliament. Among the representatives of organized workers in France was Malatesta himself, who had a mandate from the steelworkers of Amiens.

pensions for all workers, labor inspection of manufacturing, the 8-hour work-day law, etc. And I need not recall the famous agricultural program of the workers' party, regarding which, in a somewhat harsh piece in *Neue Zeit*, Engels reproached Guesde for "so many deviations and so many compromises."[89]

Jaurès continues: "Either Guesde and Vaillant will abandon this reformist program and retreat into the sterile intransigence of *doctrinal anarchism,* or they will have no right to say that the socialist party should always and at any price be an opposition party, that makes no distinction between different bourgeois elements; they have either to tear up their program or tear up their manifesto. Guesde and Vaillant would probably prefer to sacrifice a little logic in order to be free of that alternative."

And it looks as if the great majority of groups from the various French democratic socialist organizations have joined Jaurès to object to the split triggered by Guesde and Vaillant and reassert their trust in "citizen" Millerand.

And nearly every democratic socialist abroad stands by Jaurès and Millerand.

Logic will have its way.

*
**

Guesde and Vaillant remember now that socialism is the program of the proletariat struggling against the propertied classes and that it must necessarily be revolutionary.

But they themselves have transformed socialism from revolutionary to reformist and have all but renounced the class struggle, which is to say they have ceased to be true socialists, from the day they embraced the vote as the way to fight and win.

Proletarians who are aware of their position know that they cannot emancipate themselves nor make serious and lasting improvements in their conditions unless they take possession of the raw materials and instruments of production held today by the propertied class; they know that this class will never voluntarily renounce its privileges; they know that existing institutions support each other and cannot effectively be altered without stepping outside of the legal framework established for the protection of those institutions and tearing them all down—and so they are revolutionaries. And those proletarians, who are not yet aware of their rights and their needs, become revolutionary once the darkness is routed from their minds.

---

89   The agrarian program had been adopted by the French Workers' Party at the Marseilles Congress of September 1892, and extended at the Nantes Congress in September 1894. That same year Engels had criticized it in an article on the "Agrarian Question in France and Germany."

But there is another class, still more or less dissatisfied, who some-times suffers just as much as the proletarians and sometimes even more. This is the petty bourgeoisie, the class of small property owners, small merchants, employees, less fortunate professionals, shop owners, in short all those who, though finding things tight, enjoy certain privileges and hope to improve their position and perhaps grow richer by cashing in on the advantages over the proletariat that the current structure of society gives them.

This class is unhappy, it craves reforms, and may, unlike the prole-tariat, secure obtainable reforms that offer real benefits by way of leg-islation; sometimes, if the government taxes too much and favors the interests of the fat bourgeoisie too much, it becomes rebellious against the government and shows a readiness to back revolutionaries... as long as those revolutionaries can assure it that deep down they mean to rev-olutionize only those things that bother the petty bourgeoisie. Because the petty bourgeoisie, out of fear of losing their pathetic privileges, in hopes of climbing the ranks of the fat bourgeoisie, and drawing from the biases of their upbringing which teach them to scorn workers, are devot-ed to private property and become fiercely reactionary the moment that property rights are called into question.

Faced with this petty bourgeoisie, the attitude that revolutionary socialists should adopt is plain and simple: target them with propaganda, force them to understand why they should be making common cause with the proletariat, not just for reasons of justice and for the lasting and general good of humanity, but also naturally in their own interests, and then deal with them as friends or enemies depending on whether they stand with or against the workers.

But the relations between socialists and the petty bourgeoisie com-pletely change once the socialists embrace electoral tactics.

The petty bourgeoisie represents a big voting bloc; indeed it is the only bloc that can oppose, in terms of suffrage and legality, the excessive power of the government and the rich. Proletarians either have no vote, or if they have the vote they are incapable of mounting serious lawful opposition, due to the material and moral conditions in which they find themselves, when the petty bourgeoisie sides with the government and the big property owners.

Socialists know, see, experience this reality, and seek an alliance with the petty bourgeoisie; and in order to get it they tone down, hide their own program and end up forgetting about it and turning into simple democrats, in practice, representing the interests of the petty bour-geoisie. And the petty bourgeoisie embraces this socialism, revised and corrected for their use, and seizes the name of socialist and through its embrace kills off real socialism, the socialism of the proletariat.

Millerand's entry into the socialist party, and his participation in a bourgeois cabinet, plus the support he has won from most socialists represents the triumph, within the socialist party, of petty bourgeoisie reformist inclinations over revolutionary and proletarian inclinations.[90]

Guesde and Vaillant may well be saddened by these results; but they were the necessary and predictable consequence, and foreseen by anarchists, of electoral tactics. And it does not end there!

*
**

Guesde and Vaillant now say that the socialist party should not share power with the bourgeoisie. But they are members of parliament; and power is vested not just in the cabinet (executive authority), but also in parliament (legislative authority). Doesn't accepting a seat in parliament constitute sharing power with the bourgeoisie?

Guesde and Vaillant, and alongside them all the democratic socialists of all countries, want to win public power, and they want to win it gradually, little by little. They are delighted to accept minor posts in town councils, proudly counting the growing number of their representatives in parliament, and as long as the numbers grow they are not too worried about the quality... Why should they not also be happy if one of their own has begun to make inroads among the ministers?

For what reason should and could parliament, the legislative authority, be captured gradually, peacefully, and the cabinet, the executive authority, won only at a stroke, by revolution?

Besides, for many years already Guesde and his friends have striven to snuff out the revolutionary spirit of the socialists and proletarians falling under their influence... and always for electoral reasons, so as to be able to somehow capture a seat in the Parliament.

Engels openly stated in the latter years of his life that the time for violent revolutions has passed.

Three years or so ago Guesde himself said (in his speech in the Chamber on June 25, 1896): "Only by using the lawful weapon of universal suffrage, will the collectivist army inevitably, and shortly, become master of the Republic."

Deville has openly declared himself anti-revolutionary: and Lafargue replied to the bourgeois newspapers, which on May 1, 1890 accused the

---

90   In a brief note of ironic debate with *L'Avvenire Sociale,* which had described Millerand as "a manly figure who has sullied his worker's smock by bringing it close to Galliffet's blood-stained stripes," Malatesta pointed out that "rather, Millerand is a perfumed lawyer who declared at the 1896 London Congress that he wanted no relations with anarchists, not even physical proximity to them," and concluded: "Meaning: he was nostalgic for contact with the bourgeoisie and soldiers. May he stay close to Waldeck-Rousseau and Galliffet. Right where he belongs." ("I socialisti al potere," *La Questione Sociale,* December 2, 1899).

socialists of having revolutionary intentions, that considering revolution in a country which had a republic and universal suffrage would be like trying to break down an open door.

In Lille on July 11 of this year, at an anti-clerical demonstration, the director of a socialist newspaper, *Le Réveil du Nord,* called for and cheered by the crowd, said: "*At present, the socialist party is the party of order.* I therefore ask you to disperse and return quietly to your homes."

But then, if we need to conquer public authority and we need not think of revolutionary methods, how on earth could Millerand joining the Waldeck-Rousseau cabinet amount to a betrayal, rather than a step towards the goal he is pursuing?

But, say Guesde and Vaillant, (and all those who have, amid the deviations and corruption of parliamentary politics, and in defiance of logic, held on to their love for the true cause of socialism) in this manner the socialist party is placing itself in the service of the bourgeoisie and ceasing to be socialist!

Perfectly.

Given the electoral approach, what had to happen has happened, and so it is, so it shall be. Just as the anarchists, those "fools, lunatics, and spies," as Guesde used to describe them, have always said.

Unawareness and Cowardice
[by Domenico Zavattero]

Translated from "Incoscienza e viltà," *La Questione Sociale*
(Paterson, New Jersey) 5, new series, no. 8 (October 28, 1899)

[Zavattero laments the fact that the "propagandists of every party… address the people with adulation and praise," in addition to being all too ready to praise the work done by themselves and their party. However, he goes on to say, "what a painful contrast there is between the unawareness and cowardice of the masses and the 'comrades,' and the statements both use to paint us in such rosy colors!" In Zavattero's opinion, attachment to the past, ignorance, love of personal tranquility, selfishness, and fear of compromising oneself are "the merits and virtues that characterize the current generation, the people of today." As regards comrades, they admire and applaud whoever sacrifices himself, but if an attempt is made to get them to act they start complaining that "the masses are apathetic and asleep" and offer other excuses for their inaction. Zavattero concludes with an appeal to the real anarchists "to shake off their placid indifference before all is lost."]

We have published Zavattero's article because it reveals a *frame of mind* that is all the more interesting to know and study because it reveals itself in a clever and courageous comrade like Zavattero. But that is not to say we share his pessimism.

This Olympian contempt for the "cowardly and unaware masses," when it is not the posturing of supermen, is an expression to the weariness and discouragement, which periodically develop in those who periodically get excited and see everything through the prism of their own desires.

We strive to not lose sight of objective reality, we strive to retain a reasonable balance in our judgments; since our action will be good or bad, effective or useless in accordance with how correct or incorrect our judgment is.

Certainly the masses are not as we would wish, but then there would be no need for us to make propaganda, nor would we have to prepare for a violent revolution which, by changing the environment, makes the moral elevation of the people possible. But nor are the people a jumble of brutes as they are often described by those who are weary of the struggle; nor is the present generation, "the people of today," in any respect inferior to the people of the past.

It is from the masses that we have drawn our ideas; and when, having organized them, we bring these ideas back to the masses, we find a sympathetic echo from the masses, as long as we understand how to act with intelligence and muster all the patience and perseverance required.

Moreover Zavattero complains about those comrades who excuse their own inactivity by saying that the masses *are apathetic and asleep.* If his pessimism was justified, then the inertia of those comrades would be justified as well. Has Zavattero never thought about that?

Let us work actively, incessantly, to spread our ideas and prepare ourselves to perform the serious duties which the situation can thrust upon us at a moment's notice—and in this we are in perfect agreement with comrade Zavattero.

Let us remind ourselves that, as the saying goes, the world was not made in a day; but let us also bear in mind that with perseverance anything is possible.

Challenge

Translated from "Sfida," *La Questione Sociale*
(Paterson, New Jersey) 5, new series, no. 8 (October 28, 1899)

Il Proletario calls us *good people*, and how right it is.[91]

Despite our previous interactions, we were naive enough to believe that it might be possible to draw them into a serious discussion of ideas.

Instead they have answered us rather wittily, distorting our ideas in a manner perhaps appropriate in a police journal, but certainly not a socialist organ and... without even an argument.

What a way to treat us! As long as *Il Proletario* can find *good people* who are content with its approach of *non-discussion* and who fail to see how this shying away from discussion is indicative of a lack of conviction and sincerity, it can continue.

We are stubborn, though. Since we see that it is impossible to draw it into a written discussion (that is a discussion in which what has been said is on the record and cannot be denied or changed ten times during the course of a single evening) we shall make do with what *Il Proletario* cannot decently refuse us without being accused of bad faith even by the most lenient.[92] And we invite it—WE CHALLENGE IT—to enlist one of its editors to come and publicly debate with one of our editors the lies and nonsense peddled about our ideas in its issue of October 11,[93] and then to publish, as we will publish, an extensive report on the discussion, drafted jointly by the two speakers.

Our representative will be in touch with the editorial staff of *Il Proletario* to arrange the place and date for the debate.

---

91   *Il Proletario* (New York) 4, no. 27 (October 21, 1899). The short article, untitled and on the front page, revolves around the repetition of the reference to "good people" to describe the anarchists, up to the closing paragraph: "Good people, who take from socialism just enough to give themselves the authority to reject the greater part, diluting it with anarchist water, under the claim of making it authentic." The same issue of *La Questione Sociale* contained another response to *Il Proletario*, entitled "I Socialisti-Democratici 'ad usum Proletario'" (Democratic Socialists 'for the use of *Il Proletario*') and signed by "Ri-Parlachiaro," parroting *Il Proletario* by twisting the epithet "good people" against the democratic socialists.

92   The polemical reference here is to Rondani, see the untitled note dated January 6, 1900, p. 200.

93   The date is evidently a typo requiring correction to "October 21," since no issue of *Il Proletario* came out on October 11.

[Untitled]

Translated from *La Questione Sociale*
(Paterson, New Jersey) 5, new series, no. 8 (October 28, 1899)

Comrade Errico Malatesta—considering the protests being published in the Italian newspapers, as well as others that have reached us directly, regarding the slight accident that happened to him and which we believe is not even worth talking about—thanks the friends who have in such a manner expressed their sympathy with him, but begs them... to let that be the end of it.[94]

---

94 At a meeting held on September 3 in West Hoboken (New Jersey) one of the participants, Domenico Pazzaglia, had wounded Malatesta in the leg with a pistol shot. In Italy, the news appeared in the September 18, 1899 issue of *Avanti!*

SECTION IV
Against the Monarchy, Towards Anarchy

Our Financial Situation

Translated from "Il nostro bilancio," *La Questione Sociale*
(Paterson, New Jersey) 5, new series, no. 9 (November 4, 1899)

Some comrades might very well marvel that, though recently our takings have been relatively substantial, the newspaper is still under the weight of a deficit.

It will therefore be useful to give a full explanation of our financial situation. It is true that it already appears in our weekly financial statements; but we reckon it is better to err on the side of excessive clarity, rather than deficiency.

When the new series of LA QUESTIONE SOCIALE began, the position was as follows:

Apparent deficit inherited from the previous management, $58.92; but to that deficit add $10 owed to the *Biblioteca Libertaria* for pamphlets; plus $20 owed to the Paterson Committee for Revolutionary Movements; plus $12 to be paid for overdue rent on the space; which made a total deficit of $100.92.

We enlarged the paper, which leads to a greater expense for composition, paper and printing of $7.50 per week; we spent $41.23 on new printing materials, required for the larger format; we paid off $10 to the *Biblioteca Libertaria*; we paid off $12 of overdue rent; we paid off $20 to the Committee for Revolutionary Movements;—and we find ourselves with a $57 deficit, after all expenses are paid for the current issue.

Meaning that, despite the extraordinary expenses of $83.23 to acquire materials and paying off debts, and despite the ordinary increase in expenses caused by the enlargement, the deficit has diminished, over 9 issues, by $43.92.[95]

That is already a satisfying result, and we offer our congratulations to the comrades on the enthusiasm with which they support the paper.

But is still falls short: just to exist normally, the newspaper needs to pay off its deficit, cover all necessary expenses every week, and also build a surplus that will keep it safe from any temporary obstacles.

Which is why the comrades should never fail to pay their subscriptions and take it upon themselves to urge the forgetful to pay up; and they should make every possible effort (chiefly for the sake of propaganda) to widen the circle of readers and subscribers.

---

95   The final calculation contains a mistake, since the payment of debts is both included among the extraordinary expenses and deducted from the deficit, thereby being counted twice. It should have been stated that the deficit remained nearly unchanged because of extraordinary expenses, or the payments of debts should have been excluded from those expenses.

We do not think that reminders are needed to encourage comrades to put us in a position where we can not only publish the paper regularly, but also undertake other propaganda efforts.

Some localities have already done all they could, bringing their subscriptions up to date, making contributions to the donation fund, and organizing events on the paper's behalf. If other places will do likewise, the newspaper will flourish.

***

Readers will have noted that before our administrative accounts were not published with the costs of the current issue, so the deficit looked smaller than it was, or the surplus larger.

We have now corrected that error; and in every issue there will be an exact report of the newspaper's financial situation, as of the day of that issues's publication.

Police Exploits

Translated from "Gesta poliziesche," *La Questione Sociale* (Paterson, New Jersey) 5, new series, no. 9 (November 4, 1899)

In *La Tribuna* the lawyer Morello writes, concerning the unrest for the release of Cesare Batacchi, the internationalist falsely accused of having thrown a bomb in Florence in 1878, and thus despite his innocence sentenced to life imprisonment:

[In the lengthy excerpt the lawyer mentions that two witnesses had confessed that their evidence against Batacchi was false and had been given at the instigation of Florence police.]

***

Honest people shudder, and wonder how on earth so many dirty deeds could have been done to send innocent men to prison; and how, after the false witnesses confessed to their lies, and the manner in which the police secured a conviction has been revealed, could those sentenced to prison terms of up to nineteen years remain in jail, and how could Batacchi, given a life sentence, remain there today and could remain there until the end of his days, if the people's unrest fails to pull him away from his executioners!

Unfortunately his is not an isolated case. It is the general system of the police and the judiciary throughout the ages and in every country to set out to find offenders among all who fall into their hands, at any cost.

From threats to physical or psychological torture, from false evidence to fake documents, they use anything to secure a conviction. And when someone's innocence becomes apparent, the judges and police fight tooth and nail to prevent their prey from escaping. This madness for persecuting, convicting, torturing comes with the job.

Take the Frezzi and Forno cases, Acciarito's second trial, the Montjuich trial, and all cases of justice betrayed, which can be collected by the thousands.[96]

*
**

And after all this, there are still some wondering how the people could defend themselves against potential criminals if there were no longer judges and policemen!

Let them instead find ways of defending themselves against the judges and police, until they can finally be destroyed.

Open Reply to an "Intransigent" [by Domenico]

Translated from "Risposta aperta ad un 'intransigente,'" *La Questione Sociale* (Paterson, New Jersey) 5, new series, no. 9 (November 4, 1899)

[*In the open letter, addressed to "Paolo" and dated "London, October 18, 1899," "Domenico" responds to a letter in which his correspondent informed him that he absolutely felt no need for an agreement between the revolutionary parties, since "the coming revolution cannot be an anarchist revolution, hence it should be of no concern to anarchists." According to Paolo, "being anarchists, we should only be interested in what directly concerns anarchy and not, in the coming revolution, take to the streets to save someone else's bacon." The author's response is largely* ad personam.][97]

---

96   Romeo Frezzi, arrested in connection with Acciarito's assassination attempt, had died on May 2, 1897 in a prison in Rome following a beating by the police. In September that same year Andrea Forno was beaten in the Genoa police headquarters and died shortly thereafter. In the June 1899 trial of the alleged accomplices of Pietro Acciarito, who attempted to take the king's life in April 1897, it transpired that the confession by which Acciarito had compromised the accused was the product of psychological torture. Finally, torture inflicted in Spain in 1897 upon anarchists secluded in the Montjuich fortress in order to extract confessions that would have sent them to the gallows turned into an international case. On this subject see "The Judicial Crime in Barcelona," "The Barcelona Trial," and "Barcelona's Calvary" in Volume III of these *Complete Works*, p. 52, 90, and 107, respectively.

97   The author of the letter, who claims to have recently written "a lot and at length on the subject," could have been Domenico Zavattero, who in London

As is evident from this open letter, it seems as if a few comrades think there is a contradiction between staying loyal to the anarchist ideas and taking part in the coming, and any revolutionary, movement. Some, lest they betray their ideas, would rather remain neutral in an uprising from which they do not expect the immediate success of anarchy, whereas others, so as not to renounce taking part in the insurrection, show a tendency to postpone the realization of the ideal until the cows come home.

This is a very important issue upon which it would be good to open a wide-ranging debate between comrades.

As for ourselves, we believe that the alleged contradiction does not exist; and that it is precisely to serve the anarchist ideal that anarchists must take part in any movement; but take part as anarchists, on behalf of their ideas, and not to save someone else's bacon.

We will revisit this matter in the next issue.[98]

Editors' note

[Untitled]

Translated from *La Questione Sociale*
(Paterson, New Jersey) 5, new series no. 9 (November 4, 1899)

The newspapers are calling Cesare Batacchi the Dreyfus of Italy.[99]

Let's not confuse the two.

Dreyfus is a soldier who, without even the excuse of necessity, voluntarily chose to make manslaughter his profession. He certainly would have thought it his duty to command the opening of fire on workers when ordered to do so by his superiors; and, circumstances permitting, he would have made a career out of massacring people like an ordinary Galliffet. Instead, things did not go as he had hoped, and he has fallen victim to the wicked institutions he once defended.

---

in 1899 had published *I Rivoluzionari e la situazione in Italia* (Revolutionaries and the situation in Italy), in which he proposed that all revolutionary forces come together to attack the established powers.

98   In reality the matter would not be addressed further in subsequent issues. It had nevertheless been extensively addressed in "Against the Monarchy" and "Revolutionary Alliance," p. 16 and 95, respectively.

99   An article entitled "Carlo [*sic*] Batacchi: Il Dreyfus italiano!" had appeared in the September 9, 1899 issue of *Il Proletario* (New York). On the day after this article, on November 5, *Il Progresso Italo-Americano* opened with an editorial entitled "La pietosa storia di Cesare Batacchi. Il Dreyfus d'Italia" (Cesare Batacchi's pitiful tale. Italy's Dreyfus).

One might argue that the hunter has been caught in his own trap.

Batacchi on the other hand was an internationalist, an anarchist socialist; and though innocent he was sent to prison because he defended justice and freedom.

Dreyfus was pitied by us when he was cruelly tortured by his colleagues.

Cesare Batacchi, tortured by the enemies of the people, enjoys our respect, admiration, and love.

Martyrdom in Chicago.
November 11, 1887

Translated from "Il martirio di Chicago. 11 Novembre 1887," *La Questione Sociale* (Paterson, New Jersey) 5, new series, no. 10 (November 11, 1899)[100]

"The day will come when our silence will be more powerful than
the voices you strangle today"
[*Words spoken from the gallows by August Spies*][101]

And indeed the silence of those magnanimous ones, martyrs of the anarchist cause, victims of their love of humanity, was powerful: it was powerful because their martyrdom gave birth to thousands upon thousands that continue their work; and it is still powerful because when we remember them our mind ignites with a sacred passion, and we sense that, whatever we do for the cause, it will always be little compared to the splendid example of devotion and sacrifice they gave us.

Here, briefly, are the facts.

In the spring of 1886 the workers of Chicago were taking action to have the work day reduced to eight hours. Strikes, rallies, demonstrations, followed one after another and multiplied.

Anarchists, aware of and vocal about the fact that the oppression of workers will not end until there are no more property-owners nor governments, stood at their post, among the people, and encouraged them to hold strong and increase their demands. For the anarchists it was

---

100   This article is a reworked version of a flyer "Martyrdom in Chicago: A Republican Murder," published anonymously in 1890 by the group that months earlier had edited *L'Associazione*. The differences between the two versions are such that they justify their separate reprinting. The present article was republished in Luigi Fabbri's *Lotta Umana* and in other anarchist newspapers with Malatesta's signature attached to it.

101   Brackets in the original text.

important people see that when they truly want something, and trust direct action to get it, there isn't a force in the world that can stand in their way.

On May 3, at the gates of a plant, there was a demonstration by strikers, accompanied by women and children, against the master and against workers who, lacking solidarity with their comrades, went to work; and stones were thrown at the plant. The police, alerted by telephone, rushed to the scene, and were greeted with expressions of hostility from the demonstrators. In response they fired a few shots from their revolvers, to which the workers replied with stones and their own revolvers. Then the police opened live and continuous fire on the crowd, not caring that women, children, and elderly were there. Left lying on the ground were six dead and many wounded, all from the people's side.

Upset by the massacre, Spies, an editor of the German anarchist newspaper *Arbeiter Zeitung*, raced to the editorial office and wrote a manifesto entitled *Revenge Circular* which, after a few changes suggested by Fischer, was printed in twenty thousand copies, and distributed at all worker meetings. It was an invitation to come to a protest against the police in Haymarket Square on the evening of the 4th.

That meeting was indeed held, without serious incident. There were only a few hundred people still left in the square, when the police appeared and marched against the crowd, with bayonets lowered, charging.

At that point, an energetic man, who remained unknown, hurled a bomb into the police lines, killing one of them and wounding seventy.[102]

The people, who had gathered at the rally unarmed, did not know how and were unable to make the most of the effect produced by the bomb; and the police, recovering from their terror, indulged in all manner of violence. Thereafter all those who were well-known, or most feared, in the workers' movement were arrested, and the trial began.

The anarchists, who were later convicted of the act, had already left the square when the police arrived and the bomb was tossed; and the prosecution failed to show any connection between them and the unknown person who had thrown the bomb.

But the bourgeoisie was frightened, and no one is as ferocious as cowards: they wanted to stop the workers' movement which had gained such magnificent momentum, and this opportunity seemed propitious. They bought off the judges, jury members, witnesses, and sought and secured the conviction of those whom it saw as the leaders of the movement, because they were its most passionate and intelligent champions.

August SPIES, Albert R. PARSONS, Louis LINGG, Michael SCHWAB,

---

102   The final count of the victims, resulting from the bomb blast and the ensuing gunfire, was actually of seven police officers and no less than four civilians.

Samuel FIELDEN, George ENGEL, and Adolf FISCHER were sentenced to death; Oscar NEEBE, the charges against whom the public prosecutor had dropped, was sentenced to fifteen years of forced labor.

Sentenced, they were held for over a year in prison under the threat of execution; and were tormented in a thousand ways, in hopes of an act of weakness that might diminish the prestige of their martyrs' halo. But it was all useless. Right to the end these strong men remained worthy of their cause. Just as during the hearing they had stood by their principles even at the risk of their lives and turned the defendant's bench into an apostles' pulpit, so in prison they made every effort to use their hardship in service of the cause and to prevent their friends from stooping to apply for clemency, and so they died at the gallows, where they climbed up smiling, their minds cheered by the vision of a future of justice and happiness that their blood will have helped to assure for the human race.

On November 11, 1887, PARSONS, FISCHER, ENGEL, and SPIES were hanged. LINGG committed suicide—or had been forced to kill himself—in prison. FIELDEN and SCHWAB had their sentences commuted, and ended up in the penitentiary along with NEEBE.

Six years later, in June 1893, along came (a singular occurrence) a governor, ALTGELD of Illinois, who acknowledged the full disgrace of the trial, spelled it out in an unforgettable message and, exercising the rights given to him under United States law, released the three convicts in complete freedom.

People, remember! Your masters have no mercy. They have none in America, they have none in Europe; they have none under a republic, they have none under a monarchy; they have none in Chicago, they have none in Conselice nor in Milan.[103] And don't ask them for any.

You languish in misery and wretchedness—and you will remain there until you rise to rid yourselves once and for all of these greedy masters, these ignoble rulers, who live off your sweat, who quench their thirst with your blood.

For the tears of your daughters prostituted by the rich, for the groans of your brothers starving to death, for the blood of those who died for your sake, for your dignity, for your own self-interest—ready yourself for the grand struggle and as soon as you can, at the first chance you get, enter the fray to win all of the freedom, all of the wealth.

---

103   In Conselice three workers were killed during a demonstration in May 1890; the reference to Milan concerns the events of May 1898 (see note 19).

Our Organization

Translated from "La nostra organizzazione," *La Questione Sociale*
(Paterson New Jersey) 5, new series, no. 10 (November 11, 1899)

In all our propaganda, we have always insisted upon the distinction between authoritarian organization and anarchist organization.

Authoritarian organization, which is to say the type in which some command and others obey, derives from the arrogance of those who finds themselves, in some way, in a more advantageous situation than others, as well as from the submissiveness and apathy of the masses, who, unwilling and unable to manage for themselves, let themselves be dominated by someone who sets them to work in his place, with the pretext, or perhaps the sincere intention, of doing good for them. In an authoritarian organization the rulers are always, in practice, a very small number of individuals; but even if they accounted for the numerical majority of the organized, their domination would not be any less unfair and fecund with corruption and woes of every kind for the rulers and the ruled alike.

Anarchist organization is the agreement of those who, having a common aim to achieve, unite under a common interest and divide the work as they think most appropriate to achieve that goal, each having a moral responsibility only to those agreements that he freely accepted, and only for as long as he accepts them.

Organization, which is to say not casual but systematic organized cooperation, being vital to any social life, needs to be the deliberate outcome of the wishes of all of those concerned, so that it does not become oppressive. People who believe they can save their own autonomy by avoiding agreements with others, actually suffer more than anyone else from the arrogance of the social environment, as well as that of variously privileged persons. And the only way of overthrowing authority and preventing its overt or covert resurgence, is for everyone to join together with those who share the same ideas, the same interests, the same desires and seek, through voluntary cooperation with them, the means we lack alone.

And since people can agree on one thing and disagree on others, have some common interests and some contrasting ones, they cannot join together in a single gigantic association intended to meet all of life's material and moral needs; but must unite into a hundred different groupings, which can be modified according to changes in ideas and interests; tiny groups in the case of some goal shared by just a few individuals, short-lived groups in the case of short-lived interests; but the broader and more lasting goals to be achieved are shared by many people and require the participation of a large number of people and are more permanent in nature.

*
**

We have stated and repeated these things thousands of times, both about society in general, and about party organizations and any other grouping for specific purposes.

But we can only assume that such things are very hard to understand, or that we have expressed ourselves very poorly, since there are still those who, despite all our objections, continue to tell us: "The organization for which you advocate and which you say is anarchist is essentially authoritarian, since you want the members to submit to the majority, the groups to obey the Federation, the Congresses to be the party's Legislative Assemblies, and the Correspondence Committee its executive power."

Which is the exact opposite of what we want!

They allude to older organizations more or less afflicted with authoritarian residues. But what does that prove against us? If we wished to make a personal issue out of this, we could easily show that those who write this newspaper, and who have been especially called into question, bear none of the responsibility for those mistakes and indeed have played no small part in fighting against them: something that perhaps those who are calling us authoritarians may not be able to say themselves. But what does that matter? We are not writing history here; we are making propaganda: meaning that our thoughts are on the future and not the past; we advocate what we think should be done, not what has already been done.

And even if the organizations, now being created or attempted, do not turn out to be flawless models of anarchism, that would mean that ideas are slow to alter the habits all people acquire from their education and current social life, meaning that, despite the ideas, there are those among us who have a tendency to impose their will and, worse still, those who through apathy or irresponsibility let them get away with it, and suffer the will of others without responding when that will does not correspond to their own. But this does not mean that we are wrong, as we constantly preach that no one should defer to someone else's will and that everybody should play an active, direct part in the common work, unless they want others to do it for them and in their own way: and it does not mean that in order to rebuke the overbearing to show proper respect for others and in order to awaken the will of the passive ones and illuminate the consciousness of the less developed, we must encourage social disintegration, which is the chief cause of bullying by the few and of thoughtlessness of the many.

It seems to us that we have always expressed this very clearly and that it should be impossible, for anyone who reads or listens without prejudice, to misunderstand us. In any event, we shall strive to break the argument down as much as we can.

***

The organization we are dealing with here is an organization for propaganda, and for a propaganda that must lay the moral foundations for revolutionary action, and for the realization of our ideas.

Material preparation for the insurrection perhaps requires organization of a different sort, but we will not deal with that here.

So, organization for propaganda.

Since there is little one can do in isolation—and very many do nothing at all;—since the greater connections are between us the greater the means we have to not just direct propaganda toward others, but also to develop and improve ourselves, we wish to come together, into regular and ongoing relationships, with all who share the same purpose as us, and who wish to cooperate with us in achieving our goals.

To not find ourselves in the alternative—either deferring to the majority in matters of principles and general tactics, which could place us in the position of having to defend ideas other than our own and in any case would accustom us to a form of social coexistence contrary to that we want to achieve—or to split apart the day after we form a union, which would make the organization useless—we want to be sure to agree, and thus to stay united, at least until the situation changes radically and our associates alter their ideas for one reason or another. And so at the foundation of the organization we place a program that generally expresses the goals which those entering the organization seek to achieve, and the means by which they seek to achieve them.

Without believing we are obligated to automatically and without scrutiny recognize as anarchists—in the sense in which we use that term—anyone who wishes to use the name, we do not claim that our program is the only one that reflects the anarchist idea.

If not in terms of final goals, then certainly in terms of methods, there are a hundred different viewpoints, all of which are compatible with the fundamental anarchist idea, which is the idea of a society in which the means of life are accessible to all, where no one has the right to impose his will upon others, and where the entire life of society is rooted in free and voluntary agreement between individuals. But, of course, among the many possible methods more or less likely to achieve the goal, we have our own preferences and want to join together with those who share our preferences, since it is only when you agree on methods—especially upon methods to be used immediately—that cooperation is possible.

***

Organization ordinarily starts with the local group; which does not prevent the possibility of there being groups made up of people living in different locations, who join forces for a specific purpose they all share. Of course within the same location there may well be several groups for general propaganda, if this is allowed or required by the circumstances, or perhaps by personal likes and dislikes; just as there may be groups set up for particular tasks.

Within the group the individual enjoys perfect autonomy, since he joins it, not to submit to the will of others, but in order to give and receive help in those matters he holds dear; therefore he is not required to cooperate on matters which he does not approve, and can always leave the group should an incompatibility arise.

There is nothing for the majority to impose upon the minority, even should the latter consist of a single person. Only in matters unrelated to principles, and in which it is impossible, or disadvantageous, to abide by several resolutions, will the minority find it necessary or useful to adjust to the majority opinion, and will adjust to it. Thus, for instance, if there is a question of scheduling the next meeting and a majority and a minority emerge, if both groups truly want to come together, one side will give way. And if common sense does not prevail, they will not have their meeting, and will feel the practical impact of their stubbornness. All better than authority! especially since, as always, authority and imposition would make things worse rather than better.

Should the group have money, it may need to entrust that money to someone, which is to say to a *treasurer*.

To collect the money needed to cover the group's expenses, or to create a fund to be used as needed, some people prefer to give when and how much they can and want, others choose to commit to pay a set amount, unless it is beyond the realms of possibility, so that the group knows it can count on a certain minimum. And each group will do as it sees fit; and when a group cannot reach a consensus, it can also be arranged that, as has been done on several occasions, those opting for fixed dues should pay them with the rest donating whenever they want.

The group needs to write; and it charges one of its members with writing, on the group's behalf, whatever the group tells them to write. And if, as might be desired, correspondence is regular and active, it will appoint a *secretary* to handle that correspondence and report back to the group. Each member, let us be clear, retains the right to correspond directly with whomever they please, so that far from being an authority figure, the secretary is rendering a service to them all, especially to those who, not being able to write, would find themselves in the dark about everything and would have no means of communicating their thoughts beyond their local area.

The group needs to do a certain thing that they cannot all do, or which does not need to be done by all; and it appoints *Committees,* of its own choosing, or spontaneously nominated, that carry out a given mandate and cannot substitute their own wishes for those of the group.

And so, in all matters, the group will always seek to avoid the danger of authority, and to achieve the greatest possible effectiveness through voluntary agreement.

It is in the interest of all groups to remain in ongoing, active relations to share their ideas and initiatives, and to support one another morally and materially: thus they federate with one another.

This *Federation* does not require any reduction in their autonomy. Like the individual within the group so is the group within the federation, joining it not to submit to the will of others, but to secure support from those who agree with it.

Within the limits of the program, each group does what it wants; and if it departs from the program, naturally no one can stop it, but by doing so it shows that it intends to withdraw from the federation established to championing that program.

When there are many groups, it becomes impossible for each group to correspond with hundreds or thousands of groups, and even if that were feasible, it would be absurd to expend so much of the party's energy and resources on writing and reading and posting letters. Thus the need arises for *Correspondence Committees* charged with receiving communications from each affiliated group and forwarding them to all the other groups through letters or specific bulletins.

Like the group secretary, so the Correspondence Committee in the Federation does not constitute an authority, but is an institution set up for the convenience of all. The groups are always free to correspond with one another without going through the Committee; they can also never use it and therefore never contribute toward its costs; but those groups who believe it can serve them well and that cannot write or receive a large volume of letters on their own, find in it a way of keeping in regular contact with all their comrades and taking from such contacts, if nothing else, an inspiration to act, which costs them little in terms of expense or effort.

Epistolary relations are not enough. From time to time it is useful for comrades to meet, get to know each other, discuss new issues that demand the party's attention, and make arrangements for the smooth operation of the organization.

The ideal would be for everyone to come together; but since that is practically impossible, the answer lies in meetings of comrades—sent by the groups or attending as individuals—who convey to the rest the impressions from their own environments and report back to the groups from which they come, on the outcomes of discussions and the impressions they have gathered. And the more frequently such meetings—or Congresses, if you wish—are held, and the more they are held in different places in order to allow the largest possible number of comrades the opportunity to take part in them from time to time, the better.

The issue of participating with or without a group mandate has no importance beyond the statistical observation; because, in an anarchist organization, Congresses pass no laws and their resolutions are not binding to anyone. At Congresses ideas are discussed and developed, and proposals are made which are then submitted to all the groups and all the members of the organization, and are binding only to those who accept them.

*
**

This is the form of organization, based entirely upon free agreement, that we propose.

Everybody is at liberty to criticize and fight against it; but if you want to discuss it usefully, do so without attributing to us ideas and purposes contrary to those we actually have.

On August 27, the Buenos Aires anarchist communist newspaper *L'Avvenire* published:

"The meetings held last Sunday 7 [*sic*] and Tuesday 15 were impressively successful in terms both of the numbers who participated, and the subjects covered. After having calmly discussed the practicalities of propaganda methods and the effectiveness of propaganda, the following declaration was unanimously approved:

"Many comrades and constituent groups, gathered at the premises of the Social Studies Circle on last Sunday 7 and Tuesday 15, unanimously endorsed as the most effective means the organization of free groups operating autonomously, independently of one another, coming together in momentary agreement only as the needs of propaganda may require."[104]

Which seems to suggest that the comrades in the Argentine Republic have dissolved the Federation established not so long ago.[105]

We are sorry to see that; but we do not see it as an argument against our ideas.

---

104   "Cose locali. Nuova orientazione di propaganda" (Local matters. A new propaganda orientation).
105   The Federation's "Statement of Principles" and "Pact of Alliance" had been approved at an assembly held in Buenos Aires on December 28, 1898 and published in *L'Avvenire* of January 8, 1899.

If those comrades had set up an organization in which the groups were not free and did not operate autonomously, if, as others say, they had set up an "authoritarian, centralized, and bureaucratic" organization, then, they being anarchists, it is only natural they should have felt uncomfortable. Only it seems to us they would have done better to fix the bad, rather than destroy the good along with the bad.

The fact that they find it unnecessary to have a permanent agreement and propose only to *agree momentarily only as the needs of propaganda may require,* shows that they have not found a way to consistently use the strength that comes from everyone cooperating on a common project… and this reveals a weakness, not of this or that tendency, but of the anarchist movement in general.

Let us work actively and we will feel ever more the need for agreement, which is to be all the broader and more steady as our sphere of action will be broader and our activity more steady.

Life is coordination of activity; and the more intense it is, the greater the coordination.

Our Challenge to "Il Proletario"

Translated from "La nostra sfida al 'Proletario,'" *La Questione Sociale* (Paterson, New Jersey) 5, new series, no. 10 (November 11, 1899)

As readers will recall, having failed to draw *Il Proletario* into a discussion about ideas, and seeing that it responded by coarsely twisting our ideas for the use of its readership, we challenged it to a public debate, the report of which, drafted by common accord by the two parties, was to be published by LA QUESTIONE SOCIALE and *Il Proletario*.[106]

Il Proletario responds agreeing to the debate, "generously offering its meeting room" in Paterson (this *generosity* consists of wanting to keep for itself the proceeds which are always left to the owners of meeting rooms at every meeting held in Paterson); but declining to publish a report.[107] Under these conditions we are unable to accept, since publication of the report in both newspapers is essential for us, given that our objective was not to secure for ourselves the pleasure of spending an evening in debate with our more or less gracious adversaries, but to inform readers of *Il Proletario* what our ideas really are, and at the same time provide our readers with a version of the ideas of the *Il Proletario* editors, the authenticity of which could not be called into question, since it would be a work of their own.

---

106   "Challenge," p. 119.
107   "Corrispondenze. Da Paterson," *Il Proletario* (New York) 4, no. 29 (November 4, 1899).

We really cannot understand how men who say they are, and we want to believe, friends of truth and light, can turn down such a proposal—and instead reply to us with a shocking and malicious insinuation as this: "Who could stop LA QUESTIONE *from printing that it has defeated us and left us dead and buried."*

Do these gentlemen thus take their very own readers for imbeciles?

What! we are the ones who, to avoid any possible unintended mistakes in an account written by an adversary, suggest publication of a report reviewed by the concerned parties, and we are the ones *Il Proletario* suggests are capable of deliberately altering the truth!

Moreover, this notion of winning or losing in a debate shows that *Il Proletario's* editors judge the struggle of ideas by rather medieval criteria.

The relative superiority of one idea over another, of one party's program over that of another, is not something that is decided in an evening, in a debate between two more or less competent orators.

Debates, like lectures, serve only to provide food for thought to the public... and to the lecturers, too.

We do not expect anything else; but this already seems like a lot.[108]

To Anarchist Speculators [by Critico]

Translated from "Agli Anarchici Speculatori," *La Questione Sociale* (Paterson, New Jersey) 5, new series, no. 10 (November 11, 1899)

Under the title of

To Anarchist Speculators

we receive and publish:

Without lecturing anybody, it seems to us that the issue should be clearly stated.

Can an anarchist be a speculator? Or, swapping the terms, is it possible to engage in speculation while remaining, despite that, an anarchist?

---

108   Correspondence from Paterson in *La Questione Sociale* of November 25 reports that the debate, argued by Malatesta and Rondani, took place on the 15th, although the summoning procedure had been rather peculiar. On the morning of the 15th *La Questione Sociale* received an invitation to Rondani's lecture that evening, where agreements were to be made for the challenge. That evening Rondani instead expressed the wish that the challenge take place then and there. To please the audience Malatesta acquiesced. The only newspaper to publish a report of the debate was *L'Aurora* (West Hoboken) of November 25, which however limited itself to reporting and criticizing Rondani's statements. On the debate, however, see also note 126.

We have known a large number of comrades who were speculators; for that matter they only played the part of bourgeois; some (a very few) were driven by necessities of life; others (a larger number), on principle, claiming that acting like the bourgeoisie for them amounted to an immediate take-over. The latter (those who act like the bourgeoisie on principle) are today lost to the cause; the property of the bourgeoisie often being very well guarded, these neo-idealists have reached the point where they exploit their own worker brothers.

For them, anarchy boils down to the bourgeois formula of "every man for himself."

They, as Flaustier says, deserve our kicks on their behinds.[109]

As for those who, driven by necessities of existence, take to speculation, must they incur our condemnation?

We do not believe so; it would be denying them the most imprescriptible of rights: the right to life.

Should we praise them? Not at all. Theft being a bourgeois institution, it is, for this fact alone, incompatible with the anarchist ideal. If some, while remaining anarchists, resort to it because they are forced to do so by poverty, that, in our opinion, is seen as a forgivable necessity, but never as an example.

CRITICO.

*
**

The issue raised by our correspondent, which is the issue of how anarchists conduct themselves privately in present-day society, is most interesting.

There are some who, forgetting that in present-day society no one can make themselves the master of their own destiny and live in accordance with their own ideals, would like anarchists to be perfect beings and live as if we were already in anarchy... and then they themselves must adapt to their environment and endure the necessities of life.

However there are others who, because society does not allow us to live anarchistically, think any wicked action is allowed, blaming society for everything; and with the excuse of fighting the bourgeoisie with its own weapons, they themselves become bourgeois, or aspiring bourgeois.

We must find between these two extremes the correct measures to guide us.

Society dominates the individual, but it is the individual who makes society.

---

109   "Flaustier" was the pseudonym of Paul Sosset, a Belgian professor, contributor to the anarchist press and author of the pamphlet *À l'Aube d'un Siècle* (At the dawn of a century).

We must try to correct society, but at the same time we must try to correct ourselves.

We cannot entirely escape the influence of the environment; but we must resist this environment as much as possible when it pushes us toward things that are contrary to our principles.

We cannot live as we would want to; but we must strive to live as little as possible in contradiction with our ideals.

Anarchy is love, brotherhood, solidarity between men. And today, one is more or less a good anarchist, not depending on the position in which one has been placed by circumstances, but depending on the efforts one makes to live as much as possible in accordance with anarchist ideals, depending on the extent to which one feels the torment of having to live in conflict with oneself, which is to say in conflict with one's own aspirations, and depending on the energy with which one struggles to remove the obstacles standing in the way of the realization of the ideal.

Editors' note

Minority Rights and the Ballot Box Trial

Translated from "I diritti della minoranza ed il Processo delle Urne," *La Questione Sociale* (Paterson, New Jersey) 5, new series, no. 11 (November 18, 1899)

As is common knowledge, the Italian socialist deputies, after having for some time prevented, through obstructionism, approval of Corporal Pelloux's reactionary plans,[110] seeing that the President of the Chamber wanted to put an end to the obstruction by violently taking away the rights granted to them under the law and by the rules, resorted to violence smashing up the ballot boxes and coming to blows with the cabinet's pageboys.

Because of this energetic act, or using it as an excuse, the government closed the session, promulgated by royal decree the reactionary measures proposed to parliament, and intended to proceed against four socialist deputies for violation of one of the many articles, which men of the law can always find when they want to tamper with people's freedom.[111]

Then, after various events, which once more demonstrated how the judiciary is the very humble servant of the executive power, when the time came for the accused to appear in the court of assizes, the trial was

---

110   See note 87.

111   The four socialist deputies charged were Leonida Bissolati, Giuseppe De Felice Giuffrida, Oddino Morgari, and Camillo Prampolini.

deferred and the accused set free, because, once the session reopened, they once again enjoyed parliamentary immunity.

The only thing we want to retain from this is the debate it has triggered regarding the rights of minorities.

According to the government and the magistrates and the entire reactionary legion, the majority is absolutely sovereign and can commit any abuse of power, any high-handedness. The majority makes the law, and any opposition to the majority's will being carried out, is criminal.

It is an absurd, reactionary theory that, if acknowledged, after preventing any progress for a long time, would then lead to the greatest disasters; but it is logical in its brutality. Those who are in power and who aim at nothing but their own dominance, naturally seek to broaden, as much as they can, the rights of the legal majority at their disposal, because in so doing they broaden their own power. If tomorrow they were in the minority and the new majority wanted to attack their privileges, then they would change their minds and become... liberals. Nothing is simpler to understand.

The position taken by the socialists, who fight in the name of a principle, is not as clear and logical.

They say that minority rights are one of the most brilliant achievements of civilization, and that the minority that resists the high-handedness of the majority, and opposes violence with violence, is doing civilization's work.

And in order to show that "force is not always an anti-social and anti-civilized thing" and that to the contrary "there are cases in which force becomes the claimant or producer of civilization," Bissolati describes the 1892 revolution in the canton of Ticino, when the liberals, finding themselves denied by the clericalists in power, the use of legal means to revise the constitution, armed themselves and seized the government;—and he concludes:

> The example of the Ticino revolution of 1892 states in fact that at certain times in history two types of violence can collide; the violence of those who want to destroy the law because they see it used as a sword and shield by their opponents, and the violence of those who, faced with the imminent threat of being robbed of that sword and that shield, rise up, using all means at their disposal, against the despoilers. The first is the violence of reaction, the second is the violence of revolution.[112]

Therefore according to the democratic socialists, insurrection is only justifiable when it takes place in defense of the law violated by the rulers;

---

112   "Preparandomi al confiteor" (Preparing myself for the Confiteor), *Avanti!*, October 26, 1899.

and this concept of the law, which binds the majority and the minority, is the source of the contradiction in which these socialists wander.

What is the law if not the expression of violence of the majority made normal and permanent?

The socialist deputies rebelled because the president violated the rules to their detriment, and they did well to do so. But if the changes that Sonnino and Pelloux want to make to the rules are adopted and acquire the force of law, will the socialists recognize the new legality?

The monarchy and private property are certainly legal institutions. Do they mean to respect these, or at least not attack them if they do not have the legal means to do so?

As long as the socialists aspire to government of the majority (and if there must be a government, it would still be the least evil of governments), as long as they will recognize the Law, they will always be in contradiction with themselves, and they will, somewhat more hypocritically, do what everybody does: they will accept the decisions of the majority when they are in their favor, and they will reject them if they are against them.

In order to return to logic and sincerity, it would be necessary to accept the anarchist program: NOT LAW, BUT FREE AGREEMENT; FREEDOM FOR ALL MINORITIES, FOR ALL INDIVIDUALS TO DO AS THEY WANT WITH THE ONLY LIMIT OF THE EQUAL FREEDOM OF OTHERS.

Object Lesson

Translated from "Lezione delle cose," *La Questione Sociale*
(Paterson, New Jersey) 5, new series, no. 11 (November 18, 1899)

The democratic socialists have much boasted about the tactics of their Belgian comrades; and here in Paterson we have had a lot to debate with Rondani on this subject.

Twice now the Belgian socialists, after having brought the people into the streets and frightened the government with the threat of revolution, instead of taking advantage of the situation, to at least wrest genuine improvements for workers from the authorities and bourgeoisie, calmed everything down in return for simple electoral concessions, and when all is said and done, had more trust in an alliance with bourgeois parties than the people's energy.[113]

---

113   On the Belgian socialists' struggle for universal suffrage, culminating in the April 1893 general strike, see Malatesta's article "How to Get... What You Want," in Volume III of these *Complete Works*, p. 64.

And now they are beginning to experience the effects of the tactics that so delighted Rondani; he perhaps will not be displeased to hear repeated by the *Avanti!* correspondent, in the passage that we reprint below (italics added by us), some of the things that we told him:[114]

> BRUSSELS, 27 (*victor*).—The proportional representation proposed by the government, supported by the clericalists and the liberals and opposed by the socialists, radicals, and intransigent clericalists, has been approved in its first article . . .
>
> The socialists' decision to abandon obstructionism, while unexpected, came as no surprise . . . The socialist party, which did not—and perhaps could not—profit *from the times when people were in the streets* ready to do anything to win universal suffrage, suffers a setback in its surrender . . .
>
> Two lessons flow from this whole state of affairs and the story of these few months: that *after having led the people into the streets, it is a mistake to not urge them on steadfastly to direct, immediate conquest of the preestablished goals; and that it is a mistake to trust the bourgeois parties.*

To the Comrades

Translated from "Ai compagni," *La Questione Sociale*
(Paterson, New Jersey) 5, new series, no. 11 (November 18, 1899)

We learn that many groups, which are of the same frame of mind as ourselves and have notified us that they intend to join the *Federation,* have not yet sent the *Correspondence Committee* their notice of affiliation, nor their address, nor any kind of communication.[115]

If everyone were to do the same, the Federation would certainly remain a pious wish, and after a few short-lived heaves, would end up disappearing, with or without a formal death certificate.

And then our opponents would announce as a "new orientation"[116] and a step forward what would simply be the consequence of the laziness and apathy of the majority, and they would rejoice in something that should be painful for all men of good will, since the apathetic serve no cause.

---

114   "La vittoria degli anti-ostruzionisti nel Belgio" (The victory of the anti-obstructionists in Belgium), *Avanti!,* October 30, 1899; from the *Avanti!* article we are reprinting only the parts most relevant to Malatesta's argument.

115   The formation of the correspondence committee, mentioned in *La Questione Sociale* of November 23 (see "Anarchist-Socialist Federation," p. 79), had been announced in the October 7 issue.

116   For this reference see note 104.

So, if the comrades truly want to keep in constant communication with comrades, and exchange ideas, and mutually support one another and join forces to implement those initiatives they endorse—which constitutes the essence and purpose of the *Federation*—they should not delay in communicating their affiliation and address to the Correspondence Committee, writing to:

CIRCOLO DI STUDII SOCIALI
Box 299
Barre, Vermont

*
**

We receive a message that the anarchist-communist group of Yohoghany, Pa., has sent its affiliation to the Anarchist Socialist Federation.

The provisional correspondence committee of the Federation, which as the comrades are aware, is based in Barre, Vt.—informs us that within this week it will issue a circular-letter to all anarchist groups in the United States for which it has addresses.

Going Backwards like Crabs

Translated from "Come i gamberi," *La Questione Sociale*
(Paterson, New Jersey) 5, new series, no. 11 (November 18, 1899)

The council of ministers in France unanimously approved a Waldeck-Rousseau bill on workers' unions.

We do not yet know the actual text of that bill, but it is known that it is an old, slightly amended, bill by Waldeck-Rousseau, which, in exchange for acknowledgment of certain rights that workers take for themselves if they are aware and united, and that are useless if the workers do not know how to seize them, intends to subject workers' associations to continuous police supervision and strip their struggle of any revolutionary significance, confining it within the boundaries indicated by the law.

The socialists have always protested that bill, stating that "gifts" from the bourgeoisie could only be fatal to the working class.

But now Millerand is in power, and Waldeck-Rousseau becomes a friend of proletarians.

Indeed, *Avanti!*'s Parisian correspondent, speaking about the Waldeck-Rousseau bill, as if it was the work of a socialist, says:

This reform comes at a good time to show certain adversaries of social-ism how, far from carrying with it impracticable demands, socialism has today become, by the admission of the same rulers drawn from the bour-geoisie, one of the most encouraging and effective factors of progress.[117]

What in the world would be a "socialism" that has the gift of being so delightful to rulers drawn from the heart of the bourgeoisie?

Meanwhile we note that the demands of pre-parliamentary social-ism have become mere "impracticable demands" for parliamentary socialists.

And yet they do not want to acknowledge that every success of social-ists in the realm of the parliament and government represents socialism prostituting itself to bourgeois interests.

Lazio's (democratic) socialists at their recent Congress in Rome passed an agenda, from which we borrow the following passage that we dedicate to those who, in order to be controversial, say, when debating with us, that the democratic socialists also aspire to a society without government:

> The congress, reaffirming the socialist party's belief that the exercise of freedom of the press, assembly, and speech, is not compatible with the interests and methods of the current government, reaffirms *its immutable republican faith* in matters of politics.

Maybe the republic is no longer a form of government!

[Untitled]

Translated from *La Questione Sociale*
(Paterson, New Jersey) 5, new series, no. 11 (November 18, 1899)

Freedom, the organ of our London comrades, mentioning the debates that culminated in the withdrawal of some comrades from the *La Questione Sociale* group and the establishment of *L'Aurora* says that this concerns the famous issue: Organization versus free initiative.[118]

---

117   "Pei sindacati operai: Il nuovo disegno di legge Waldeck-Rousseau" (For the workers' unions: the new Waldeck-Rousseau bill), *Avanti!*, October 29, 1899.
118   "International Notes," *Freedom* (London) 13, no. 142 (October 1899).

We leave it to the readers to evaluate the differences between us and *L'Aurora*; we do not want to speak of them lest we reopen a debate which we believe is inappropriate.

We are only anxious to protest the way our friends from London present the issue, which is ultimately the way our adversaries use to present it.

We are not against *free initiative*, or *individual initiative* if you want to call it that: instead we want to get organized and encourage everybody to get organized precisely so that the right of initiative ceases to be the privilege of those few who are able to organize others beneath them, and becomes a reality for all.

And we are confirmed in our ideas seeing every day that, when our opponents want to pursue an initiative of their own, they do exactly what we do: they get organized.

"The Two Freedoms"

Translated from "'Le due libertà,'" *La Questione Sociale*
(Paterson, New Jersey) 5, new series, no. 12 (November 25, 1899)

With this title and with the signature of Constant Martin, *Le Libertaire* of Paris publishes the following article, which we think requires our comment, to clearly establish our opinion in opposition to a tendency that, despite being called anarchist, contains the seed of a whole authoritarian theory and authoritarian practice.

> Everyone speaks in the name of freedom, royalists and clericalists, anti-Semites and Jews alike, masters and workers alike, rich and poor alike.
>
> And it is not unusual to find socialists, revolutionaries, and anarchists, overcome by sentimentality, who right now, "in present-day society," seek freedom for all—while they have none themselves.
>
> This principle, or rather this general thesis, necessarily leads them to not deny the priest's freedom to say Mass and to suborn the youth in churches, in schools, in confessionals; the royalists' freedom to try to be our rulers; the masters' right to exploit us; the anti-Semites' right to slaughter Jews and drive them out of France.
>
> It is with this word, freedom, which seems to have become the important term in the clerical world, that attempts are now being made to put a stop to revolutionary efforts.
>
> What, you don't approve of freedom for all, they tell us, you who call yourselves anarchists? You are nothing more than sectarians and horrible Jacobins.

Such opposition willingly, or deliberately, confuses present-day society, full of privilege and social inequality, with the egalitarian society of the future; they argue from the perspective of present-day society that they want to preserve.

But anarchists cannot accept this point of view, unless they wish to commit suicide, without denying their own reason for existing.

What, they reply in turn, you have grabbed all the wealth, government and religious power; you have fabricated laws to uphold all your privileges, you keep us subjugated with hunger and with violence, and you demand freedom! And we are supposed to recognize your freedom to starve us to death, to make us be soldiers, to exploit us, to educate our children with the goal of securing your perpetual domination over us?

No, we do not agree. Let us settle accounts first, let us divide things up, let us reassess the wealth: "let us become socially and economically equal" and then we will talk about freedom, since whoever lacks bread cannot be free.

We accept freedom as one of the principles of the future society that we want to establish; but in present-day society we scoff at this principle, when it makes us perish: we deny our enemies all freedoms, all rights.

We cannot practice anarchist principles in present-day society, which enslaves us, abuses us, kills us: doing so would be committing suicide.

It is a clever move on the part of the priests and the wealthy to preach freedom today based on their "established rights," and to say to us: why dispossess the clergy and strip them of their freedom to educate the youth? Freedom is like the sun: it shines on everyone. Therefore freedom for royalists, for capitalists, for anti-Semites, for masters, etc.

The only thing left for the oppressed is the freedom to revolt: the efforts of their masters intend to take that away from them, creating confusion between the society of tomorrow and that of today. They will not succeed.

Let the people organize for civil war, the necessary prelude to their liberation, and let them be merciless with their enemies.

Now, let them call us sentimentalists as much as they want (the writer has heard that for twenty years alongside the other charge of "authoritarian" and it has not done his health any harm), but we cannot do less than to strongly protest against this reactionary, authoritarian, liberticidal theory that asserts freedom as a good principle for a future society and denies it in the present.

It is in the name of this theory that today's tyrannies were established; and it is in its name, if the people let themselves be persuaded, that future tyrannies will be established.

The historian of the Great French Revolution, Louis Blanc, attempting to explain and justify the contradiction between the vaunted humanitarian and liberal aspirations of the Jacobins and the fierce tyranny they exercised when they were in power, drew a precise distinction between "the republic," which was an institution yet to come in which the principles would be fully implemented, and "the revolution," which was the present and helped justify every tyranny as a means of bringing about the triumph of freedom and justice.[119] What came about was the guillotining of the best revolutionaries, as well as masses of the wretched, the consolidation of bourgeois power, the Empire and the Restoration.

And the democratic socialists, these modern-day Jacobins, in the name of *future* freedom and as a means of reaching it, are preparing to seize power and force their tyranny upon us.

We know well that the priests, the masters, the anti-Semites, the royalists and, may Constant Martin permit us to say, the republicans, are lying when they talk about freedom, since they only want freedom for themselves, because it serves to keep them or put them in power. We are well aware that there is no freedom for those who are economically subjugated and for those who must submit to the rule of the state.

But in order to fight our enemies, and fight effectively, we do not need to deny the principle of freedom, not even for a moment: it is enough for us to want true freedom and want it for everyone, for ourselves just as others.

We want to expropriate the owners, and to expropriate them with violence, since they hold on to society's wealth with violence and use it to exploit the workers, not because freedom is a good thing for the future, but because it is always good, today as much as tomorrow, and the owners deprive us of it by depriving us of the means of exercising it.

We want to overthrow the government, all governments—and to overthrow them with force since force is what they use to compel us to obey—not because, once again, we laugh at freedom when it does not serve our interests; but because governments are the negation of freedom and we cannot be free without having overthrown them.

In France we will oppose, and with force, attempts by the anti-Semites and royalists, because they want to use force to violate the freedom of the Jews and to impose their domination over us.

We want to use force to strip the priests of their privileges, since it is with such privileges, guaranteed to them by the force of the State, that they take from others the right, which is to say the means, to the same freedom to propagate their ideas and beliefs.

119   Louis Blanc (1811–1882), author of *Histoire de la Révolution française,* 12 volumes (1847–1862), was an exponent of "Jacobin socialism" and member of the provisional government of the Second French Republic established with the revolution of 1848.

The freedom to oppress, to exploit, to compel people to undergo military service, to pay taxes, etc., is the negation of freedom; and the fact that our enemies use the word freedom so excessively and so hypocritically, is not enough for us to deny the principle of freedom, which is the distinctive characteristic of our party, which is the eternal, constant, necessary factor of life and progress of humanity.

Equal freedom for all and therefore the right to resist any violation of freedom, and to use brute force to resist, when violence is based upon brute force and there is no better way to successfully oppose it.

And this principle is true today and holds true forever, since if anyone in some future society sought to oppress someone else, the latter would have the right to resist them and to fight force with force.

Moreover, when does today's society end and the future begin? when can one say that the revolution is definitively finished and that the unchallenged triumph of a free and egalitarian society has begun? If people are awarded the right to violate anyone's freedom with the excuse of paving the way for the triumph of freedom, surely it will always be found that the people are not yet mature, that there are still dangers of a reaction, that education is not yet complete, and with this excuse an attempt will be made to cling to power:—power that could have begun as the force of a risen people, but that unregulated by a deep-seated feeling of respect for everyone's freedom, would become a proper government, just like the governments that exist today.

*
**

But, they will say to us, do you then want the priests to continue brutalizing children with their lies?

No, we believe it is necessary, urgent, to destroy the vile influence of the priest, but we believe that the only means of doing so is freedom— freedom for us and for them.

With force we want, and one day or another we will be able, to strip the priests of all privileges, all advantages that they owe to the protection of the State, and to the conditions of misery and subjugation in which proletarians find themselves; but this done, we rely on, and can only rely on the power of the truth, which is to say, on propaganda.

We believe—and this is why we are anarchists—that authority cannot do anything good, or if it can do something relatively good, it does damage a hundred times worse in exchange.

There is talk about the right to prevent the spread of mistakes. But with what means?

If the strongest current of opinion is on the side of the priests, it will be the priests who will prevent our propaganda; if on the other hand opinion is on our side, then what need will there be to deny freedom to combat a decaying influence and to risk arousing sympathy for it by persecuting it?

Every other consideration aside, it always suits us to stand for freedom, since, as a minority, we will have, if we demand freedom for all, greater moral strength to have our own freedom respected, and as a majority we will have no reason, if we truly do not aim at our own domination, to violate the freedom of others.

And then, who is to say what is truth and what is error? Will we then establish a ministry of public education with its licensed professors, approved text books, school inspectors, etc.? And all this in the name of the "people," just as the democratic socialists want to attain power in the name of the "proletariat"?

And what about the corruption that power exerts, which consists in assuming the right to impose one's will over others and being in a condition to do so?

We rightly say that by entering parliament the democratic socialists practically cease being socialists. But this certainly does not depend on the material act of taking a seat in an assembly called parliament; but, rather, from the power attached to the title "member of parliament."

If we, in one way or another, dominate others and prevent them from doing what they want, we would practically cease being anarchists.

Freedom then, freedom for all and in everything, with no limit other than the equal freedom of others: which does not mean—and even having to say this is ridiculous—that we embrace and wish to respect the "freedom" to exploit, oppress, command, which is oppression and not freedom.[120]

The Crisis of Anarchism

Translated from "La crisi dell'anarchismo," *La Questione Sociale* (Paterson, New Jersey) 5, new series, no. 12 (November 25, 1899)

Some friends insist that I respond to an article published by one E. Leone in *Presente e Avvenire* of Rome entitled: *The Crisis of Anarchism*, which discusses the disagreements that have arisen among the Paterson anarchists and mentions my name.

I agree to do so, but reluctantly; because such is the state of ignorance of this E. Leone concerning anarchists' ideas and the history of anarchism that I really do not know where to begin.

---

120   On this subject see also "For Freedom," in Volume III of these *Complete Works*, p. 201.

Indeed he believes that we have been calling ourselves anarchist socialists only since 1897 (a mistake of 25 years in a movement that has only existed for little more than 30 years!), and clearly shows, throughout his piece, that he knows little more about our movement than a few issues of *La Questione Sociale* and *L'Aurora*, and perhaps not even firsthand!

This is too little for him to set to writing about the "Crisis of Anarchism" and to position himself as a judge between the competitors; and it explains how the writer could create such odd confusion in describing the differences separating us from anarchists of different leanings and in attributing to me ideas that are the very opposite of those I profess.

However, we cannot repeat the general presentation of our program and retell our history every time somebody gets it into his head to talk about our matters without knowing anything about them!

In any case, since I have taken to reply, I will try, as briefly as possible, to set the record straight.

We, anarchist socialists, have existed as a separate party, with essentially the same program, since 1867, when Bakunin founded the *Alliance,* which (oh, irony of words!) began by being called the *Alliance of Socialist Democracy,* and then changed its name to *Revolutionary Socialist Alliance*: and we were the founders and soul of the anti-authoritarian wing of the "International Working Men's Association."[121]

Since then we have been socialist, anarchist, and revolutionary in the same sense as we are today. In Italy for many years we were simply referred to as *socialists,* because at that time there were no other socialists in Italy than ourselves, but we were anarchist socialists and called ourselves that any time there was any danger of misunderstanding.

There have been divergences among us over our conception of the future society. At the start of the movement we were all *collectivist,* and then many of us (almost all in Italy and in France) became *communist*; then finally the differences began to diminish and almost vanished in the face of the notion of free organization and free social

---

121   The International Alliance of Socialist Democracy was made up of dissident members of the League of Peace and Freedom—Bakunin had participated in the latter's congresses of September 1867 in Geneva and September 1868 in Bern. It then merged into the already existing International, thereby triggering the dispute between anarchists and marxists within that organization. The Alliance's program was set out in seven points concerning: atheism; abolition of inheritance rights and collective ownership of the means of production; equality of development resources for all children; rejection of all political action not designed to bring about labor's direct triumph over capital; the staged phasing-out of political and authoritarian States; rejection of patriotism; free association from the bottom up. In terms of both the number of points as well as the content, there is a persistent similarity between this program and Malatesta's 1899 program (See "An Anarchist Programme," p. 43).

experimentation, which is essential to the anarchist program.[122] But during these theoretical debates concerning the more or less distant future, we have always remained what we still are today, which is to say anarchist socialists.

Meanwhile, in parallel to us, sometimes from within our very own ranks, other currents have developed that although describing themselves as anarchist were different from our current and opposed to it; and we constantly fought against them, just as we always fight against the democratic socialists and the various bourgeois parties, as every man and every party combats those ideas that they believe to be mistaken and harmful.

Nevertheless, despite our unrelenting objection, it happened that the public, mainly due to noisy incidents that briefly drowned out the voices of the propagandists, lost the correct differential criteria, and confused as one, with serious damage to our propaganda, individualists and anarchist socialists, organizationists and antiorganizationists, revolutionaries and terrorists, men committed to fighting and sacrificing for the general good and men who openly declared that they sought nothing more than their own advantage, even at the expense of others. And then some of us, realizing the damage already done and the greater danger threatening our party's future, shouted louder than usual, and managed to clearly break away from the others and draw the public's attention to the differences that separate us from them.[123]

If ever, it is referring to that period of battles, more intense than usual, and new in some respects, between individuals and groups of different leanings, laying claim to the common name "anarchist," that one can truly speak of a crisis of anarchism.

The battles prior to that intense period and the battles subsequent to it, including the ones fought in Paterson, are merely the ongoing, normal unfolding of our propaganda. And it is ridiculous to talk about a *crisis* when we are dealing with two fractions that have long gone their separate ways, which in the course of their work encounter one another and, of course, fight it out.

But, crisis or no crisis, what is important for me is that I am not credited with ideas other than the ones I hold.

Leone says that "the key concepts tying together the fabric of the individualists' views are *free* initiative, *free* competition, mutuality, voluntariness" and he implies that my views run counter to these.

---

122 For Malatesta's determining contribution to this turning point, see "Appeal" and "Our Plans. I. Union between communists and collectivists," in Volume II of these *Complete Works*.

123 See, for instance, "A bit of theory" and "Errors and Remedies," in Volume II of these *Complete Works*.

Now, the real difference that separates us from the individualists (I am referring to the doctrinal individualists) is the issue of *conscious and deliberate* solidarity between men, of organized and continuous social cooperation, and has nothing at all to do with the principle of *free initiative,* to which we pay homage, and nothing at all to do with the principle of *voluntariness* which is at the core of our entire doctrine.

That Leone then believes that we must "either agree (with those he calls pure anarchists) that any organization is to be avoided, or embrace democratic forms of organization with the sound logic that *majorities* make decisions and minorities obey them," simply shows that he is completely saturated in the most antiquated authoritarian prejudices, and belongs among the ranks of people (alas there are so many!) who believe that four people cannot gather together without subjugation to a corporal, and perhaps a slave-driver armed with a whip.

Let him nurture within himself the concepts of freedom and human dignity, and then he will be prepared to study anarchism with some chance of understanding it.

ERRICO MALATESTA.

What We Have to Say to "Il Proletario"

Translated from "Quello che diciamo noi al 'Proletario,'" *La Questione Sociale* (Paterson, New Jersey) 5, new series, no. 12 (November 25, 1899)

We take this from New York's *Il Proletario*:

"France, England, Germany, and the United States, the world's four most advanced countries, proceeding in agreement although in the interest *of capitalists,* but also in the interest of civilization! What a beautiful dream for human progress! May the democracy of the four countries make a reality of it, *with the end of exploitation,* and the establishment of peace in the human family."

Thus and not otherwise the editorial of *Il Progresso italo-americano* ended on the 11th of this month.

Now, as I detest rhetoric and lofty style, I wanted to break down the prose above and I have come up with the following construct: *working in the interests of the capitalists, the four great powers may very well put an end to exploitation, etc...*

For a newspaper that brags of being *forward-looking and libertarian,* not bad, I say. What do the libertarians from *L'Aurora* and *La Questione Sociale* have to say about it?[124]

What we say is that whoever penned the passage above is dishonest, if not a fool who writes without understanding what he is saying. We say this because he tends to make his readers believe that *La Questione Sociale* and *L'Aurora*—which, no matter what one thinks of the theories they advocate, are known to be anti-capitalist propaganda publications made in the exclusive interest of propaganda—may be associated with Sir Barsotti's paper, which is a mouthpiece for bourgeois interests produced for the sole purpose of making money.

That aside, let us point out that for socialists such as those of *Il Proletario*, who claim that the triumph of socialism must be preceded by a flourishing capitalist development, what *Il Progresso italo-americano* says must look like the most evident of truths.

It's a shame!

Translated from "È una vergogna!" *La Questione Sociale*
(Paterson, New Jersey) 5, new series, no. 12 (November 25, 1899)

We are not patriots.

The worker, the oppressed, Chinese or Russian or from any other country, is our brother, just as the property-owner, the oppressor, is our enemy, even if he is born in our home town.

And yet we cannot help but feel a particularly stinging sense of shame, when we see how so many Italian proletarian immigrants act in this country—and in others.

Not a strike happens without Italians going to break it, or trying to break it. And everywhere, in every trade, our countrymen content themselves with the lowest pay.

You could say that Italians have a psychological need for low earnings... when it comes to earning from labor and not exploiting the labor of others.

It is the deep-seated ignorance of their own rights, it is the long-ingrained habit of servility that robs Italian workers of the boldness to demand what more civilized workers barely consider a decent wage. It is

---

124   Somebody, "Sotto le forche caudine" (Running the gauntlet), *Il Proletario* (New York) 4, no. 31 (November 18, 1899). The editorial in *Il Progresso Italo-Americano* was entitled "England and Germany." The italics were inserted by the *Proletario* writer.

narrow, stupid, improvident selfishness that prevents them from feeling the solidarity that binds them to other workers, and pushes them, for the immediate gain of a meager pay, to betray the cause of their comrades and serve the interests of the masters.

Sometimes, it is true, they are driven by harsh necessity, by hunger, to accept work under any condition, and then they are simply to be pitied. But, unfortunately, this is not generally the case.

We have recently seen in New Haven, Conn., and we see today in Orange Valley, N.J., Italians leaving the work they have so that they can go take the place of strikers out of sheer greed to earn a few more cents!

And the Italian typesetters provide us with another despicable spectacle, even though, by virtue of their profession, they should be more developed, more aware than other workers.

Let us leave aside those who cannot even grasp the usefulness, the duty, of uniting with their comrades to defend common interests, and let us talk about those who have formed resistance societies. They have introduced a *pay rate*, but they set the pay lower than that of the American Typesetters' Union. Why? Italian typesetters in the United States are few in number, they are much sought after and the work that they do cannot be put off because it is nearly all newspaper work; nor can they be replaced by Americans who don't know the language. Is it really their passion then to want to be less than other workers of other nationalities in the same profession?

LA QUESTIONE SOCIALE of course pays its typesetters according to the pay rate. Yet, would you believe it? there is always some compositor who, offering to do it for less, tries to steal the work away from those who do it now. And they do this with such unawareness that they are taken aback when we respond that we do not want scabs.

Let our comrades and all Italian-speaking workers with any sense of dignity and understanding of their own interests set out to eliminate this shameful behavior, which has made the name "Italian" despised and mocked everywhere.

We are told that New York's *Il Proletario*, organ of the democratic socialists, is composed by a poor devil they have by the throat and pay under the union rate.

That would be a terrible example to set and would reduce the efficacy of *Il Proletario*'s propaganda on behalf of workers' resistance.

Let us hope we have been misinformed. Should it turn out to be true, let us ask the Typesetters' Union why it has not blacklisted *Il Proletario* for being produced by scab labour.

The Taxpayers' Strike in Spain

Translated from "Lo sciopero dei contribuenti in Spagna," *La Questione Sociale* (Paterson, New Jersey) 5, new series, no. 12 (November 25, 1899)

Something of great importance is happening in Spain, due to the consequences that may result.

Businessmen and industrialists are refusing to pay taxes and prefer to risk the seizure and sale of their property by bailiffs, rather than willingly give in to the insatiable demands of the tax authorities.

In Barcelona especially, the movement has become widespread, so much so that the government there has proclaimed a state of siege and declared non-payers guilty of sedition, to be judged by court martial. In reality few people have been jailed and the threats have failed to scare anyone.

It pains us that the news reaches us so late and so incompletely that it is impossible for us to keep our readers up-to-date on the events. However, we want to make a few remarks about this situation, since it is not impossible that a similar situation may occur in Italy someday. The memory is still fresh of the 1897 protest led by Roman shopkeepers in opposition to the assessment of taxable income during which... a worker was killed![125]

Fed up with a government that takes from them much of what they themselves take from the workers, the bourgeoisie seem, especially in Catalonia, determined to resist until the end. But it is evident that unless the workers become involved everything will end peacefully: either the government or the capitalists will surrender, or, more likely, a compromise will be made between them both for the greater glory of their shared rule. Wolf does not eat wolf—and the state of siege in Barcelona must have been prompted, more than anything else, by the very fear that the workers might become involved in the conflict.

But what should workers aware of their rights and their interests do?

Save the businessmen's and industrialists' bacon, certainly not.

The industrialists exploit and kill the workers with excessive and unhealthy labor: no human consideration prevails over their greed for increased profits. Businessmen exploit them as consumers and, to enrich themselves, do not hesitate before systematically poisoning the population. The prosperity of both, and the entire bourgeoisie, is founded on the misery and enslavement of the workers. And all the bourgeois always side with each other and with the government, when it comes to keeping the people oppressed, even through slaughter.

---

125   See "The Carnage in Rome," in Volume III of these *Complete Works*, p. 329.

Why should workers ever side with the bourgeoisie in their conflicts with the government?

They should rather intervene in the situation, but on their own behalf, to profit from the division presently existing between their enemies.

And since the issue is refusal to pay they may take their example from the bourgeoisie, and they should not pay their rents nor anything else they can avoid paying.

The things that fill the warehouses are things produced by the people and that rightfully belong to the people. The force of the government is the only reason preventing the people from touching these things. Now the bourgeoisie, who have stolen these things and hold on to them thanks to the government's protection, find that this protection is too expensive and are rebelling.

Very well; but let them return the stuff.

Better yet: let the workers take it back... and by force.

Social Movement. United States

Translated from "Mouvement Social. États Unis," *Germinal*
(Paterson, New Jersey) 1, no. 5 (November 30, 1899)

PATERSON.—Below we carry a report on a conference organized by the socialists of Paterson. Rondani, the former socialist member of the Italian parliament, opened the conference.[126]

He began with the claim that the distinction between socialism and anarchism relates only to collectivism and communism. His language seemed to lean towards communism but after some sophistry it leaned toward collectivism. The socialists, he said, are very logical in that they know how to profit from the right to vote; the only so-called practical means of winning social emancipation. Besides, he added, the socialists are gaining ground whereas the anarchists are dying out. He also claims that progress and science will kill off the anarchist epic entirely and argues that anarchist ideas attract many followers in the more impoverished and ignorant countries such as Italy and Spain, whereas they are only a minority in France, Switzerland, Germany, etc. He then claims that the real socialists are the socialists from the Labor Party.

Our comrade Malatesta rises to his feet with a smile, like a self-confident man. We know, he says, that at first the anarchists referred to themselves simply

---

126   The date of the lecture is not given. However, since *Germinal* was published fortnightly in Paterson, we can assume that the lecture was given during the two preceding weeks. It is therefore probable that this was the Malatesta–Rondani debate held in Paterson on November 15 (see note 108).

ERRICO MALATESTA NEL 1899

*quando era redattore della nostra Questione Sociale,
ora Era Nuova. Urgenti richiami a Londra non gli
permisero che un troppo breve soggiorno fra noi per
aver l'agio di campiere il vasto lavoro di propaganda
che si era prefisso.*

(Da una fotografia dell'epoca)

"ERRICO MALATESTA IN 1899, when he was the editor of our
Questione Sociale, now *Era Nuova*. Urgent calls from London
prevented him from staying long enough among us to be able
to complete the broad propaganda work that he had planned.
(From a photograph of the period)"
Source: *L'Era Nuova* (Paterson), July 17, 1915

as socialists and, shortly afterwards, politicians came to the fore who claimed the name of socialists for themselves. But, not content with calling themselves socialists, those politicians sought to add, not one, but many labels to that name: we have seen thereafter religious socialists, democratic socialists, parliamentary socialists, etc.

He points out especially the unfeasibility of collectivism, when it comes to the measurement of work, and at the same time the difficulties of communism; and he states that the free agreement alone can produce true organization by means of ongoing experimentation with production and social consumption. But to get to the point of free agreement, authority, which stands in the way of proper social organization, must to be destroyed: authority, the great beast which Rondani has avoided to discuss. Herein lies the ultimate kernel of the anarchist philosophy: it is not a question of setting boundaries to social organization; what matters is that the authority, which prevents the unfettered growth of that organization, must be abolished.

Malatesta then reviews the history of the International, so as to show that socialism was introduced into both Italy and Spain by anarchists. Contrary to Rondani's assertion that the anarchists are making no headway, he goes into a lengthy explanation of the advances being made by their idea everywhere, adding that we have a splendid example before our very eyes right here in Paterson where two Italian anarchist newspapers, a Spanish one and a French one are being published, while, when we got here, there was only one, the Q. S., publishing twice a month.[127] He remarks that while the anarchists might not be progressing as fast as they would like, this is because their idea does not take bourgeois into their ranks like the socialists do, because they know all too well that they could not keep their privileges.

Next, he offers a splendid critique of electoral action and shows that voting does not build a socialist consciousness. He presents lots of examples and forcefully attacks Rondani's contention that the social question can be resolved by means of parliamentarianism.

Rondani attempts to reply but drifts off into digressions, after having lost himself in rhetorical flourishes, which lead him to conclude that laws may always be needed in a civilized society, trying to argue that law is the same thing as free agreement. Here Malatesta proved very eloquent and mounted a very successful rebuttal. In the end, Rondani was left not knowing how to respond; he was caught in his own snare. The impression left on the audience was entirely in favor of our ideas. It was a splendid evening for the cause.

---

127   Besides *L'Aurora* and *Germinal*, which had begun publishing on October 1, the other paper to which Malatesta refers is the Spanish-language *El Despertar*, which had already been out for some time, but whose typographical material had been recently transferred by its editor Pedro Esteve to Paterson (see the article "Personal Matter" of December 23, 1899, p. 190), although that newspaper was formally based in New York.

The Anarchists' Task

Translated from "Il compito degli anarchici," *La Questione Sociale*
(Paterson, New Jersey) 5, new series, no. 13 (December 2, 1899)[128]

What should we do?

That is the question facing us, as indeed it does all who have ideas to put into effect and interests to defend, in every moment of our party life.

We want to do away with private ownership and authority, which is to say we are out to expropriate those who cling to the land and capital, and to overthrow government, and place society's wealth at the disposal of everyone so that everyone may live as he pleases with no other restriction than those imposed by natural and social necessity, *freely* and *voluntarily* recognized and accepted. In short, we are out to implement the anarchist-socialist program. And we are convinced (and day to day experience confirms us in this belief) that the propertied and governments use physical force to protect their ascendancy, so, in order to defeat them, we must of necessity resort to physical force, to violent revolution.

As a result, we are the foes of all privileged classes and all governments, and inimical to all who, albeit with the best of intentions, tend, by their endeavors, to sap the people's revolutionary energy and substitute one government for another.

But what should we do to ensure that we are up to making our revolution, a revolution against all privilege and every authority and that we win?

The best tactic would be for us to spread our ideas always and everywhere; to use all possible means to nurture in proletarians the spirit of combination and resistance and to egg them on to ever greater demands; to be unrelenting in our opposition to every bourgeois party and every authoritarian party and remain unmoved by their complaints; to organize among those who have been won over and are being won over to our ideas and to provide ourselves with the material means needed for struggle; and, once we have built up enough strength to win, to rise up alone, on our own exclusive behalf, to implement our program in its entirety, or, to be more exact, to secure for every single person unrestricted freedom to experiment, practice and progressively amend that form of social living that he may feel is best.

---

128   This article was reprinted in *L'Iconoclasta* (Paris) on December 25, 1924, which had in turn borrowed it from *Umanità Nova* (Brooklyn) no. 3 of November 15, 1924. The reprint makes no mention of the original edition and presents the article as contemporary, amending a few references to the monarchy by apposite comments about fascist rule.

But, unfortunately, this tactic cannot always be strictly adhered to and there is no way that it can achieve our purpose. The effectiveness of propaganda is, to say the least, limited, and when, in any given context, all individuals likely, by virtue of their moral and material conditions, to understand and embrace a given set of ideas have been brought on board, there is little more to be achieved by means of the spoken and written word until such time as an alteration in the context elevates a fresh stratum of the population to a position where it can value those ideas. Likewise, the effectiveness of labor organization is limited by the very same factors as inhibit the indefinite spread of propaganda; as well as by broad economic and moral factors that weaken or entirely neutralize the impact of resistance by conscious workers. Our having a strong, vast organization of our own for the purposes of propaganda and struggle runs into a thousand hurdles in ourselves, our lack of resources, and, above all, government repression. And even if it were possible, over time, to arrive by means of propaganda and organization at sufficient strength for us to make the revolution, striking out directly in the direction of anarchist socialism, every passing day, well ahead of our reaching that point of strength, throws up political situations in which we are obliged to take a hand lest we not only lose the benefits to be reaped from them, but indeed lose all sway over the people, thwart part of the work done thus far, and render future work the more daunting.

The problem therefore is to come up with some means whereby, insofar as we can, we bring about those changes in the social environment that are needed if our propaganda is to make headway, and to profit from the conflicts between the various political parties and from every opportunity that presents itself, without surrendering any part of our program, and doing this in such a way as to render victory easier and more imminent.

In Italy, for instance, the situation is such that there is the possibility, the probability sooner or later of an insurrection against the Monarchy. But it is equally certain that the outcome of the next insurrection is not going to be anarchist socialism.

Should we take part in laying the groundwork for, or in mounting, this insurrection? And how?

There are some comrades who reckon that it is not in our interest to engage with a rising that will leave the institution of private property untouched and will simply replace one government with another, that is to say, establish a republic, that would be every bit as bourgeois and oppressive as the monarchy. They say: let us leave the bourgeois and would-be governors to lock horns with one another, while we carry on down our own path, by keeping up our anti-property and anti-authoritarian propaganda.

Now, the upshot of any such abstention on our part would be, first, that in the absence of our contribution, the uprising's chances of success would be lessened and that therefore it might be because of us if the monarchy wins—this monarchy that, particularly at the present moment, when it is fighting for its survival and rendered fierce by fear, bars the way to propaganda and to all progress. What is more, if the rising went ahead without our contribution, we would have no influence over subsequent developments, we would not be able to extract any advantages from the opportunities that always crop up during the period of transition from one regime to the next, we would be discredited as a party of action, and it would take us many a long year before we could accomplish anything of note.

It is not a case of leaving the bourgeois to fight it out among themselves, because in any insurrection the source of strength, material strength at any rate, is always the people and if we are not in on the rising, sharing in the dangers and successes and striving to turn a political upheaval into a social revolution, the people will be merely a tool in the hands of ambitious types eager to lord it over them.

Whereas, by taking part in the insurrection (an insurrection we would never be strong enough to mount on our own), and playing as large a part as we can, we would earn the sympathy of the risen people and would be in a position to push things as far as possible.

We know only too well and never weary of saying so and proving it, that republic and monarchy are equally bad and that all governments have the same tendency to expand their powers and to oppress their subjects more and more. We also know, however, that the weaker a government is, the stronger the resistance to it from among the people, and the wider the freedom available and the chances of progress are. By making an effective contribution to the overthrow of the monarchy, we would be in a position to oppose more or less effectively the establishment or consolidation of a republic, we could remain armed and refuse to obey the new government, and we would be able, here and there, to carry out attempts at expropriation and organization of society along anarchist and communist lines. We could prevent the revolution from being halted at step one, and the people's energies, roused by the insurrection, from being lulled back to sleep. All of these things we would not be able to do, for obvious reasons of popular psychology, by stepping in afterwards, once the insurrection against the monarchy had been mounted and succeeded in our absence.

On the back of these arguments, other comrades would have us set aside our anarchist propaganda for the moment in order to concentrate solely on the fight against the monarchy, and then resume our specifically anarchist endeavors once the insurrection has succeeded. It does not occur to them that if we were to mingle today with the republicans, we would be working for the sake of the coming republic, throw our own ranks into disarray, send the minds of our supporters spinning, and when we wanted to would then not be strong enough to stop the republic from being established and from embedding itself.

Between these two opposite errors, the course to be followed seems quite clear to us.

We must cooperate with the republicans, the democratic socialists, and any other anti-monarchy party to bring down the monarchy; but we must do so as anarchists, in the interests of anarchy, without disbanding our forces or mixing them in with others' forces, and without making any commitment beyond cooperation on military action.

Only thus, as we see it, can we, in the coming events, reap all the benefits of an alliance with the other anti-monarchy parties without surrendering any part of our own program.

"Le Journal du Peuple"

Translated from "Le journal du peuple," *La Questione Sociale* (Paterson, New Jersey) 5, new series, no. 13 (December 2, 1899)

We are among those who believe that the group of French anarchists, which heads *Le Journal du Peuple* and among whom Sébastien Faure is the most well-known figure, during the recent crisis, has drawn too close to the anti-monarchist and anti-clerical bourgeois parties and has, out of fear of reaction, become overly forgetful of the war against republican institutions that nevertheless serve capitalist interests so well.[129]

Indeed it is not that we believe the greater of lesser measure of freedom that can be extracted from the State is unimportant, and that a clerical and monarchist reaction in France would not be damaging.

But we believe that anarchists (who are either proletarians or have embraced the cause of the proletariat), even if using where possible the efforts of others in the fight for freedom and well-being, must always battle as a distinct party opposed to all authoritarian parties, and as a distinct class at war with the bourgeoisie en masse and against any bourgeois fraction. We believe that in the middle of all the fortuity of the struggle and while tailoring our methods of action to suit the changing circumstances, we must always maintain our program and remind ourselves that our purpose, to which every resource must be subjected, is: Total freedom for all; all wealth accessible to all.

---

129   On the French crisis see also "Dreyfus's Conviction," p. 108.

And it seems to us that the *Journal du Peuple* group has not done so, or has not done so sufficiently; and this also appears to be the opinion of many French comrades, who have voiced their objections publicly.

Sébastien Faure in turn voices his own objections and defends himself. Below we reproduce the most interesting part of his defense—both in respect to objectivity, and because it might be true, and we would be very glad, that we were mistaken, having judged from facts that may have been incorrectly reported and interviews that may not have been authentic.

In any event here is what Sébastien Faure says in no. 2 (third series) of *Le Libertaire,* which is certainly an eloquent reaffirmation of his long-standing anarchist belief.

[*In the article Faure rejects the charge that* Le Journal du Peuple *is anti-anarchist. In order to be such, he contends, a newspaper would have to champion some sort of government, private ownership, religion, or patriotism. Faure argues in detail that* Le Journal du Peuple *is, by contrast, anti-parliamentary, anti-capitalist, anti-religious, and anti-patriotic, and concludes that not only is it anarchist, but it is in fact the only daily paper that is such.*]

The "Wicked Laws" in France

Translated from "Le 'leggi scellerate' in Francia," *La Questione Sociale* (Paterson, New Jersey) 5, new series, no. 13 (December 2, 1899)

A few years back, in the wake of the fear that Vaillant's bomb and Caserio's dagger struck into the hearts of the bourgeoisie, the government proposed special laws against anarchists that, because of their ferocity, were qualified as the "wicked laws."[130]

They sought to sentence people to lengthy prison terms or deportation for life for a mere thought crime.

The socialist members of parliament fought fiercely against these laws, but the laws were passed; and several dozen anarchists, and alleged anarchists, were convicted, some for having posted a bill, some for words uttered in a café, some for no reason, simply because a policeman had made a report against them.[131]

---

130 See note 87.
131 One of the consequences of these laws was the so-called "trial of the thirty" in August 1894, in which anarchist exponents and intellectuals such as Jean Grave, Sébastien Faure, Paul Reclus, and Émile Pouget were brought before a court along with a number of illegalist anarchists.

Later, a radical prime minister by the name of Bourgeois came to power, he needed the support of the socialists, and he obtained it. It was a good opportunity for the socialist members of parliament to force the repeal of the "wicked laws," and there were plenty who tried to persuade them to perform what seemed to all men of good faith to be an elementary duty of justice and reason.

But by then the socialists in parliament were no longer an opposition group with no connections to the men in power: they were already officially recognized, interacted as equals with ministers, and were already thinking about the chances of securing a few portfolios. And so, they forgot about the splendid campaign they had supported a short time before, they refused to propose that the anti-anarchist laws be repealed *lest it cause embarrassment to the cabinet,* as they cynically admitted.

Recently, at the time of the turmoil over Dreyfus, the socialists, radicals, and liberals, in order to win the support of the anarchists and popular components in the struggle on behalf of an unjustly convicted bourgeois, promised that, once Dreyfus was set free, they would contribute to the agitation for the release of the anarchists and repeal of the wicked laws.

But Dreyfus has already been set free; and, with very few exceptions, those who, among the bourgeoisie, were so enthusiastic about justice when the cause was that of a bourgeois, have completely forgotten the anarchists innocently suffering in the prisons of Guiana and New Caledonia.

And the socialists, now that they have two of their own in power, will want less than ever to create embarrassment for the cabinet!

Of the anarchists convicted during the reactionary period when these special laws were created, some died massacred during a rebellion, others died because of the climate and despair; and the survivors are all reduced to a bad state.[132]

In an eloquent appeal, the lawyer Leyret states that unless we hurry up to free them, there will soon be no one left to free.

But the President of the Republic and his ministers, socialists included, are in no hurry.

In recent days Loubet has pardoned Monod, one of the anarchists whose conviction seemed most outrageous: he pardoned him three months after Monod's little daughter, weeping, managed to make him promise to do so.[133]

---

132 At that time a pamphlet had recently been published against the wicked laws, consisting of three articles, in the last of which anarchist Émile Pouget reviewed the history of persecuted anarchists (Francis de Pressensé, Un Juriste [Léon Blum] and Émile Pouget, *Les Lois Scélérates de 1893–1894,* Paris, Éditions de la Revue Blanche, 1899).

133 Gabriel Monod had been arrested at the time of the killing of President Carnot, for apologia of the crime during a conversation in a café.

Towards Anarchy

Man! (San Francisco) 1, no. 1 (April 1933)[138]
Translated from "Verso l'anarchia," *La Questione Sociale*
(Paterson, New Jersey) 5, new series, no. 14 (December 9, 1899)

It is a general opinion that we, because we call ourselves revolutionists, expect Anarchy to come with one stroke—as the immediate result of an insurrection that violently attacks all that which exists and which replaces it with institutions that are really new. And to say the truth this idea is not lacking among some comrades who also conceive the revolution in such a manner.

This prejudice explains why so many honest opponents believe Anarchy a thing impossible; and it also explains why some comrades, disgusted with the present moral condition of the people and seeing that Anarchy cannot come about soon, waver between an extreme dogmatism which blinds them to the realities of life and an opportunism which practically makes them forget that they are Anarchists and that for Anarchy they should struggle.

Of course the triumph of Anarchy cannot be the consequence of a miracle; it cannot come about in contradiction to the laws of development (an axiom of evolution that nothing occurs without sufficient cause), and nothing can be accomplished without the adequate means.

If we should want to substitute one government for another, that is impose our desires upon others, it would only be necessary to combine the material forces needed to resist the actual oppressors and put ourselves in their place.

But we do not want this; we want Anarchy which is a society based on free and voluntary accord—a society in which no one can force his wishes on another and in which everyone can do as he pleases and together all will voluntarily contribute to the well-being of the community. But because of this Anarchy will not have definitively and universally triumphed until all men will not only not want to be commanded but will not want to command; nor will Anarchy have succeeded unless they will have understood the advantages of solidarity and know how to organize

---

138   The actual title of *Man!*'s edition and all successive reprints is "Toward anarchism." We have replaced "anarchism" with "anarchy" in the title and throughout the text to rectify a gross mistranslation. The whole article is based on the distinction between "anarchy," the ultimate ideal, and the incessant effort to approach that ideal, which is what "anarchism" is about. Thus translating "anarchia" as "anarchism" completely obfuscates the article's main thrust. We have also made changes in a few places where the translation was unclear or incorrect.

a plan of social life wherein there will no longer be traces of violence and imposition.

And as the conscience, determination, and capacity of men continuously develop and find means of expression in the gradual modification of the new environment and in the realization of the desires in proportion to their being formed and becoming imperious, so it is with Anarchy; Anarchy cannot come but little by little—slowly, but surely, growing in intensity and extension.

Therefore, the subject is not whether we accomplish Anarchy today, tomorrow, or within ten centuries, but that we walk toward Anarchy today, tomorrow, and always.

Anarchy is the abolition of exploitation and oppression of man by man, that is the abolition of private property and government; Anarchy is the destruction of misery, of superstitions, of hatred. Therefore, every blow given to the institutions of private property and to the government, every exaltation of the conscience of man, every disruption of the present conditions, every lie unmasked, every part of human activity taken away from the control of the authority, every augmentation of the spirit of solidarity and initiative, is a step towards Anarchy.

The problem lies in knowing how to choose the road that really approaches the realization of the ideal and in not confusing the real progress with hypocritical reforms. For with the pretext of obtaining immediate ameliorations these false reforms tend to distract the masses from the struggle against authority and capitalism; they serve to paralyze their actions and make them hope that something can be attained through the kindness of the exploiters and governments. The problem lies in knowing how to use the little power we have—that we go on achieving, in the most economical way, more prestige for our goal.

There is in every country a government which, with brutal force, imposes its laws on all; it compels all to be subjected to exploitation and to maintain, whether they like it or not, the existing institutions. It forbids the minority groups to actuate their ideas, and prevents the social organizations in general from modifying themselves according to, and with, the modifications of public opinion. The normal peaceful course of evolution is arrested by violence, and thus with violence it is necessary to reopen that course. It is for this reason that we want a violent revolution today; and we shall want it always—so long as man is subject to the imposition of things contrary to his natural desires. Take away the governmental violence, ours would have no reason to exist.

We cannot as yet overthrow the prevailing government; perhaps tomorrow from the ruins of the present government we cannot prevent the arising of another similar one. But this does not hinder us, nor will it tomorrow, from resisting whatever form of authority—refusing always to submit to its laws whenever possible, and constantly using force to oppose force.

Every weakening of whatever kind of authority, each accession of liberty will be a progress toward Anarchy; always it should be conquered—never asked for; always it should serve to give us greater strength in the struggle; always it should make us consider the state as an enemy with whom we should never make peace; always it should make us remember well that the decrease of the ills produced by the government consists in the decrease of its attributions and powers, not in increasing the number of rulers or in having them chosen by the ruled. By government we mean any person or group of persons in the state, country, community, or association who has the right to make laws and inflict them upon those who do not want them.

We cannot as yet abolish private property; we cannot regulate the means of production that is necessary to work freely; perhaps we shall not be able to do so in the next insurrectional movement. But this does not prevent us now, or will it in the future, from continually opposing capitalism. And each victory, however small, gained by the workers against their exploiters, each decrease of profit, every bit of wealth taken from the individual owners and put to the disposal of all, shall be a progress—a forward step toward Anarchy. Always it should serve to enlarge the claims of the workers and to intensify the struggle; always it should be accepted as a victory over an enemy and not as a concession for which we should be thankful; always we should remain firm in our resolution to take with force, as soon as it will be possible, those means which the private owners, protected by the government, have stolen from the workers.

The right of force having disappeared, the means of production being placed under the management of whomever wants to produce, the rest must be the fruit of a peaceful evolution.

It would not be Anarchy, yet, or it would be only for those few who want it, and only in those things they can accomplish without the cooperation of the non-anarchists. This does not necessarily mean that the ideal of Anarchy will make little or no progress, for little by little its ideas will extend to more men and more things until it will have embraced all mankind and all life's manifestations.

Having overthrown the government and all the existing dangerous institutions which with force it defends, having conquered complete freedom for all and with it the right to the means of production, without which liberty would be a lie, and while we are struggling to arrive to this point, we do not intend to destroy those things which we little by little will reconstruct.

For example, there functions in the present society the service of supplying food. This is being done badly, chaotically, with great waste of energy and material and in view of capitalist interests; but after all, one way or another we must eat. It would be absurd to want to disorganize the system of producing and distributing food unless we could substitute it with something better and more just.

There exists a postal service. We have thousands of criticisms to make, but in the meantime we use it to send our letters, and shall continue to use it, suffering all its faults, until we shall be able to correct or replace it.

There are schools, but how badly they function. But because of this we do not allow our children to remain in ignorance—refusing their learning to read and write. Meanwhile we wait and struggle for a time when we shall be able to organize a system of model schools to accommodate all.

From this we can see that, to arrive at Anarchy, material force is not the only thing to make a revolution; it is essential that the workers, grouped according to the various branches of production, place themselves in a position that will insure the proper functioning of their social life—without the aid or need of capitalists or governments.

And we see also that the Anarchist ideals are far from being in contradiction, as the "scientific socialists" claim, to the laws of evolution as proved by science; they are a conception which fits these laws perfectly; they are the experimental system brought from the field of research to that of social realization.

The Milan Elections.
The Anarchists' Conduct

Translated from "Le elezioni a Milano. La condotta degli anarchici,"
La Questione Sociale (Paterson, New Jersey) 5, new series, no. 14
(December 9, 1899)

On December 10 the general local elections will take place in Milan.

After the massacres in May, the state of siege, the Turati election, etc., we can understand the government's great interest in convincing everyone that the people of Milan support the reaction.[139]

And its activity is proportionate to its interest.

By means of certain allegedly independent socialists, who are actually policemen who publish a self-proclaimed socialist newspaper in Rome, *La Riscossa*, the government tried to use the abstentionist propaganda

---

139   The parliamentary mandate of the foremost socialist Filippo Turati had been declared lost due to his conviction for the events of May 1898. However he had been reelected in the Milan by-elections of March 1899.

of anarchist socialists for its own purposes. And somebody from *La Riscossa* turned up in Milan, got in touch with our comrades, and offered them money to rent space, publish manifestos, etc.

But the comrades immediately realized who they were dealing with, and thus ignominiously shooed away this shady middleman, and through comrade Pandiani Sisinio communicated the affair to the public, writing a letter to *Avanti!* in which, stating the facts, they concluded "that anarchist socialists neither have nor want to have anything in common with the independent socialists of *La Riscossa*, that they remain steadfast in fighting for their ideal, but do not want to play into anyone's hands and much less damage the reputation or slander the intentions of the democratic socialists."

Can you imagine anything more natural, more consistent with the conduct that anarchist socialists have always advocated?

Yet this overjoyed those fine minds at *Il Proletario*, who believe they can pit against us, who criticize the program and tactics of democratic socialists, the conduct of our comrades in Milan... who do just as much.[140]

So, gentlemen from *Il Proletario*, do you believe that faced with a choice between democratic socialists and the government, we would choose the government? We would get angry and treat you harshly, were it not clear that this is nonsense said with no bad intentions, only because of the embarrassment in which *Il Proletario* finds itself at having to debate us yet having no good argument to use against us.

According to *Il Proletario* we would say that all the evil of the reaction is the work of the socialists and their deputies!!!

But that is sick of them! What we are saying is that the socialists will make the reaction, they will be condemned to do it, the day they become the government, due to the necessity that, as we see it, requires any government to do harm, even if it is made up of honest and well-intentioned people. Today certainly the democratic socialists fight against the government and for the good of the people with complete sincerity, and utter devotion. Only, in our opinion, they are going the wrong way, and that is why we seek to propagate a different tactic. That is all.

But those at *Il Proletario* struggle to understand how one can angrily refuse any contact with those who preach abstention on the government's behalf, and then turn around and preach abstention anyway!

Let them listen to us and try to understand.

Preaching abstention alongside the reactionaries, funded by reactionaries and therefore, like it or not, with reactionary attitudes, would mean playing into the reaction's hands, and naturally we do not want to smell

---

140   "Le elezioni a Milano," *Il Proletario* (New York) 4, no. 33 (December 2, 1899). The article verbatim reprints Pandiani's letter from *Avanti!* of November 6.

of it, even setting aside our repugnance at dealing with police reptiles and the danger of appearing to be sellouts.

On the other hand, preaching abstention with our criteria, in opposition to the government and all bourgeois and authoritarian parties, is doing the work of educating the people, work of revolutionary preparation.

Should the socialist-republican-radical coalition be beaten in Milan by the strength of the moderates and clericalists, or by the people's indifference, that would certainly be a triumph for the government, which we would be the first to regret.

But if this coalition were to be beaten thanks to the efforts of anarchists, which is to say, due to aware, active, militant abstention by those who want more forceful methods than elections, then, no matter who wins the election, the government and the bourgeoisie would be mortally wounded worse than by a thousand electoral defeats. And the government knows this: the proof is the viciousness with which the police have always ripped up our abstentionist flyers during election times, and the months and years of imprisonment that so many of our comrades have suffered due to those flyers.

Do the gentlemen at *Il Proletario* understand now?

Falsification

Translated from "Falsificazione," *La Questione Sociale*
(Paterson, New Jersey) 5, new series, no. 14 (December 9, 1899)

In no. 80 of Buenos Aires's *L'Avvenire* we find an article by G. Ciancabilla dated Paterson, August '99, in which there are such... things, that, despite our desire to avoid certain arguments, we cannot help but bring to the attention of our comrades.[141]

According to Ciancabilla, we, the advocates of organization, tend to "exclusively organize the masses in the struggle against capital, showing them that their only path to salvation lies in economic emancipation, in the abolition of private property, *from which everything else will follow.*" Whereas according to him (as if we did not say the same thing) "it is necessary that the people understand that anarchy, besides meaning their economic emancipation, must be for us also freedom, which is to

---

141   "Due tendenze in lotta" (Two contending tendencies), October 7, 1899. This
       was the follow-up to an article that had appeared in issue no. 74 of July 16,
       1899, dated Paterson, June 1899.

say, aware and permanent rebellion against every kind of authority, until there is not a trace left, no matter how faint."

The comrades, organizationists or not, will wonder where Ciancabilla ever met these strange anarchists who wage war solely against capital and not also against authority? And if any existed, would Ciancabilla recognize them as anarchists? We certainly would not.

Ciancabilla knows us, reads us, attends our lectures... how are we to explain him attributing to us ideas that are the opposite of what we profess?

We are continually debating with the democratic socialists, precisely because we hold that individual ownership and government are two manifestations of the same fundamental fact: the dominion of man over man; that, if private property was abolished without abolishing the government (supposing it were possible), the government then, unable to survive without the support of a privileged class, would recreate it again, just as, on the other hand, if government was abolished without abolishing private property, the property-owners would immediately recreate it to defend their privileges: and, as a result, we hold that we need to combat property and authority simultaneously. And Ciancabilla knows this, since he says he agrees with us on the points where we disagree with the democratic socialists.

Why does he try to make out that we are so different from what we are?

Falsehoods are not a good way "to create conscious minds"; but they are great for obfuscating them.

Aside from the foregoing, the article contains abstruse comments that seem designed to complicate the simplest things, and to confuse the ideas to anyone who lacks the time and practice to see through sentences that appear to say a lot but really say nothing.

For instance, what does it mean "that economic emancipation is the indispensable means of obtaining anarchy, and political freedom is the goal"?

The goal is life, happiness. And living a happy life means abundantly satisfying all one's material, moral, and intellectual needs: it means having bread, freedom, love, knowledge.

Therefore, economic well-being, freedom, moral, and intellectual development do not stand in a means–ends relation, but are integral parts of the goal for which we struggle.

Anarchists in the Labor Unions

Translated from "Gli anarchici nelle Unioni operaje," *La Questione Sociale*
(Paterson, New Jersey) 5 new series, no. 14 (December 9, 1899)

In Havana, Cuba, the labor Unions have celebrated the anniversary of the Chicago martyrdom.[142]

This fact, which is an eloquent indication of the anarchist leanings of those workers, was made possible because Spanish and Cuban anarchists have always been active and enthusiastic unionists, and all of the anarchist newspapers that have been and are being published in Cuba have always been and are champions of the labor movement.

Had the anarchists instead opposed or scorned the organization of worker resistance because it was insufficient, and had they limited themselves to theoretically preaching anarchist ideas, would the Cuban workers be more advanced, and would they have done anything more practically revolutionary than celebrating November 11?

We greatly doubt it: indeed we are afraid that they would have looked upon anarchists as damaging to the workers' cause, and would have made McKinley an honorary member of one of their unions... to the great delight of the republican socialists at *Il Proletario*.[143]

Provoked

Translated from "Provocati," *La Questione Sociale*
(Paterson, New Jersey) 5, new series, no. 14 (December 9, 1899)

L'Aurora has grown tired of explaining its ideas and letting us explain ours, leaving it to the readers to judge and make their choice. Now it feels the need to indulge in gossip.

In fact in its latest issue it publishes the following:[144]

UNIONISM AND SPECULATION

We receive and publish here in its entirety, correcting only spelling:

---

142   On the events in Chicago see "Martyrdom in Chicago. November 11, 1887," p. 127.
143   See "Buffoonery," p. 92.
144   The issue of *L'Aurora* is that of December 2.

Paterson, November 26, 1899.

Dear AURORA,

I seek your hospitality for the publication of this text of mine, having every reason to doubt that it would be well-received in the columns of *La Questione Sociale*.

The latter, in its last issue, attacked New York's *Il Proletario* for ripping off its typesetter, paying him below the going rate; and it was right to do so because whoever preaches union resistance to the workers should start by setting a good example.[145]

The Q. S. boasts of paying its workers the going rate. That too is true, and indeed the rate is unduly high; but what the Q. S. has the fault to hold back, in my opinion, is that its typesetter, paid at the Union rate, is not however a member of the Union; so that he enjoys all the benefits of the Union without bearing any burden, such as dues, strike donations, etc.

This seems to me therefore to be acting a bit like Father Zappata: not practicing what you preach.[146] In my opinion, I think that when one is working for propaganda among *comrades*, there should be no speculation, and no question of the rate, but one should only take what is strictly necessary for the needs of life.

Or, even if one wanted to keep up the appearances of the rate, anyone calling himself a *comrade* should hand over a certain amount for propaganda, especially when propaganda is in the state of *deficit* in which the Q. S. currently is.

Otherwise it could be very well presumed that the fanatical unionism of certain anarchists is simply a speculative unionism.

That's all.[147]

Yours and for the cause

A PATERSON ANARCHIST.

The letter is anonymous, or was published anonymously, and so we must believe that *L'Aurora* assumes responsibility for it. So much the worse for them.

Let us analyze at this document from an "anarchist" who makes personal attacks without giving his name: let us analyze it not for benefit of the writer, since it is not our habit to heed anonymous insults and

---

145   "It's a Shame!" p. 153.
146   The reference is to the Tuscan proverbial phrase "acting like Father Zappata, who did not practice what he preached."
147   In English in the source text.

accusations, but for the benefit of the comrades, so they can see to what base and petty ground a disagreement is brought, which should only be founded on differences of ideas honestly professed by both sides.

"We pay our typesetters the going rate." Could we decently do otherwise? If we did not have printing material and were forced to have our printing done at a capitalist print shop, we certainly would not go to a scab print shop under Union boycott; we would go to a print shop where the workers are paid the going rate. Possessing the material and paying the workers directly, we cannot treat them worse than would the capitalist we would otherwise use.

"The rate is too high." Why? are we now supposed to believe that workers have set their sights too high and fight to reduce the rate?

"Our typesetter is not a Union member." It would be more accurate to say our typesetters, since it is true that we have directly employed just one typesetter, but it is known that, being him unable to handle the work on his own, he employed additional people, whom he pays himself at the going rate, making absolutely no profit. If they were not Union members, they would be at fault, when there were no material obstacles preventing them from joining; but that does not concern the newspaper. In any case let us point out that not being able to join the Union, for whatever reason, is no justification for acting like a scab and helping lower wages.

"When one is working for propaganda among comrades one should only take what is strictly necessary for the needs of life." Let's see. Our typesetters work at composing just like the aforementioned "anarchist" works at some other trade, and they are paid for their work just like he is paid for his. If they did not work for LA QUESTIONE SOCIALE they would work in a different print shop and earn the same pay. Why, being comrades, should they be obliged to donate to propaganda anything beyond "what is strictly necessary for the needs of life," when there is no such obligation for other comrades? And then what exactly is strictly necessary? We are sure that, even paid the going rate, our typesetters, like all workers, go without much of what would be strictly necessary to live as men. To be sure, if our typesetters would and could give up all their pay to be used for propaganda and also add a certain amount from their pockets, we would admire their devotion; but this holds for them as it holds for any other anarchist, and one cannot ask them for a sacrifice that is not asked of others and he does not do himself.

"If our typesetters do not donate a certain amount towards propaganda, it would mean that their unionism is speculative." What does this language mean? The worker trying to keep up working wages for himself and for others is therefore a speculator? Maybe so; but then we are all speculators, because we are anarchists to win freedom and well-being for ourselves as well as others. We are not accustomed to moral blackmail: anyone who can contribute to cover the deficit and ensure that the paper flourishes is doing good work, others no more and no less than the comrades working in our printing house.

Let us leave it there: let the comrades judge.

*
**

The typesetters have passed us the following letter that they addressed to *L'Aurora*:

[*There follows a letter of protest signed by Pedro Esteve, A. Guabello, and B. Mazzotta, dated "Paterson, N.J., December 1899," in which the allegations are described as "unjustified" and it is requested that* L'Aurora *publish the letter itself.*]

[Untitled]

Translated from La Questione Sociale
(Paterson, New Jersey) 5, new series, no. 14 (December 9, 1899)

SOMEBODY from "Il Proletario," the one we described as dishonest or foolish, because, in his attack against "Il Progresso"—mistaken, by the way—he insinuated that we might have something in common with Sir Barsotti's paper, replies that the columnists for that paper have often described themselves as "forward-looking and libertarian."[148] Meaning that since the writers for "Il Rospo Volante" and "La Riscossa" in Rome declared themselves socialists, there would be grounds, without being dishonest, to insinuate that the writers of "Il Proletario" could be mixed up with them.[149]

But this would be nothing: it still has some semblance of an argument.

The thing is that SOMEBODY, perhaps realizing the weakness of his excuse, resorted immediately to telling lies—for example that we described ourselves as forward-looking, individualist, amorphous, and switch names with "every moon phase"—and nonsense about the universal "bang" and humanity's redemption on the strength of one word:—all to make people laugh.

---

148   "What We Have to Say to 'Il Proletario,'" p. 152; Somebody, "Sotto le forche caudine" (Running the gauntlet), *Il Proletario* (New York) 4, no. 33 (December 2, 1899).

149   Regarding *La Riscossa* see the article "The Milan Elections. The Anarchists' Conduct," p. 170. The newspaper was started after its predecessor *Il Rospo Volante* was shut down.

So why argue with him further?

He is making an insinuation, malicious or stupid, the choice is his; and when called upon to justify it, he starts telling jokes, and performing somersaults and smirks like a clown that tripped.

Let him play the clown if he pleases.

Electoral Struggle and Direct Struggle

Translated from "Lotta elettorale e lotta diretta," *La Questione Sociale* (Paterson, New Jersey) 5, new series, no. 15 (December 16, 1899)

The fundamental reason for which we refuse to delegate to others or, given the case, accept legislative roles ourselves, and for which we preach abstention from voting in political and local elections, is the fact that we do not acknowledge that anybody has the right to make laws, and we want the agreement required for the smooth functioning of society to derive, not from the imposition of the few over the many and not even the many over the few, but from the free consent of all those concerned. Consequently, we consider any methods that lead the people to believe that progress consists in a change of governing individuals, and revolution in a change of government form, to be dangerous, and directly counter to our purposes.

But this reason, of course, only holds true for anarchists.

Others, those who believe in the right of majorities and in the parliamentary system, are right to want people to get used to abandoning their interests to the luck of the ballot box. Besides, the bulk of the dissatisfied public has no interest in matters of principle, they do not think about distant consequences and side-effects, and look only at the direct practical results.

By electing good deputies and good council members one can obtain a reduction in taxes, an increase in freedom, laws favoring the workers, etc.—say those who are interested only in immediate improvements.

Through elections one might perhaps transform society gradually and peacefully, or, if that cannot be done due to the government's contrary violence, one can, at any rate, draw closer and facilitate socialism's triumph, using these elections to make propaganda and agitation, conquering those freedoms that are the necessary tools for educating the people and getting them used to participating in public life, and preparing our people to exercise public office—say the democratic socialists, who aspire to "conquer public powers," which is to say to enter government.

And here and there, when the reaction is most pressing, some anarchists, who want to act and don't know where to find the means of doing so, or who are weary of the struggle and looking for an honorable way to withdraw, come out to say: "There is no need to be exclusivist, we need to know how to adapt to circumstances. So, in times when persecution denies us the possibility of any sort of activity, it is good to vote—not so much to send anyone to the legislature, but as a way of protesting, on behalf of the convicted and persecuted, to find an opportunity to make propaganda, to let it be known that we are alive and assert ourselves as a party."

And so from an issue of principle, which it fundamentally is, the issue of elections is presented as a mere tactical issue.

Well then, let us leave principles aside, let us for a moment disregard the final goal we pursue and consider the issue as a purely tactical one, in view of the improvements that can be immediately obtained, and the gains propaganda can make.

We maintain that electoral tactics are an obstacle to potential improvements, and damaging to propaganda and agitation.

In assessing the results of their method, the *electionists* make two mistakes which are at the root of persistent illusions. First, they mistake effect for cause, and attribute to the effectiveness of the electoral struggle and the parliamentary system what little good (oh, how little it is!) at rare times (oh, how rarely!) is done by elected bodies, while this is really the effect of popular pressure, to which the rulers concede what little they think is necessary to calm the people, anesthetize their energy and prevent them from demanding more. Second, they compare what is done in the electoral struggle with what would happen if nothing were done; while instead they should compare the results obtained from the fight at the ballot box against those obtained when other methods are followed, and with what might be achieved if all effort used to send representatives to power, from whom they expect reforms or proposed reforms, were employed in the fight to directly achieve what is desired.

The whole of history, the whole of contemporary experience is a confutation of these errors; and if they have taken root in the consciousness of so many men of good will it is because they suit the intellectual laziness of the public, which loves to stop at the first appearance of things, and because the desire for honors and power has induced so many socialists, even though they fight sincerely for the good of all, to more or less unwittingly misrepresent the facts and misdirect the minds of their friends and followers.

Abstract reasoning alone would be enough to prove our argument.

The government—this much is obvious—only possesses whatever power it draws from the people. If the mass of the people is unaware, passive, submissive, the government will absolutely do as it pleases in its own interest and in that of the ruling class, and will use the people themselves, transformed into soldiers, to keep the recalcitrant down. If the masses start making demands and showing a willingness to assert themselves, then the government, if it is clever and has foresight, will yield bit by bit to avoid the worst; and if it is stupidly stubborn, or if the demands are such as to make the matter a life-or-death issue for the government and for the class upon which it relies, it will resist until it has been overthrown by revolution. In any event, it may well be able to exploit the strength of the community for the benefit of one class, but it cannot do a thing for the people that the people do not do for themselves.

The illusion that the government does good for the people is perhaps a little less stupid but nevertheless akin to the illusion of the worker who, receiving from his employer a small part of what he has himself produced, thinks that the employer is putting food on his table.

The fact that the government in question is a representative one does not affect our argument. Even supposing (and we have often shown this to be false) that it genuinely does represent the "will of the people," in order to make any reform whatsoever, this would need to exist and be strong enough to overcome any resistance. So, why wait for the deputies to ensure that this will triumphs, through a thousand legal impediments and thousands of delaying formalities? Why do not people implement that will directly, by simply doing what they want and are strong enough to do?

Now, let us remember a few facts.

It is a proven and generally accepted truth, even by the most parliamentary of socialists, that parliaments are actually nothing more than registry offices; that when it comes to social reforms, all they do is legalize what has become or is becoming enshrined in custom. If they want to do something else, their resolutions remain unenforced, because they have no strength.

There is much talk about labor protection laws. Yet everybody knows that these laws usually pass only when the people force them, which is to say when there is no need for them. And if a few times they have passed before the workers were strong enough to demand them, it was merely to silence the opposition, divert public attention away from the political mess behind the scenes, and make them think that the government looks out for the people's interests: and rest assured that they are then left unenforced. As evidence the Italian law on child labor.[150] In England itself, where labor protection laws were extracted from the bourgeoisie

---

150   The law on child labor, which set the minimum working age at nine years old, was approved in February 1886. Remarking upon an incident that had occurred in Turin, *La Stampa* of September 26, 1899 observed: "That law does indeed exist: but, it seems, it is not always enforced." And *Avanti!* of September 29, in the article "Contro la legge: Il lavoro delle donne e dei fanciulli" (Against the law: Female and child labor), stressed: "This is a law that, though it has been around for many years, can be regarded as stillborn; since it was never or hardly ever enforced, as can be deduced from the official statistics."

by force, often extremely violent, of organized workers, they are not really enforced other than for those trades that stand ever-ready to fight to defend themselves.

And what of freedom?

Which freedom has not been forcefully extracted? Which freedom has survived if the people were not ready to rush to arms to defend it?

The whole history of the parliamentary age (not to mention more ancient times) is an alternation of progress and reaction: whenever the people have risen up or threatened to rise up, when they have agitated vigorously and directly, progress has been made; when they have placed their trust in the work of elected leaders they have more or less slowly lost what they had achieved.

What reform, what act of justice has really been achieved through parliamentary action?

In France there has been a republic with universal suffrage for nearly thirty years. But when justice was sought for Dreyfus, when they sought to defend themselves against the menace of clericalism, they were forced to resort to direct popular action. Parliament was, and would still be, on the side of the general staff and the clericalists.

Let us look at what is happening in Barcelona. The issue involves the bourgeoisie, but the method can still be used by the workers. The businessmen and industrialists find that the tax burden is too heavy. Instead of thinking to appoint members of parliament, who would then not have been able to do anything because they would have been a tiny minority in the *Cortes*, they simply refused to pay. The government threatened the debtors with seizure, but they persisted with their refusal to pay; and seizing the things of so many people became impossible. The government proclaimed a state of siege, said that refusal to pay taxes constituted rebellion, and put a few people in prison. The taxpayers held firm, the prisoners received the population's applause; and the government had to stop the arrests and seek another gimmick. It tried closing a few shops, but all the stores immediately closed in protest; and the government was more embarrassed than ever. How will this end? Probably with a compromise, because neither the government nor the bourgeoisie are interested in pushing matters too far: but it is clear they will achieve more with this resistance than they would have with a hundred years of elections.[151]

To be sure, until the revolution has swept aside all the current authoritarian organization, there are lots of things that cannot be done without passing through the government's mechanisms. In order to abolish a liberticidal law, until it can be abolished by force, we must look to parliament. To feed poor children in the schools, until wealth can be taken

---

151   On the events in Barcelona, see "The Taxpayers' Strike in Spain," p. 155.

into common ownership, we must rely upon the municipality that has or can find the resources. But parliaments and municipal councils will pass measures favoring the people only when the people force them to do so; they will abolish harmful laws and regulations only when the people refuse to obey them. And it is not a good war tactic to send our friends into their ranks, as they will serve as shields from attacks.

If those socialists who were elected as deputies had instead remained among the people, to preach direct popular action, their action would have been more effective, even on parliament itself, without the party having to suffer parliamentarianism's corrupting influence. The part they now play in parliament, would have been performed by radicals, and there would not have been any need for them to transform into radicals and republicans.

But what if the reaction does not allow us to agitate through means other than elections!—they say.

Oh how did they manage when there was no right to vote? How did they manage to win that right? And what would they do if the government were to take it away?

The truth is that the illusion of doing something by electoral means and of doing it without danger and with little effort, prevents us from finding the right methods to resist the reaction.

Let this be considered by those anarchists—fortunately very few in number—who are inclined to go out and vote... because "there is nothing better to do."

Unjustified Criticism

Translated from "Critiche ingiustificate," *La Questione Sociale*
(Paterson, New Jersey) 5, new series, no. 16 (December 16, 1899)

The Provisional Correspondence Committee (residing in Barre, Vt.) of the Anarchist Socialist Federation wrote in its circular to comrades in the United States that "it will see to the dissemination to all groups of any proposals received from any group and pertaining to propaganda."[152]

The phrase *and pertaining to propaganda* was clearly intended by the Committee to convey that it assumed the responsibility for disseminating messages concerning propaganda, and not things of a private interest.

However *L'Aurora*, in search of an argument to support its cherished thesis, interpreted that phrase to mean that the Committee intends to

---

152   The circular had been published in *La Questione Sociale* of December 2, under the title "Federazione Socialista-Anarchica."

judge what is and what is not relevant to propaganda, and so goes to war against it, voicing the very same criticisms we would make if *L'Aurora's* interpretation was correct.[153]

We will not raise a philological issue and argue that *pertaining to something* means *regarding it, having relevance to it*; and, since anything regarding propaganda *pertains to it*, whether it be deemed useful or harmful, good or bad, so the expression used by the committee does not imply any intention to *judge*.

Let us concede though that the expression used may not have been fitting. What matters is the spirit and not the letter; the intention and not the more or less correct form of expression; the facts and not the more or less exact words.

The intention of the committee that offers us its services, and our intention in accepting, is to establish a transmission office that, as such, has no judgments of its own to champion, and is merely an affordable and steady method of correspondence. The members who constitute it are certainly entitled to express their judgments and take whatever initiatives they please, but they must do so as individuals, or as members of some group, and not as the correspondence committee.

We want a correspondence committee because, among other reasons, we know that without one it is the newspaper that becomes the agency that connects comrades and correspondence is centralized in the hands of the newspaper's editors; and neither the paper nor the editors can disregard their own judgments since their task is precisely to uphold and champion those judgments. There are always reasons of space and literary quality (which cannot be entirely ignored) that allow or actually force the editor of a newspaper to choose among a range of contributions— and, of course, they base their selection on their own judgment.

But will the reality live up to the words? That remains to be seen.

To be sure it may happen that someone who takes on a given role may not perform it well, or may seek to distort it. But there is no great harm done when people are free not to use the services of that functionary.

What turns a role, a delegated task, into power, into authority, is the fact that, as happens in societies organized along authoritarian lines, everyone is obliged to suffer the will of the individuals in these roles and can only get rid of them (when they can at all) by having a majority on their side. That danger does not exist among us. The fact of having a correspondence committee deprives no one of the right to correspond directly with anyone they wish: that committee is simply another means of communication made available to comrades, and if perchance it does not perform its assigned task well, the comrades will not have

---

153   "La lotta politica" (The political struggle), part 6, *L'Aurora* (West Hoboken) 1, no. 11 (December 9, 1899).

the hoped-for advantage, but will have lost nothing of their individual resources.

Does that mean that there is no danger of authoritarianism within our organization, and that everything will function as it would in an ideal anarchist society?

Of course not! There are always dangers, but they don't depend upon organization: rather they depend upon the apathy of those who should do their part and instead leave it to others to do everything.

Whoever seeks a boss, whoever seeks a master can always find one; and more so outside of the organization than within it, since the energetic person who, rather than use their energy to arouse the energy of others and work together for the common good, aspires to give orders and impose their will, meets with more success when they are not hampered by being held accountable for assignments, and when they are dealing with isolated individuals rather than organized groups.

On a Personal Matter

Translated from "Per una questione personale," *La Questione Sociale* (Paterson, New Jersey) 5, new series, no. 15 (December 16, 1899)

Ciancabilla has privately responded with the following letter to the letter that our typesetters addressed to *L'Aurora* and that we published in the last issue:[154]

West Hoboken, December 8, 1899.

TO THE TYPESETTERS OF THE Q. S.

[*In the first three paragraphs Ciancabilla takes full responsibility for the published letter and reiterates the charges against the typesetter, although, he claims, his assistant typesetters are now coming to defend him "due to a petty solidarity of interests. He addresses these assistants in the following part.*]

I can only note their consistency, recalling that right up until my last day residing in Paterson, they were continuously complaining to me about the system of exploitation, payment, and division of labor, to which their *boss*[155] was subjecting them. That *boss* was so much a *boss* that he would take on other anarchist orders—always in tribute to the *apostolate* and

---

154   The letter from the typesetters had been published as an appendix to the article "Provoked," p. 174.

155   In English in the source text throughout the paragraph.

abnegation which he proclaims... in words only, quoting Bakunin and others—charging the master's rate (50 cents) and instead paying his employees the worker's rate, while, by his right to be the *boss*, he makes no sacrifices—as in regard to unionism—not even that of paying rent for his printing house.

For all of these considerations I do not find it strange that the Paterson comrade—who exists, whether you like it or not—spoke of *the typesetter* rather than *the typesetters* of the Q. S. And the latter should have considered themselves out of the matter.

L'AURORA's purpose is not to attack so-called comrades—a very elastic term; but it does not refuse to warn comrades making sacrifices for propaganda about those who profit from it, preaching morality and zealous puritanism. Besides, all attacks coming from me have this difference from those that certain people have mounted against me from the shadows: I make my attacks based on truth, and do not resort to poisonous insinuations and cowardly lies; I attack head-on, openly lashing out, frankly, and I am not a follower of the arts of the sons of Loyola who jesuitically hit from behind, slithering like reptiles.

Permit me to find it strange that you *demand* (!) publication of your protest in L'AURORA. In the face of *factual* accusations only *factual* defenses and corrections can be acceptable. For bombastic protests, such as your own, you have *your* newspaper, and you can use it.

I have nothing more to say to you. I just caution you that, as far as I am concerned, this epistolary debate is also over, because I do not have time to waste.

Should you seek some other satisfaction, you can come and get it. You know where I live.

G. CIANCABILLA.
419 Courtland St. II floor
WEST HOBOKEN N.J.

We the undersigned believed it fitting to publish this letter because it paints a portrait of this man.

Ciancabilla lies knowing he is lying. Thus far we had refrained from attacking him personally because we did not want a personal issue to get mixed up with matters of ideas and come to change the composure of the discussion.

But since he has not been able to resist the nasty impulses of his temperament and he himself provides us with the proof that he intends to lead a campaign of insults and slander, we believe it is necessary to set our reservations aside and say once and for all that for us Ciancabilla is not a comrade.

Let the comrades who agree with Ciancabilla's ideas take care to not misunderstand us. We respect all ideas and believe them all worthy of examination and discussion. We are attacking Ciancabilla not for his ideas, but for his dishonest behavior.

Aquadro L., Besso G., Bianco S., Boffa C., Cominetti B., Casale G., Castelli G., Casale A., Cavallo G., Cerino A., Cerino S., Cerruti A., Cravello E., Cravello V., Ferro P., Foschini G., Frattini Lucia, Frattini Luigi, Gallo F., Gillia E., Magliocco C., Mainardi S., Malatesta E., Mazzotta B., Mercandino Giuseppe, Mercandino Giacomo, Minero Re L., Motta Marcello, Perino L., Picco G., Porrino F., Porrino M., Prina Q., Raveggi P. (Evening), Rivetti S., Robino P., Roda C., Rolli G., Sanguinetti B., Sella G., Simone A., Sola A., Tamaroglio Amedeo, Tamaroglio Antonio, Tamaroglio G., Tognetti E., Verolet L., Vineis E., Vineis G., Widmar F.

[*There follows a statement from the administrator of* La Questione Sociale, *Widmar, who attests that the typesetter Pedro Esteve is paid at the workers' rate of forty cents, and a statement from the typesetters Guabello and Mazzotta, attesting that they are paid by Esteve at the same rate.*]

The Long Way and the Short Way

Translated from "La via lunga e la via breve," *La Questione Sociale* (Paterson, New Jersey) 5, new series no. 16 (December 23, 1899)

Many people, and some of the best, out of a genuine love for the common good, have the habit of saying to us:

"Your ideas are just and sacrosanct; but why do you want to implement them by means of a violent revolution? Revolution could be the shortest way to get to the goal; but you cannot have a revolution without facing pain and sacrifice and without a more or less large amount of bloodshed. Would it not be wiser, more humane, to take the undoubtedly longer, but gentler way of gradual and peaceful evolution?"

And the legalitarians purposely capitalize upon this noble desire to spare human suffering to bang the drum for their parliamentary program.

We too would be in favor of the long but peaceful way, if it were an issue of our own personal satisfaction; in fact we would even and forever renounce this satisfaction, if doing so would prevent the shedding of a single tear or a single drop of blood. However this is precisely an issue of abolishing the social causes of human suffering, and we support the violent revolution, done as soon as possible, because we believe it is necessary to save blood and tears.

Those who talk about the *long way* to avoid suffering must never have reflected on the actual conditions of the proletariat in present-day society: otherwise they would understand that every additional day that the current state of affairs continues, produces more suffering and more sacrifice of life than a hundred of the bloodiest revolutions.

In the city of New York alone there are many tens of thousands of women who sell their bodies every night for bread. Tens of thousands of men are homeless or jobless and to satisfy their hunger they must beg or steal... when they manage.

Mrs. Leonora Barry, in a survey performed on behalf of the Knights of Labor[156] found in Newark, N.J., a girdle factory in which women and kids, paid starvation wages, were not allowed to talk, laugh, sing, nor eat a bite during work, and were fined 10 cents for every transgression.

Does thus strangling laughter and song in the throats of the youngsters, day after day, year upon year, for an entire lifetime, not amount to murdering the human being and reducing it to a simple cog in a machine?

In Bordentown, N.J., Mrs. Barry found women who were competing with prison inmates, who were making shirts at a price of 17 to 25 cents per dozen.

In Auburn, N.J., she visited a factory making women's and children's clothing, in which the female workers had to purchase the machine from the master and pay for it 50 cents per week if they earned three dollars, and 75 cents if they earned four dollars; and if they were fired or fell ill, they lost what they had paid for the machine, which remained the property of the master, who sold it to another female worker at the same price as before.

In Paterson, N.J., in the yarn factories, she found that the women were working in their bare feet on a stone floor with their chests drenched by a continuous spray of water, and in summer and winter were forced to go home soaking wet because, once work was over, the master did not let them stay in the factory long enough to change their clothes.

And this, and worse, is happening in America, where people from all over the world stream in fleeing from even worse suffering!

What can we say about the millions of peasants living in animal-like conditions and dying of prolonged malnutrition? What about the hundreds of thousands dying of acute starvation?

---

156   The Knights of Labor were a pioneering workers' organization especially strong during the 1880s. The survey by Leonora Barry, one of the organization's national officers, dated from 1887.

And what about the victims of the mines, the railways, sailing, insalubrious work, all of them victims of the capitalists' greed and indifference?

And the children dying by the millions from lack of food and medical treatment?

What of the famines? and the epidemics? and the wars?

Maintaining this state of affairs longer to save the few victims who would regrettably perish in a violent conflict, is that what is meant by sparing bloodshed and pain?

*
**

But it gets even worse.

Rejecting violent methods and consequently not preparing to use them to one's advantage, does not prevent violent outbreaks of popular anger: it simply makes the people's victory unlikely, and gives governments the means to periodically carouse in blood and persecution.

Keeping demands low, preaching that we should make do with taking things a step at a time, means deliberately multiplying violent revolutions with little or no benefit for the sufferers.

The only way to spare the bloodshed and suffering is to strike hard and in the name of all human demands.

*
**

A few days ago, a comrade, Pietro Cane from New York, told us an anecdote he swears is true.

In Palermo, there was a shoemaker who, having had a puppy, conceived the idea of raising it without a tail. To achieve this goal he cut off a small piece of the animal's tail every day; one can easily imagine how much torture this caused the poor little animal.

The neighbors, tired of the continual yelping and having realized the cause, complained to the shoemaker. And he apologized saying that he wanted to raise the dog without a tail.

—Then why not lop the entire tail off at one go? the neighbors said.

—Because I'm afraid of hurting him, the shoemaker answered.

What a strange sensitivity! But this is what the democratic socialists want to do, like all who would want to have a little revolution to make a little conservative republic, and then another one to make a radical republic... and so on until centuries are consumed.

Socialist Congress?

Translated from "Congresso... socialista?" *La Questione Sociale*
(Paterson, New Jersey) 5, new series, no. 16 (December 23, 1899)

We have news from the first sessions of the French legalitarian socialist congress in Paris.

Even a quick glance at the agenda reveals what kind of socialists they are.

1. The class struggle *and the conquest of public powers*.

2. Stance to be adopted in conflicts between various bourgeois fractions.

3. Socialist unity.

The economic issues of greatest concern to workers are of no concern to these "socialists"... except in regard to whether they may or may not provide a pathway to power.

It is interesting to note (and comforting to us) that, aside from the delegates of the electoral committees, few workers attend this congress. Barely sixty corporative groups were represented, and in general they were not represented by one of their worker members, but by a prominent politician.

All members of parliament and council members and those who aspire to be such are present. Under the pretext of socialism they address the conditions under which a "socialist" might accept a ministerial portfolio. Millerand's laurels are disturbing the sleep of these gentlemen.

There are two fractions in the Congress.

On the one side there are the *Guesdists* and the *Blanquists* who take on the air of guardians of the sacrosanct tradition of scientific (?) socialism, which, it seems, is against one of its members serving in the government. They are the revolutionary (!) part of the Congress.

On this occasion, they support the argument that the anarchists have always supported, namely that once one sets out on the slope of concessions, one must go on to the end; and they scold their friends from yesterday for doing what they themselves have not ceased to do to gain seats in parliament or on municipal councils.

On the other side we have the *independents* with Jaurès and "his recruits from the universities and bourgeois circles" who, more logically, applauded Millerand's entry into a bourgeois cabinet, taking their theory of conquering public powers to its last consequences, and inevitably ending up as nothing more than faint radicals.

The Congress is nothing but a battle between these two groups.

We shall keep our readers informed of the conclusions reached by the Congress.

Personal Matter

Translated from "Questione personale," *La Questione Sociale*
(Paterson, New Jersey) 5, new series, no. 16 (December 23, 1899)

In *L'Aurora,* Ciancabilla continues his dirty campaign of insults and slander.

And, of course, he says that he is doing so as a matter of principle and… in the interest of LA QUESTIONE SOCIALE![157]

To the question of principle we respond that sacrifices for the cause must be voluntary, or, when they are mandatory, should be equal for all, according to the resources of each person, of course.

Why should the typesetter who composes LA QUESTIONE SOCIALE be required to make a sacrifice that is not demanded of fellow typesetters working elsewhere and of comrades plying other trades?

The typesetter is in a different position than an editor or a lecturer. These are tasks that are done as anarchists, which offer their own reward in themselves, indeed they are a privilege and should be done free of charge, or better not to do them; except when help from comrades is necessary to pay the expenses required, which one may not be able to arrange for otherwise.[158]

On the other hand, the work of the typesetter is manual labor that one does not need to be an anarchist to perform, and which could as easily be taken on by a comrade as by any other worker.

When comrade Pedro Esteve, invited by comrades from the group, who found themselves without a typesetter, took on the task of composing *La Questione Sociale,* he certainly had no intention of sacrificing for the cause, but was simply plying his trade, just as he had done in other printing houses.

He makes his share of sacrifice (if we may call it a sacrifice)—and it is no less than that of others—through his activities as a propagandist and lecturer and by devoting a lot of time for free to the paper, time that takes away from his paid work, as well as contributing financially within the limits of his means.

As to Ciancabilla's concern for the interests of *La Questione Sociale,* they are laughable for anyone who really knows the man.[159] But, if that

---

157   "Speculazioni anarchiche," *L'Aurora* (West Hoboken) 1, no. 12 (December 16, 1899).

158   For a discussion of this subject see "Wages in Socialist Enterprises and Workers' Organizations," in Volume III of these *Complete Works*, p. 158.

159   Ciancabilla had written that "having excited the comrades of *La Questione Sociale* to provide for the newspaper's budget at a point when it is in a deficit, amounts to wanting the newspaper to prosper and quickly regain stability, in the interest of propaganda."

were the case, why did he ignite a public scandal and not invite the author of the anonymous letter to bring his concerns before the group?

And is it also in the interest of *La Questione Sociale* and propaganda that he informs the public that we reduced our circulation when he knows that the number of our readers in the United States and elsewhere has been growing and that the reduction in circulation was due to the fact that we have had to suspend much of our shipment to Italy because the police sequester our packages at the border?

But enough of these hypocrisies.

Ciancabilla KNOWS all of the devotion Pedro Esteve has to the cause and the services he has rendered it in Spain, Cuba, and the United States; he KNOWS that Esteve not only doesn't make any profit off the labor of the other typesetters, but that because of the time dedicated to taking care of the newspaper and because of so many small expenses that unofficially fall upon him, he comes to earn much less than he would earn in a capitalist print shop; he KNOWS that Esteve, to his own disadvantage, printed the first issue of *L'Aurora* yielding to Ciancabilla's insistent *pleas* and to provide proof of tolerance; he KNOWS that Esteve's type was brought to the premises of LA QUESTIONE SOCIALE at the behest of the group and of Ciancabilla himself in order to facilitate other anarchist publications, such as *El Despertar, Germinal,* and *L'Aurora* itself, which Ciancabilla maintained could only be produced in Paterson; he KNOWS that, when he was a member of our group and an editor with the Q. S., matters at the printing house were as they are now and not only did he not find fault with anything but he had fun ridiculing a fellow who was forever counting the leads and criticizing Esteve when he showed up for work an hour late without realizing when he worked the whole night through to get the paper out on time; he KNOWS all the good that (hypocritically, of course) he used to say to Esteve when Esteve was in the same current position—he KNOWS all this, and he knowingly lies.

We could seek the interest that has driven him in this attempt to sow division and suspicion among comrades. We prefer to leave him to wallow in his mud and not worry ourselves anymore with him and what he might say—unless he truly drags us into it.

Always, when propaganda work begins well and the highest hopes smile upon us, people come forth who, affecting to be more anarchist than the others, seek through slander and insinuations to disgust the most active comrades and do the greatest possible damage to the cause of anarchy.

Ordinarily, this dissolution work was done through anonymous manifestos.[160] This time someone has the sad courage to say his name.

---

160   The reference is to a series of manifestos published in London by the so-called "anonymous group." In this regard, see the two "Filth" articles and the articles

The comrades will know to whom to attribute the harm done... or attempted.

[Untitled]

Translated from *La Questione Sociale*
(Paterson, New Jersey) 5, new series, no. 16 (December 23, 1899)

Dear Comrades,

Wishing to respond to the article "Falsification," *L'Aurora* recalls a note that Grave added to a correspondence that Ciancabilla sent to *Les Temps Nouveaux* in November '97 regarding the anarchist movement in Italy.[161]

The note read exactly as follows: "We do not entirely share the *author's* outlook on the need for a centralization of propaganda; rather, our social movement must take heed of all mindsets that are expressed." (See *Les Temps Nouveaux* of November 20–26, '97.)[162]

I do not want to get into a discussion with Ciancabilla. But it is important to me to state that, given how Ciancabilla described our affairs in Italy, I would have had and I would have exactly the same reservations as Grave, since I was and I am against the centralization of propaganda, and I have always urged and urge comrades to make their own propaganda and multiply initiatives and activities.

Ciancabilla (while approving me and singing my praises) used to give the same misrepresentation of the ideas and aims of the men of *L'Agitazione* as he is today trying to give of the ideas and aims of LA QUESTIONE SOCIALE. With the difference that back then, when he was new to the anarchist movement, the mistake might have been attributed to error, whereas today, when he knows our ideas and our people well, it is obviously a deliberate and planned falsehood.

Now on to other matters.

"Our Correspondence" and "A Mystification Ended," in Volume III of these *Complete Works*, p. 104, 161, 187 and 415, respectively.

161 The article "Falsification" appears on p. 172. Ciancabilla replied with an article of the same title in *L'Aurora*, no. 12 (December 16). In the article Ciancabilla disputed what he in turn considered a falsification contained in a note in *La Questione Sociale* of December 9, in the "Fatti e opinioni" column. The note concerned a comment in the November 1899 issue of *Freedom* (London), which mentioned an article, appeared in the July 1899 issue of the same paper, in which Jean Grave wrote in support of organization. Ciancabilla countered that Grave was actually opposed to organization and to this end brought up the 1897 editorial note in *Les Temps Nouveaux*.

162 At that time Ciancabilla had not yet adopted an anti-organizationist position.

I learned that Ciancabilla, concerning the statement from many comrades, including myself, that he is not our comrade, intends to ask in this week's issue of *L'Aurora* whether he is not considered a comrade because of his campaign, supposedly against the typesetter but actually against LA QUESTIONE SOCIALE, or because of other more serious things that have been whispered about his conduct in Europe, and that he intends to address the question to me in particular.[163] It is probable that most of the signatories to the statement are judging him especially based on his conduct in America; but that is for them to say if they want.

As for me, I preempt my reply.

When I got back from *domicilio coatto*, comrades whom I had mostly known for many years and whom I hold in the highest esteem, as do all comrades who know them, told me things about Ciancabilla that were very dishonorable for an anarchist and a revolutionary... even allowing for possible exaggeration due to emotion. These were matters of which I did not have direct knowledge, since I had played no part in them, indeed when they happened I was in prison or on the island. But the comrades who told me are trustworthy people, and I believed them, as I believe them now.

Although one of those concerned is now unfortunately in prison, the others are alive and free and will certainly not refuse, if Ciancabilla so wishes, to repeat what they told me.

Furthermore, they had me read a letter from Ciancabilla that for me was enough to judge the man. If Ciancabilla so wishes, I believe I can arrange for its publication.

All of this of course prepared me to end any relationship with Ciancabilla and to publicly explain the reasons—as much as it is always tiresome to assert facts that one does not know directly and for certain.

But there was a problem.

Ciancabilla had long purported to have a brand of ideas of his own to argue, and it looked as if he wanted to argue them against me, since he dubbed *malatestian* anyone who disagreed with him.

I could plainly see that he had no such ideas, and I saw in all of his word tinkering the intention to sow confusion in order to create a prominent position for himself. But that was my opinion and others might not agree; and then Ciancabilla is well-versed in the art of coloring a phrase, something that easily dazzles comrades, who are not generally scholars.

---

163   For the declaration by Malatesta and others against Ciancabilla see "On a Personal Matter," p. 184. Ciancabilla's question anticipated by Malatesta actually appeared in the article "Per una questione personale. La scomunica" (On a personal matter. The excommunication), *L'Aurora* (West Hoboken) 1, no. 13 (December 23, 1899).

It was necessary to resolve the matter of ideas, to induce comrades who were undecided to reflect, to not let themselves be deceived by phrases; and for that to happen any personal conflict needed to be eliminated.

Had I attacked Ciancabilla on personal grounds, there would have been those who claimed that I was "excommunicating" him because he did not think like me; and Ciancabilla would have benefited from this. So I decided to focus only on the question of ideas, and strictly avoid any personal attacks.

I was pleased when, after the parting of the ways, the comrades from the "Diritto all'Esistenza" group, even the ones most hostile to Ciancabilla, helped him financially to launch a newspaper in which he could set out his ideas. I never uttered a word against him; and when, in locations where I went to give talks, comrades asked me about Ciancabilla, I without fail replied that I did not want to say anything about him, that they should read both newspapers and choose the ideas they found more persuasive regardless of the personalities presenting the ideas. When, at my lectures, money was collected and comrades asked if it would be all right with me to divide the proceeds between LA QUESTIONE SOCIALE and *L'Aurora,* I always answered that they should do as they wished. In short, I always avoided any sort of opposition to Ciancabilla, outside of the field of a pure debate of ideas. And I was determined to continue in this manner, even though I was not unaware of the insinuations that he spread and the poisonous letters that he wrote, as long as, at least in public, he kept to the field of a debate of ideas.

But Ciancabilla could not continue in that field, since ideas were the very thing he lacked, and he found himself in the humiliating position of having to repeat, in slightly different words, what he had understood from his adversary the previous day, to present it to the public as a truth he had discovered and that his opponent rejected. And unwilling to abandon his personal objectives, he found himself reduced to resorting to insults and slander. That authorized and forced me to set aside my reservations. Now no one could reasonably suspect me of attacking Ciancabilla because he does not think like me. Besides, the sight of him resolutely lying about things, which this time I know for certain and first-hand, banishes any remaining doubts I may have had as to what I had heard about him and shows me, beyond any doubt, that he is capable of dirty deeds.

Therefore, I declare with a completely clear conscience that, as far as I am concerned, Ciancabilla is not a comrade.

Yours
ERRICO MALATESTA.

The Malatesta Lectures[164]

Translated from "Le conferenze Malatesta," *Il Proletario*
(New York) 4, no. 35 (December 23, 1899)

Not many of our comrades attended the four lectures given in the Tirelli Hall of New York by the anarchist Malatesta, maybe because they mostly live far away and were not overwhelmingly attracted by the novelty of what was going to be said. However, comrades Rondani, Cianfarra, and others, refuted all of Malatesta's scientific heresies with which anarchist propaganda necessarily decorates itself and spelled out the nature of the international Socialist party's program.[165]

Malatesta admits that government and property are the two links in the oppression of the proletariat. Every so often—in his presentation—a third link crops up, religion; but as to the importance of the latter, Malatesta is very far from having, shall we say, a permanent judgment.

In Barre, Vermont, just a few months back, it appeared that religion was the capstone of capitalist rule. Now it seems that it is rather from government—which allegedly created and upholds private ownership of the means of production and exchange—that the present enslavement of wage-earners derives. All the weakness and illusions of anarchism are nestled in this half-Saint-Simonian, half-Marxist, half-Spencerian uncertainty.

. . .

To All Comrades

Translated from "Ai compagni tutti," *La Questione Sociale*
(Paterson, New Jersey) 5, new series, no. 17 (December 30, 1899)

Outraged by the dishonest behavior practiced by Ciancabilla, in appearances toward our comrade, while really against LA QUESTIONE SOCIALE, we publicly stated in no. 15 of this newspaper that for us Ciancabilla was not a comrade.[166] Now, for this reason only, in the latest issue of *L'Aurora* Ciancabilla presents us with a barrage of insults. We are idiots, screwballs, drunkards, crooks... is it not enough?[167]

---

164   This excerpt was inserted here because the subsequent untitled note on p. 208 refers to it.

165   *Il Progresso Italo-Americano,* in its issues of December 15–17, mentions these lectures were held daily from December 13 to December 16 and that the topics of the last two were, in order, "Fatherland, Religion, and Family" and "How and when Anarchy will triumph."

166   "On a Personal Matter," p. 184.

167   For Ciancabilla's article see note 163.

In the face of such insults, we, the signatories of the above-mentioned protest, must declare that if we had had any doubts about the timeliness of our statement, Ciancabilla's method of *judging* would have removed it.[168]

And we want to believe that all comrades will think the same as we do, since lots and lots of them have expressed their displeasure at not having known about our statement soon enough to be able to add their names alongside ours.

The Signatories.

That declaration had already gone to the press when the following letter reached us from the Spring Valley comrades:

[*There follows the text of the letter signed individually by members of the "Germinal Club, who protest against the behavior of Ciancabilla, who "does not shrink from personally attacking comrades," and against* L'Aurora, *which "out of mercenary jealousy, does nothing but sow discord and grudges between organizationist and antiorganizationist comrades," and finally invite* La Questione Sociale *to refrain from any personal controversies.*]

In addition to this, we have received other letters from various locations, in which comrades tell us about the plots Ciancabilla is orchestrating against "La Questione Sociale." We do not publish these because, as the Spring Valley comrades correctly say, we seek the most rapid possible end to this mudslinging in which others are so happy to engage.

From Orange Valley they write us that Ciancabilla and his followers even tried to use violence against comrades who tried to settle the dispute at a meeting called by Ciancabilla himself.

Malatesta on the Problem of Love

Clipping from unidentified periodical[169]
Translated from "Le problème de l'amour," *L'Unique*
(Orléans), no. 5 (November 1945)

Originally published as "Il problema dell'amore," *La Questione Sociale*
(Paterson, New Jersey) 6, new series, no. 18 (January 6, 1900)

---

168   The emphasis upon the word "judging" is probably meant to be a dig at the antiorganizationists, theoretically hostile to the right to judge. See "The Right to Judge," p. 251.

169   The clipping consulted is in Vernon Richards Papers, International Institute for Social History, Amsterdam. We have restored the paragraph division of Malatesta's original text and silently amended some mistranslations and omissions.

At first sight it may appear strange, but it is undoubtedly true that the question of love between the sexes, and all the subsidiary issues arising from it, occupies a great part of most people's thinking, even when problems, which if not more important, are certainly more urgent, seem to call for the undivided attention of those who seek to end social wrongs.

Every day we meet people crushed down by poverty and the fear of poverty; who, steeped in degradation by eternal want, have scarcely the right to love and parenthood, and yet these people would not listen to the means whereby we propose that they should be liberated from political and economic serfdom unless, at the same time, we explain how we should satisfy the need for love, and how we would organize the family. And, of course, this preoccupation grows bigger in those who have in their own cases solved the pressing problem of hunger, and blinds them to the existence of the other basic questions.

The importance of this fact is explained by the major rôle played by love in the material and moral life of mankind. It is in order to build an independent family around himself that man extends the greater and best portion of his life and energies.

Again, this fact is explained by that tendency towards the ideal which has illuminated the human spirit right from the time when man first owned the sway of conscience. When man suffers without measuring the wrongs he is undergoing, without looking for the remedy, without thought of revolt, he is living the life of an animal; but from the time he perceives that life's evils do not depend on incontrovertible decrees of fate, but on human causes removable by human means; from that time he is filled with a need for perfection, and desires (ideally, at least) to enjoy a society which would know nothing but harmony and from which all misery would be forever eradicated. This tendency is very useful when pressing forward to its ideal, but not so when it encourages lethargy, and approves the *status quo* because even in achievable progress faults and shortcomings might still persist.

Now, let us openly admit it; we have no nostrums for all those evils which can and do arise from the phenomenon of love, because they cannot be destroyed by social reform, nor by a change in customs. They derive from obscure psychological motives, and are immutable—or, if mutable at all, then only by a slow evolution the process and outcome of which we cannot foresee.

We stand for liberty. We hold that all men and women have the inalienable right to unite freely with each other for no other reason than that of mutual love, and without any physical, legal, or economic coercion. But while this is the only solution we are willing and able to offer, this freedom will not do away with one fundamental fact—that love must depend on two harmonizing free-wills. And, then as now, it may happen that they do not harmonize in anything. Consider also that the liberty to do as one pleases means nothing if one has no clear objectives.

It is all very well to say "When a man and a woman are in love let them 'marry' and when their love ceases, let them part." But for this principle to be a sure and certain source of satisfaction it is necessary that both should begin to love—and stop loving—at the same time! What if one should love, but not be loved in return? If the partner who does not love wishes to follow new affections? Or if someone should love several persons simultaneously, and if these do not know how to adapt themselves to such a position?

"I am ugly," one might say, "What shall I do if no woman is willing to love me?" A silly question perhaps—but not a whit less applicable to certain tragic situations.

Another one, concerned with the same problem, was heard to say, "Today, if I can find no love, I can economize on good—and buy it. What shall I do when there are no more women for sale?" The attitude is a deplorable one, but it shows what a vested interest there can be in poverty.

Some say the remedy lies in the complete extirpation of the family—the abolition of any regularized cohabitation; the reduction of "love" to a simple physical act, or at best its transformation (with the addition of sexual intercourse) into a sentiment scarcely distinguishable from the "friendship" which admits of a multiplicity, variety, and simultaneity of affections. And the children?—why, they would belong to everybody.

But is it possible to abolish the family? Is it desirable?

And above all, remember that, without forgetting the régime of lies and coercion now built into the structure of the family under present conditions, it will remain the potentially and actually greatest factor in the improvement of human character. It is the only sphere in which man normally sacrifices himself for others, does good for the sake of good without expecting any reward other than the affection of his partner and children.[170]

Certainly there are cases of noble self-sacrifice; of martyrdoms submitted to for the good of society as a whole, but these are always exceptional and cannot be compared to the constant sacrificing of a couple who devote themselves to the education and upbringing of their children.

But, it will be argued, questions of interest being removed, all men will become brothers and love one another.

---

170   On this note, compare "An Anarchist Programme," p. 43, where the seventh and final point in the program consists of the "reconstruction of the family" on fresh foundations.

Certainly they will stop hating each other. The feeling of solidarity and sympathy will be greatly increased. The idea of the general good will become a powerful influence on each individual. But that is not love.

Loving everybody is much the same as loving no one.

We will sometimes be able to alleviate distress, but we cannot mourn with everyone in trouble, else all our life would be spent in tears; and yet a tear of sympathy is a great consolation to a suffering heart.

Statistics of births and deaths provide valuable indices of social needs, but they can mean little to our feelings. We cannot regret every man that dies. We cannot celebrate the birth of every child.

And if we loved no one more intensely than all the others, there would be no one for whom we would be specially disposed to sacrifice ourselves. And would not life be less rich, less creative and less beautiful if we knew no love beyond a tedious, moderate, almost theoretical sentiment extended to all alike? Wouldn't the best of human instincts be perpetually hobbled? Wouldn't life be deprived of its best felt joys? Wouldn't we be unhappier?

Love, then, will remain love. When someone is very much in love, he feels the need of constant contact with and eventually exclusive possession of the beloved. Jealousy, in the better sense of the word, would seem to be necessarily co-existent with love. One can regret the fact, but the tendency cannot be modified.

In my opinion, then, love is a passion naturally productive of tragic situations, which, however, when a general freedom prevails, will not express themselves as to-day, in acts of violence or displays of brute force. And in a free society, public opinion will no longer exhibit its present misguided and sentimental sympathy for so-called "crimes of passion." These factors will assist the growth of harmony, but meanwhile, love's tragedies will be no less painful.

However, let us not make the seeming immutability of the difficulties arising from sexual relationships deter us from struggling against a form of society which aggravates them. To do so would be rather like going naked because we cannot dress in the finest furs.[171]

Remove the exploitation of man by man, destroy the brutal claims of the male to dominate over the female, oppose all prejudices, whether social, sexual or religious, and guarantee to all the right to live and enjoy life in freedom! Spread this teaching and we shall one day congratulate ourselves that the only problems on earth are those arising from the insoluble mystery of love!

---

171   This paragraph loosely summarizes two paragraphs of the original article.

And when all else fails, those whose sexual life cannot be made to function harmoniously can eventually find due compensation in other spheres—whereas to-day love, along with alcohol, is the sole consolation of the greater part of the human race.

[Untitled]

Translated from *La Questione Sociale*
(Paterson, New Jersey) 6, new series, no. 18 (January 6, 1900)

Il Proletario devotes an article to the four lectures that Malatesta delivered recently in New York.[172] And since it wanted to cover them, it should have honestly presented what Malatesta said and put forth its own objections, so that its readers might judge on a basis of knowledge.

But that is not the habit of *Il Proletario*. That would be too dangerous, for those who chase votes and nothing else!

Instead the author in *Il Proletario* produces a jumble of words, which simply reveal that he did not understand—or does not want to understand—anything of what Malatesta said in New York or of what he had said earlier in Barre. But he makes do with speaking of "science" and citing Marx, Spencer, and Saint-Simon (with whom we are beginning to think he is only vaguely familiar) to provide the illusion that people take him for a man of learning. Good for him!

Fixing the blunders that *Il Proletario* says, and makes Malatesta say, would require printing Malatesta's lectures just as he delivered them. But that is useless, since Malatesta writes in LA QUESTIONE SOCIALE, and everybody knows that anarchist lecturers are not in the habit of saying things different from what they write.

We would rather hear the opinion of the audience that attended the lectures on Rondani's habit of contradicting himself ten times in the same evening.

By and large, the audience did not seem to be very favorable for the democratic socialist champion.

Of Cianfarra we shall say nothing, because we received the impression that even his own friends pulled at his coat to silence him and not compromise their cause any more than it deserves.

---

172   "The Malatesta Lectures," p. 195.

[Untitled]

Translated from *La Questione Sociale*
(Paterson, New Jersey) 6, new series, no. 18 (January 6, 1900)

The peak… no, a perfectly normal thing for a socialist, who could even be the hilarious *Somebody* from *Il Proletario*.

To find something absurd because it comes from the mouth of Errico Malatesta, the very same thing he would have accepted as gospel, if he knew that it had already been said by Enrico Ferri at an anthropologists' congress.[173]

Personal Matter

Translated from "Questione personale," *La Questione Sociale*
(Paterson, New Jersey) 6, new series, no. 18 (January 6, 1900)

Pittsburgh, Pa. 28-12-99

In accordance with what I was told, Ciancabilla wants to know, from me especially, the reasons why I do not consider him a comrade.[174]

I have already provided him with my answer in advance.[175] Let him delve as deeply as he likes into the issue: I will help him insofar as I can to shine light on the truth as it is.

For me, his behavior towards *La Questione Sociale* and its typesetter, which I know for a fact to be dishonest, because it is in bad faith, means that the opinion I have reached regarding his moral character will be hard to change, even if this or that fact ascribed to him is incorrect.

Allow me to add that Ciancabilla shows that he intends to use a very convenient method for his defense. He has started an entire campaign of

---

173 In his "Sotto le force caudine" column, in *Il Proletario* of December 23, 1899, Somebody had written:

> The peak for an anarchist speaker who could even be Errico Malatesta:
> Confounding Lombroso's theory with figures from attorney Bartolo Longo!!!

Longo, a devout Catholic, was devoted to projects designed to rescue the children of prisoners, in defiance of biological theories of criminality. Even though he was a disciple of Lombroso, the socialist criminologist Enrico Ferri also emphasized the social factors of criminality.

174 See note 163.

175 See the untitled open letter of December 23, p. 192.

slander against comrade Esteve putting forward as his only evidence the word of an individual he fails to name, paying no heed to the statement from 40 or 50 honest workers, who have made and are making ongoing sacrifices for the cause, and he thinks he can get out of this awkward predicament by attacking them with harsh words! If he goes on to also treat comrades in Europe, who have things to say against him, as *witless, crooks, drunkards, and lunatics*, he will have quickly dealt with the matter, but by no means will he be cleansed... and he will have tarnished no one's reputation.

And let me finish with a wish: that *La Questione Sociale* pay no more attention, or as little attention as possible, to this personal controversy. Our newspaper is made for propaganda. Ciancabilla has tried to forcefully drag us into personal issues; but, having clearly stated our case, we must not follow his example and allow him to turn an anarchist organ into a rag for gossip. If he wants to do that with his *L'Aurora*, he is free to do so; but *La Questione Sociale* must remain the impersonal propaganda organ it has always been.

As for the personal matters, they will be dealt with, independently of the newspaper, by anyone who is involved and by all comrades who, knowing the men and the facts, or being able to gather information about the former and verify the latter, can come to their own informed opinions.

Errico MALATESTA.

Consequences of Commercialism

Translated from "Conseguenze del Commercialismo," *La Questione Sociale* (Paterson, New Jersey) 6, new series, no. 19 (January 13, 1900)

In the trial taking place in Pittsburgh against four Italians charged with having killed an American in a drunken brawl, Judge J. W. F. White had the chance to speak several times on the effect that American beer produces on the drinker. He advised those wishing to drink beer to buy imported beer. German beer, he said, is the only real thing: American beer does not just intoxicate, but makes brutes of men. Beer, he added, is the cause of more crimes than any other liquor: it would be better to drink whiskey. And then he added: "No good beer has ever been made in this country, and I believe it has gotten worse than ever since the breweries united in a consortium. This is the inescapable consequence of monopolies. The only remedy would be to drink no more beer."

—Bah!—one American beer drinker said—He must be a partner in a firm importing German beer, and is using his position as judge to advertise his product.

And yet that judge was probably absolutely honest and disinterested in his opinion.

However, this is one of the consequences, and not the least damaging, of the commercial system derived from private property. One cannot say something good about a product without being suspected of advertising for the manufacturer, nor can one say anything bad about it without being suspected of putting it down for reasons of commercial competition. And one cannot believe what he hears or reads without first checking that he is not falling victim to advertising.

And how can we be sure of that?

Advertising appears everywhere and makes any sincerity, any mutual trust in social interactions impossible.

Science itself, which should be the sanctuary of truth, is infested with it.

A hygienist recommends an item to you; a doctor recommends a medicine to you and advises you to buy it at a given pharmacy telling you that you will find the genuine product there. But how can you be sure that such advice, instead of science, is not inspired by dirty profit? How can you believe, when you see other hygienists and other doctors giving the opposite advice? How can you know if you are dealing with differences of opinion honestly held regarding scientific issues yet to be definitively determined, or with mere business matters?

Under the system of "everyone for themselves," and therefore of private property and competition in trade and in work, which are the results of the individualist principle, deceit and lies become ordinary and often necessary activities, not just to in order to prevail, but also to simply survive.

The industrialist, the merchant lie about the quality of their goods, unless they want to be crushed by the lies of their competitors. Before publishing a truth, the scientist must consider if it will bring him fortune or ruin him. The worker rather than worrying about the excellence of the product ponders how they can earn the greatest amount with the least effort, and does not care about the rest.

If someone is not able to do something, but his livelihood depends on doing it, he will claim to be very good at it; and if he works as a doctor he will kill the sick, if he is an architect he will crush people beneath collapsing houses, if he is a lawyer he will have his clients jailed or ruined, and if he plies any trade he will botch his work in a thousand ways.

In order to get work the builder lowers his prices, and then builds bridges and homes that fall down due to bad materials; the producer of food products poisons the public, the pharmacist gives medicine different from what the doctor prescribed (with regards to quinine sulfate alone, a few years ago fourteen counterfeit versions were found), the tailor passes cotton off as wool, and so it goes for all products.

A discovery, an invention which in itself would be a blessing upon humanity, boosting wealth produced and reducing human effort, turns out instead to harm the workers, who are left jobless, and the industrialists and merchants who see the value of their machinery and their merchandise reduced.

Often, no matter how beneficial something new might be, it is not adopted because too much capital is invested in the old system.

It is in the interest of the doctor and the pharmacist for there to be many sick people, and they are damaged by public health laws. At a gathering of Italian doctors in New York City there was protest voiced against the destruction of a particularly unhealthy block in Mulberry Street because, according to one of them, "those homes keep us alive."[176]

The innkeeper has an interest in there being lots of drunkards, and he serves up stimulating food that may ruin the stomach, but "makes people drink."

Police and judges have an interest in there being many criminals. The professional military, the arms manufacturers, the supply contractors desire war. And the priests promote the degradation of the masses, which is necessary for them to live.

Everywhere there is rivalry, hatred, deceit, and unrelenting battles to snatch the bread out of each other's mouths.

And this happens at a time when bread, which is to say all that man requires, could easily be produced in abundant quantities for all; this happens when, with just a little cooperation, life could be beautiful and happy for everyone!

This state of affairs, which tends to get worse as production develops and dealings between men increase, cannot change unless we change the foundations upon which human society is based. The system of "everyone for themselves" needs to be replaced by solidarity between people, through the abolition of private property, business, and competition, and their replacement with common ownership and free association between workers.

The 1900 Socialist Congresses in Paris

Translated from "I congressi socialisti del 1900 a Parigi," *La Questione Sociale* (Paterson, New Jersey) 6, new series, no. 19 (January 13, 1900)

---

176   Mulberry Street was the main street in Manhattan's "Little Italy."

This year, as is well-known, two international socialist congresses will be held in Paris: one of the democratic, legalitarian, parliamentary socialists, in short the ones who advocate "the proletariat's conquest of public power by means of parliamentary and legislative action;" and the other of the anti-parliamentary, revolutionary, and anarchist socialists.

Recent past international socialist congresses were the scene of a struggle between the anarchists and democrats, with the anarchists asserting their right to take part in a congress entitled socialist and pro-worker, and the democrats wishing to deny anarchists that right, and to drive them out. The last of the series, the 1896 congress in London, spent four of its six days over this struggle, to arrive at the fine result of expelling us as anarchists... but letting us in as representatives of workers' societies.[177]

Being in the majority, the democratic socialists tried to argue that the anarchists insisted on attending their congresses for the pleasure of hindering their work; but they should know that is not true. We wanted to take part in those congresses because they were announced and organized as *socialist and workers' congresses* without further restriction; and we could not allow the democratic socialists to appear to be the only representatives of socialism and the workers' movement. Being socialists—and much more than them—and workers ourselves, we have the right to be wherever socialists and workers gather.

In London, through Domela Nieuwenhuis, we told them: "Up until now we have come to your congresses because you claimed to be holding *workers' congresses*; and since we do not want you to look like the representatives of the revolutionary world, we come to your gatherings in order to assert that you are not the embodiments of the revolution. Just say that from now on you will only hold congresses that only admit democratic socialists, and you will see us no more."

They have followed this advice, and this year they convene the congress by clearly stating that the only people who will be admitted will be:

1. Representatives of groups seeking the replacement of capitalist ownership by socialist ownership and which consider legislative and parliamentary action as one of the necessary means of achieving that goal.
2. Pure labor organizations which, although they may not engage in militant politics, declare that they acknowledge the necessity of legislative and parliamentary action. *Consequently anarchists are excluded.*

This is therefore a politicians' congress, and surely no anarchist will want to attend.

---

177   On the London Congress, see note 27.

Instead, anarchists will take part in the anti-parliamentary revolutionary socialist congress, at which laws are neither made nor drafted, but where ideas will be discussed, and perhaps agreements will be proposed which, in accordance with libertarian principles, will be binding only to those who accept them, and only for as long as they accept them.

While we propose to later study the various issues placed on the agenda of the upcoming revolutionary socialist congress, we think it might be useful to publish in this and subsequent issues a study that Peter Kropotkin published in French about the London Congress of 1896.[178]

[There follows the first part of Kropotkin's article "The International Congresses and the 1896 London Congress."]

Concerning the "Problem of Love" (The Other Side) [by Beniamino Mazzotta]

Translated from "Intorno al 'problema dell'amore' (L'altra campana)," *La Questione Sociale* (Paterson, New Jersey) 6, new series, no. 19 (January 13, 1900)

[In the article, Mazzotta rejects the claim that the pains of love depend on man's deep-seated and almost physiological feelings. If that claim was true, he argues, "we should naturally have to have uniformity of customs," in contrast with the variety of sexual customs observed. Mazzotta stresses that the moral sphere is directly influenced by the economic sphere, asserts that the "family institution" should be fought against, because in favoring one's family "one acquires exclusiveness and selfishness," and instead he invokes "complete autonomy, which is achievable only without co-habitation." He identifies love with the sexual function: "love is nothing but the physical act." The highest degree of love is simply desire at its most intense, and is exhausted once the desire is appeased. Any other theory about the caducity of love, Mazzotta concludes, is a form of fatalism.]

The author of the article, which the above intends to contradict, has little to offer in terms of a reply. He professes a profound ignorance on the subject, which he thinks is shared by everyone, or nearly so. If Mazzotta is an exception, and is sure that he has found the cure for the

---

178   The International Revolutionary Workers' Congress in Paris, which should have taken place from September 19 to 22, 1900, was later prohibited by the Waldeck-Rousseau government under the 1894 "wicked laws."

pains of love by preaching that "love is nothing but the physical act" he must have his good reasons... which will possibly not survive the first experience of falling in love.

Just one observation on an issue that goes beyond the exclusive field of the problem of love.

Indeed the economic factor influences—to a degree—the moral factor; but influencing does not mean encompassing.

Be that as it may, admitting the influence, in whatever degree, of the economic factor upon moral sentiments, and even assuming, for the sake of argument, that *everything* hinges upon the economic factor, it clearly follows that, changing the economic position of men, their sentiments will change; but it does not follow that they will change in the way Mazzotta anticipates.

For example, with the release of man from misery and the fear of misery, and with the elimination of all the anxiety produced by the present struggle for existence, one could suppose that sentiments may become more developed, refined, and lofty, and love may become, even more than it is today, a much more complex feeling than mere copulation.

In the end, on this topic everyone passes judgment based on his own feelings and experience: the debate accomplishes little.

So let us leave it there.

To the Comrades

Translated from "Ai compagni," *La Questione Sociale*
(Paterson, New Jersey) 6, new series, no. 20 (January 20, 1900)

For some time we have been receiving persistent complaints regarding the irregularity with which the post office forwards our shipments of newspapers. Last week not a single copy of LA QUESTIONE SOCIALE was delivered in the entire state of Pennsylvania. Such a setback, of which we do not know the cause, leaves us greatly astonished, all the more so since we know for sure that shipments of bourgeois newspapers are forwarded regularly and arrive at their destinations on schedule.

Not that we are the only ones to lament this disruption. Some time ago "Freiheit" of New York, a German-language anarchist-socialist propaganda organ, run by comrade John Most, had the same complaints to advance regarding the irregularity of shipments made by the U.S. Post Office.

Given this state of affairs, which can only be explained by the assumption that "free America" seeks to ape the "beautiful kingdom of

Italy" in the most hateful and repulsive aspects of its Administration, we urge all comrades to complain vigorously to the post offices in the areas where they live and notify us at the same time, so we can resend whatever issues were not received.

We would like to believe that by doing this, those people with evil intentions will be convinced of the uselessness of their dark ploys to block the free circulation of our propaganda organ and will in the end abandon their dishonest plans.

May comrades therefore show their energy and write to us every time they do not receive the newspaper. For our part, we will make a firm complaint as well.

Federalism and Anarchy

Translated from "Federalismo e Anarchia," *La Questione Sociale*
(Paterson, New Jersey) 6, new series, no. 20 (January 20, 1900)

Years ago, in the times of the International, the word federalism was often used as a synonym for anarchy; and the anarchist fraction of that great Association (which its opponents—who, being infused with the authoritarian spirit, are in the habit of lowering broad questions of ideas to petty personal issues—called the *Bakuninist International*), was called indifferently by friends either the *Anarchist International* or the *Federalist International.*

Those were the days when "unity" was in fashion in Europe; and not just among the bourgeoisie.

The most listened-to representatives of the authoritarian socialist school preached centralization of everything, and they thundered against the federalist school, which they described as reactionary. And even within the International, the General Council, made up of Marx, Engels, and democratic socialist comrades, attempted to impose its authority over the workers of every country, centralizing in its hands complete control over the association's entire life, and insisted on reducing to obedience, or driving away, rebel Federations, which did not want to acknowledge any legislative attribution and proclaimed that the International had to be a confederation of autonomous individuals, groups, and federations, linked to each other through a pact of solidarity in the struggle against capitalism.

In those days therefore the word federalism, while not absolutely free from ambiguity, represented rather well—were it not for the meaning the opposition of the authoritarians gave it—the idea of free association between free individuals, which is the basis of the anarchist concept.

But now things have quite changed. The authoritarian socialists, formerly ferociously unitarian and centralist, pressed by anarchist criticism, gladly describe themselves as federalists, just as most republicans have begun calling themselves federalists. And it is therefore important to keep one's eyes open, and not be fooled by words.

Logically federalism, taken to its final consequences, applied not just to the various places where people live, but also to the various functions they perform in society, and extended to the commune, to the association for any purpose, and to the individual person, means the same thing as anarchy:—free and sovereign units that federate with each other for the common benefit.

But this is not how non-anarchists understand federalism.

We need not concern ourselves now with republicans proper, which is to say bourgeois republicans. Be they unitarian or federalist, they want to preserve private property and class division in society; and therefore, however their republic is organized, freedom and autonomy would still be a lie for the majority:—the poor is always dependent, slave to the rich. Bourgeois federalism would simply mean increased independence and increased liberty for the lords of the various regions, but no less force to oppress the workers, since federal troops would always be ready to restrain the people and defend the lords.

Let us talk about federalism as a political form regardless of the economic institutions.

For non-anarchists federalism boils down to some measure of regional and municipal administrative decentralization, always without prejudice to the supreme authority of the "Federation." Membership in the Federation is mandatory; and it is mandatory to obey federal laws, which should regulate the "shared" business of the various confederated bodies. The entity that determines which issues must be left to the autonomy of the various localities, and which ones are common to all and must be governed by federal laws, is again the Federation, which is to say it is the central government. A government that must limit its own authority!... obviously it will limit that authority as little as possible and will continually try to go beyond the limits it was initially forced—when it was weak—to impose upon itself.

Besides, this greater or lesser autonomy applies to the various municipal, regional, and central governments in their dealings with one another. The individual, the person, always remains governable and exploitable at discretion,—with the right to say who he would like to be governed by, but duty-bound to obey any parliament that may emerge from the electoral alembic.

In this sense, which is the sense in which it exists in some countries and is pursued by the most forward-looking republicans and democratic socialists, federalism is a government that, like every other government, is founded on the denial of individual freedom, and tends to become increasingly oppressive, with no boundary to its authoritarian demands other than resistance from the governed. Therefore we are opponents of federalism just as we are against any other form of government.

We will instead accept the name of federalists, when it is understood that every locality, every guild, every association, every individual is free to federate with whom they please or not federate at all, that everyone is free to leave any federation they have joined when they please, that a federation represents an association of forces for the greater benefit of its members and does not have, as a group, anything to impose upon the individual federated members, and that any group just like any individual must not accept any collective resolution unless it is worthwhile and agreeable to them. But in this sense federalism ceases to be a form of government: it is just another word for anarchy.

And this is true for federations in the future society, as it is for federations formed between anarchist comrades for the purposes of propaganda and struggle.

To Conclude

Translated from "Per finire," *La Questione Sociale*
(Paterson, New Jersey) 6, new series, no. 21 (January 27, 1900)

We receive and publish:

[*First published is a long undated letter from Pedro Esteve to* La Questione Sociale, *in which he defends himself, with a wealth of technical details, from the accusations leveled against him. Then the following letter from Malatesta is published.*]

SPRING VALLEY, ILL. JANUARY 21
I am looking over the *L'Aurora* from the 13th.[179]

---

179 Under the title "Questione personale" (Personal matter) *L'Aurora* gathered an article by Ciancabilla, in response to the article of the same name dated January 6, 1900 and published on p. 201, and various letters of support. In the meantime the controversy had continued without direct intervention by Malatesta: another article "Questione personale" had appeared in the January

Ciancabilla is greatly deceived if he believes I want to drop the matter; and he is even more deceived if he believes that by vomiting foolish insults and making ridiculous threats he will manage to dissuade me from proving what I have stated.

I wished, and still do, that LA QUESTIONE SOCIALE not dwell, or dwell as little as possible, upon this; but I added that personal issues would be settled between the persons concerned with the aid of comrades who are, or may become, capable of judging with knowledge of the matter. I said "let Ciancabilla delve as deeply as he likes into the issue," since he was shouting about wanting to *get to the bottom of it*, but I also said that I would help him bring the truth to light. Let him rest assured that he will be served.

It is simply a question of seeking the best way to verify the truth, without using up the space of propaganda newspapers and printing matters that might prove compromising.

And it seems to me indeed that the best way would be a JURY of comrades, although (I am not sure why) Ciancabilla, while also suggesting it, calls it "a bourgeois method." Instead it seems to me that the bourgeois method of settling personal conflicts is the court, just as the feudal method is the duel, and the savage method is the exchange of fists and stabs; whereas the jury of comrades is the best, most civilized, and most anarchist method available, when it comes to issues that cannot be brought before the public, or about which the public is not competent.

At any rate, since Ciancabilla is willing to accept the jury, and I am, too, let us settle on the jury.

If Ciancabilla wants this jury to be made up of comrades living in Europe, where the events to which I refer occurred and where the individuals who are familiar and involved with these events are found, let him say so and I am ready to appoint my representatives just as he will appoint his.

Or if he prefers the jury to be established in America, representatives from both parties will be chosen from comrades living in America. The location is wholly irrelevant to me.

Of course this jury should deal with the entire issue; meaning it should examine not only what I said against Ciancabilla, but also what Ciancabilla said against Esteve, against me, and against others during

---

6 issue of *L'Aurora*; *La Questione Sociale* of January 13 carried "Dichiarazioni" (Statements) from several Paterson anarchists called into question by Ciancabilla. Following the aforementioned article of January 13, to which Malatesta is replying here, *L'Aurora* of January 20 published several further statements, under the title "Speculazioni anarchiche" (Anarchist speculation). We were unable to consult the subsequent issues of *L'Aurora*, the first series of which continued until no. 23 of May 24, 1900.

this whole controversy. It will collect the facts and the evidence, and then will publish, together with the conclusions it will have reached, everything that can be published without anyone being compromised to the authorities.

And now let me re-establish the facts that Ciancabilla tries to complicate.

Ciancabilla is trying to make people believe that I am the one who attacked him as a way of waging war on *L'Aurora*.

To make such a claim he must rely heavily on people's bad memory! The truth is—and it is well known—that I never opposed *L'Aurora* other than purely in the field of ideas; that indeed I supported its emergence and, to avoid personal issues getting mixed up with issues of ideas and clouding the serenity of the discussion, I forced myself to keep cordial relations with Ciancabilla, even if the information received from my friends made me have a low opinion of him.

It was Ciancabilla who, abandoning the field of ideas, began slanderous attacks against comrade Esteve: slander, be it noted, which was brought forth by an anonymous person, and which Ciancabilla supports without any other evidence than his gratuitous claim, in contrast with the statements made by all those familiar with the facts, whom he himself dragged into the dispute.

This behavior provoked outrage among the Paterson comrades, who published their well-known statement against him.[180]

Ciancabilla then expressed the intention of asking, particularly of me (who was among the signatories of that statement) the reasons why I did not consider him a comrade. And I responded to him that for me the dishonest, slanderous attack brought against Esteve was confirmation that he, Ciancabilla, was morally capable of the dishonorable behavior earlier attributed to him by comrades, whom I regard as trustworthy and who are considered as such by all who know them.[181]

Consequently, Ciancabilla set aside the accusations he had made against Esteve—and demanded proof of what had been said against him.

If I just acted out of spite instead of seeking the truth, I could do what he did to Esteve and say: I do not want to name the accusers.

But Ciancabilla should not have this fear... or this hope.

I will provide the names and all evidence available to me; and I am convinced that Ciancabilla will have no reason to be happy. He will try to dig his way out, as he has believed he could do thus far, by showering insults upon all who will have anything to say against him; but this is a method of defense which is for comrades to judge.

And now I should deal with the insults that Ciancabilla directs at me,

---

180   "On a Personal Matter," p. 184.
181   Untitled open letter of December 23, p. 192.

since he realizes that I know him and am no longer willing to remain silent on his account.

But is it really worth the trouble?

He says that I make authoritarian, centralizing, 1848-style propaganda. My propaganda is what it is, and if I make it, this means that I believe it to be good and useful. Ciancabilla calls it authoritarian, etc. He might as well call it monarchist or clerical, since everyone knows, or can ascertain from reading and listening to me, what ideas I champion. Ciancabilla merely demonstrates, in a manner evident to everyone, his bad faith and the dubious interest he has in sowing confusion among anarchists by attributing to me—and thus to the comrades at LA QUESTIONE SOCIALE with whom I agree—ideas which are the opposites of those we actually have and propagate.

Only one thing I would like to point out.

Recalling the principle that a trouble shared is a trouble halved, Ciancabilla says that "more than one person who has known Malatesta for a long time" has assured him that it has always been his tactic to personally attack "those who made the mistake of thinking differently from him." If it is true that someone said this, they have done him a disservice. Since the fact remains—and this is easily proved—that I have NEVER had any personal issue over matters of ideas, and that indeed I count among my dearest friends many whose ideas oppose my own in various ways.

Until this current case, the ONLY times I have directed personal accusations publicly against someone was when it concerned spies. Then too I was regarded as a pope, excommunicator, inquisitor, authoritarian, etc., and then too I received all sorts of threats and insults; but then the spies returned to the police to report their defeat, and I continued to give to the anarchist cause the modest contribution of my work. But do not misunderstand me: I sincerely hope that Ciancabilla does not wish to fraternize with the likes of Azzati-Terzaghi, Castagneto-Prete, and a few other spies with double or triple names, whom I have had the luck to help uncover and drive out of our ranks.[182]

Thus I await Ciancabilla's further decisions regarding the jury.

Comrades must forgive me if things can not progress as fast as would be desired: the persons concerned are scattered across several countries in Europe and I myself, still busy with my propaganda tour, can only

---

182   For Carlo Castagneto's denunciation see Malatesta's correspondence of October 18–19, 1884 in *Il Comune* (Ravenna), in Volume I of these *Complete Works*. Because of that denunciation, Malatesta was sentenced in absentia for defamation by the Ravenna court in June 1885. On the denunciation of Carlo Terzaghi, who introduced himself under the false name Azzati, see "Azzati-Terzaghi. A Spy Unmasked," in Volume II of these *Complete Works*.

complete the necessary procedures when the relevant communications reach me. Let them rest assured however that, sooner or later, the whole truth will come out.

Errico MALATESTA.

[*A note from the editors follows stating that, from then on, the columns of the newspaper will be closed to any personal controversies; moreover clarification concerning Giuseppe Granotti, mentioned in Esteve's letter, is provided.*]

SECTION V
Cuba and Farewell

[Untitled]

Translated from *La Questione Sociale*
(Paterson, New Jersey) 6, new series, no. 24 (February 17, 1900)

Errico Malatesta reports to us from Tampa, Fla., that he has written friends asking them to represent him in the dispute with Ciancabilla. As soon as he receives a positive response, he will make their names known.[183]

[Untitled]

Translated from *La Questione Sociale*
(Paterson, New Jersey) 6, new series, no. 25 (February 24, 1900)

Comrade Errico Malatesta writes us from Tampa, Fla., that he has chosen comrades B. Sanguinetti and F. Widmar as his representatives, and they have accepted the task of representing him in the dispute with Ciancabilla.

For his part, Ciancabilla having appointed comrades N. Quintavalle and G. Della Barile as his representatives, they will reach an agreement amongst themselves to set the date and location for the thus established jury to meet.

---

183 Malatesta's trip to Tampa, Florida is part of the "Spanish" portion of his American stay. Already on October 20, 1899 *El Despertar* had reported on a lecture given by Malatesta at the Circulo de Trabajadores in Brooklyn. On January 30, 1900 the same paper announced that Malatesta had been commissioned by the Sociedad de Torcedores de Tabaco de New York (New York Cigar Makers' Association) to promote the idea of a federation for all cigar workers in the United States, and to that end he would shortly be visiting Tampa, where the tobacco industry was booming. According to what was announced by *La Federación* (Ibor City, Tampa) of February 16, Malatesta gave a lecture in Italian in Tampa on February 18 on the topic "Italy's future"; the next day he held a meeting proposing a cigar workers' federation; and on February 20 he gave a lecture in Spanish on anarchy and its development. In order to resolve lingering divisions between the workers, Malatesta agreed to extend his stay in Tampa by three days (See "Por la posta," *El Despertar,* May 20, 1900). Then, after a stay in Key West (Cayo Hueso, in Spanish) he set sail for Cuba. For a short account of Malatesta's stay in Tampa, see "At the Workers' Circle. A Lecture by Malatesta," p. 253.

Anarchist Propaganda

Translated from "Propaganda anarquista," *La Discusión*
(Havana), March 1, 1900

ENRICO MALATESTA IN HAVANA.—INTERVIEW WITH A REPORTER.
—IMPORTANT STATEMENTS.

The noted anarchist agitator Enrico Malatesta arrived in this capital yesterday on board the steamship *Mascotte*.[184]

Yesterday evening we reached the Centro Obrero at Monte, 56[185] and shortly thereafter we were introduced to the Italian propagandist.

A 47-year-old native of Naples, he has thick, black beard and he is a very pleasant conversationalist. He speaks flawless Spanish.

He was a medical student at the time of the Benevento uprising, of which Malatesta himself was an instigator; he was sought by the police together with those who had taken part in the insurrection, but managed to escape to London.[186]

He later returned to Italy where he published a newspaper championing his ideals and this triggered an active crusade by the authorities.[187]

Despite the intense investigation made to find him and prevent the publication of his newspaper, which continued to circulate, Malatesta could not be found. Eventually, after being reported to the police, he was arrested and banished to *domicilio coatto*, but after a short while he escaped from confinement with the help of a fisherman, who provided him with the means to escape.

He went to London, then moved on to New York. He has visited several American localities, including Tampa and Key West, where he recently delivered some lectures.

Enrico Malatesta's articles are known throughout the world. Like Kropotkin's, they have always found readers even among those who do not share their ideas, because, regardless of their beliefs, they are educated men and profound thinkers.

---

184   Adrián Del Valle, editor of the Cuban anarchist newspaper *El Nuevo Ideal*, whom Malatesta had met in 1891, thus explained the reasons behind the latter's trip to Cuba in a commemorative article (Palmiro de Lidia [pseud.], "Malatesta's Visit to Havana in 1900," *La Revista Blanca*, December 1, 1932): "At the request of the group that published the libertarian weekly *El Nuevo Ideal*, Malatesta stated his readiness to visit Havana to give some lectures there. We believed that it was a suitable time, since Cuba had been liberated from Spanish rule—although at the time it was still momentarily under the control of the United States—and the political ideal of independence no longer preoccupied the Cuban proletariat, therefore the times might prove better suited to the propaganda of the libertarian socialist ideal."

185   The full name of the street is "Calzada del Monte."

186   Malatesta was actually arrested, tried, and acquitted in the wake of the Benevento incidents in 1877. His first period in exile in London dated back to 1881.

187   The reference is to 1897 and the publication of *L'Agitazione*.

*
**

Mr. Malatesta greets us politely.

We express to him our intention to talk with him so we can offer the readers of LA DISCUSIÓN the impressions we get from the encounter.

— Do you believe that your propaganda will be warmly received by Havana's *socialists*?

— I am not a *socialist;* I am an anarchist. With respect to the local workers, I cannot make a judgment about what they think, yet, as I arrived a few hours ago. Apart from this, I believe that the worker in Cuba is completely absorbed by the political question, since they are a diverse people, and it is only natural that everyone should be concerned with securing first what they have suffered for.[188]

— In Cuba—we tell him—the word "anarchist" frightens. Could you explain us what this word means on the whole?

— Tomorrow evening I will be giving a lecture that will explain it; if anything remains unclear after my explanation, feel free to let me know. I also welcome a debate, should anyone want to discuss my ideas.

— Otherwise, the Anarchist Party is like every other party. Its enemies oppose it. It fights back, in turn; a struggle arises and everything else springs from that. Yourself, the Cubans, have demanded freedom; it was not granted to you, and so you fought with every means at your disposal, you burnt, you killed; because that is what happens in war. We anarchists do not want any government because in our opinion they are all the same.

— Do you think that the Cuban government elected through popular suffrage is the same as all the rest? ·

— Yes, it is the same. We all know that elections are a fraud; the only difference is that some people say so openly, while others keep it to themselves. People do everything they can to gain power and, once they get it, they rule as despotically as the people allows. Believe me. Do you know why there is a difference in daily wages between workers in Italy, in Cuba and elsewhere? Well, quite simply because when an Italian was offered ten cents for his day's work, he accepted it, perhaps reluctantly, but in the end he accepted it. Offer a Cuban that wage and he will refuse to work.

At this point our interview was interrupted by a group of workers who had gathered around us and our job was over.

Mr. Malatesta believes that the Cuban war broke out because the people were oppressed; the people had its agitators who capitalized upon the opportunity with which they were presented.

---

188   The original Spanish sentence, rather muddled, is as follows: "Pero á pesar de eso, creo que el obrero en Cuba, está distraido completamente con la cuestión politica y como existe un pueblo heterogeneo, se empeñan todos y es natural en llegar primero á lo que por tanto han sufrido."

He says that the Cubans who have accepted appointments from the Americans should be considered traitors, because they are helping the government that today is their oppressor; if, instead of cooperating with the invaders, they had created the vacuum around them, the military occupation would leave, because there is no nation, however powerful, that could stand against the passive resistance of the million and a half people that Cuba can count on.

He acknowledges that there are traitors everywhere, just as the Cuban autonomists who sided with the Spanish during the war were traitors.

He believes the Americans will not leave Cuba.

To a worker who asked why he believed this, he replied: "Oh! By the time we are able to prove it, they will already be standing on top of our heads. It's like a thief who enters your house; I spot him and warn you, and then you ask me what proof I have that the fellow is there to steal; the proof is that they entered your home against your will! But you certainly won't thank me if I wait until after the robbery has taken place before I warn you."

He says that in the United States he has witnessed the sad spectacle of a people applauding and looking up to Dewey just because he sank three or four wooden vessels from the Spanish navy—the very same Dewey who is trying to force onto the Filipinos the protection of his neo-colonialist nation.[189]

He also states that should the English beat the Boers, they will never succeed in staying there, precisely because the people do not want them...

Mr. Enrico Malatesta is to spend a week in Havana before moving on to England.

The anarchist leader will give a talk at 7:30 this evening at the Centro Obrero, Monte 56.

Malatesta Lectures

Translated from "Conferencias Malatesta," *Nuevo Ideal* (Havana) 2, no. 56 (March 9, 1900)

With his talks, comrade Enrico Malatesta has succeeded in arousing widespread interest, of both his sympathizers and his opponents, in the ideals of anarchist socialism, which are much feared by some and little understood by many.

Workers came in considerable numbers to listen to his eloquent speeches and cheered them with enthusiasm; all the press has dealt with our comrade and his ideas, some papers reporting impartially, while others such as *El Cubano, Diario de la Marina* and *El Comercio* have reported with notable hostility, the

---

189   George Dewey commanded the US fleet in the victorious Battle of Manila Bay, during the Spanish-American War of 1898. A triumphal arch was erected in New York to welcome him back in September 1899.

sort of hostility typical of a dog who—as a token of gratitude to his master for tossing him a bone—snarls to defend his master's property; and the authorities, as always creatures of the bourgeois class, did all they could to prevent Malatesta from freely expressing his thoughts, forbidding him from speaking about *anarchy* on the grounds of a Spanish law that is no longer enforced in Spain itself, to the shame and disgrace of the revolution that freed Cuba from the Spanish yoke.

It is impossible to listen to Malatesta and not identify with what he says. His simple and energetic words, despite the difficulty of fully mastering our language; the solid arguments, the accurate reasoning, and the rigorously precise inferences; the abundance of facts he cites in support of his arguments: all of this allows one to listen for hours pleasurably and effortlessly. Even his opponents are won over by his irrefutable logic.

Below we publish an account of his

FIRST LECTURE[190]

The Cuban people are among the most prepared to carry on and accomplish the pursuit of freedom.

The Cuban people's economic situation is the same as that of any other people. The social problem is the same everywhere.

The first notable characteristic of modern society is poverty, which is not general, because, while some have nothing, others possess everything.

Nowhere is life secure for workers. In Italy, the peasant works for ten cents a day and a loaf of bread costs him eight cents. In Russia, the workers are literally starving to death, something that also happens in the most developed countries.

The mortality statistics for Brussels, the capital of Belgium, one of the most liberal countries, show that in wealthier neighborhoods the mortality rate is ten per one thousand, while in the poorer neighborhoods the figure is ninety-two per one thousand. It thus turns out that eighty-two out of a thousand die on account of their miserable conditions. And this is a widespread fact in both Europe and America.

In the Italian neighborhoods of New York, the death rate is horrific, due to the complete absence of sanitation. It was proposed to demolish the area, but

---

190   The lecture was given on March 1. As Adrian Del Valle recalled: "Just moments before the lecture was to start the police sent a suspension order issued by the civil governor, which was greeted with resounding demonstrations of disapproval. A committee from the Circle immediately went to the governor, succeeding in making him rescind the order and thereby allowing Malatesta to speak, on condition that he not touch upon the topic of anarchism, 'banned by the current legislation' (dating back to colonial times)." A rather detailed account of the lecture can also be found in the March 2 issue of *El Diario de la Marina* (Havana), evening edition. However, it adds no new details to the report in *El Nuevo Ideal*.

there were doctors who opposed the proposal, due to the fact that they benefit from the spread of diseases.[191]

Ignorance is one consequence of poverty; the bourgeois and the rulers have a vested interest in the poor's remaining brutes so that they can be exploited and dominated more easily.

Prostitution, crime, vice in all its forms, and race hatred, these are all the fruits of poverty.

If poverty was an unavoidable fact of nature, like lightning bolts, we would have no choice but to accept it and we could only study how to limit its consequences, just as we have sought to limit the consequences of lightning by using lightning rods; but poverty is not a fact of nature and there are ways to prevent it.

If the stronger crew members of a ship set adrift, rudderless and lost in the middle of the ocean with limited supplies, were to kill the weaker ones in order to take all the rations instead of sharing them equally with all, we would say that they are wicked, but their actions, the product of their instinct to survive, might be understandable.

But if we were to read that the crew and passengers of a great ocean liner—like the ones that make the crossing from continent to continent in eight days and carry enough provisions to last a hundred—in the absence of danger, stabbed each other to get their hands on the food, we would certainly say that they had gone mad.

These facts reflect exactly what happens in present society.

If nature did not produce enough and human labor did not suffice to meet everyone's needs, then it would be understandable for people to fight over products, although it would be fair to share them equally, or at least to leave their enjoyment to whoever produced them; but if it can be shown that the world produces enough to amply satisfy everybody's needs and still we stab each other, then we must agree that this is a society of lunatics.

The statistics released by the United States Board of Trade show that in that country they produce enough to sustain sixty million people more than its current population, but that does not prevent thousands of people from starving to death every year.

In Italy, many peasants live on corn flour, when they get to eat anything; and this is not caused by lack of land, given that there are thousands of uncultivated acres and enough manpower to farm them.

Nevertheless, whenever the hungry ask for bread, the Italian government sends soldiers to give them lead. In Milan, five hundred workers were killed in a riot driven by hunger. And even as that was happening, trains in the stations and ships in the docks were loaded with grain that could not be unloaded because of the increased custom tariffs imposed by the government.

The result is that the land lies fallow, the import of wheat is restricted, and meanwhile the people perish of hunger. Is that not madness?

---

191   On this example, see also "Consequences of Commercialism," p. 202.

Año II. Número 56. | **HABANA, 9 MARZO DE 1900** | **Precio: 5 Centavos**

CONFERENCIAS MALATESTA

El compañero Enrique Malatesta ha logrado con sus conferencias despertar el interés general, tanto de simpatizadores como de adversarios, por los ideales del socialismo anarquista, tan temidos por algunos y poco comprendidos por muchos.

Los trabajadores han acudido en número considerable á oir sus elocuentes peroraciones, que han aplaudido con entusiasmo; la prensa toda se ha ocupado de nuestro compañero y de las ideas que sustenta, algunos periódicos con imparcialidad, otros, como *El Cubano*, *El Diario de la Marina* y *El Comercio*, con marcada animosidad, propia de todo perro que, en agradecimiento al hueso que le tira el amo, defiende, á ladridos, los intereses de éste; y las autoridades, hechura, como todas, del elemento burgués, han hecho cuanto han podido para impedir á Malatesta la libre emisión del pensamiento, prohibiéndole que hablara de *anarquía*, amparándose en una ley española—que en la misma España ya no se aplica—para vergüenza y escarnio de la revolución que libertó á Cuba del yugo español.

Imposible es oir hablar á Malatesta sin identificarse con lo que él dice. Su palabra fácil y enérgica, aun con la dificultad de no dominar por completo nuestro idioma; su argumentación sólida, su certero raciocinio y sus deducciones rigurosamente exactas; la abundancia de hechos que expone en apoyo de sus afirmaciones, todo contribuye á que se le oiga horas enteras con agrado y sin cansancio, venciendo á los mismos adversarios por su lógica incontravertible.

A continuación publicamos una reseña de su

PRIMERA CONFERENCIA

El pueblo de Cuba es uno de los más preparados para proseguir y concluir la obra de libertad.

La situación económica en que se encuentra el pueblo cubano, es idéntica á la que se observa en todos los pueblos. El problema social es igual en todas partes.

El primer fenómeno que en la sociedad se apercibe, es la miseria, que no es general, pues mientras unos de todo carecen, otros todo lo poseen.

El trabajador no tiene seguridad de vida en parte alguna. En Italia, el campesino trabaja por 20 centavos al día y una libra de pan le cuesta 8 centavos. En Rusia, los obreros mueren materialmente de hambre, lo que también sucede en los mejores países.

La estadística de la mortalidad en Bruselas, capital de Bélgica, uno de los países más liberales, muestra que se hace morir sicos muertos 10 por mil, en tanto que en los barrios pobres la relación es de 93 por mil, resultando que 83 por cada millar mueren á causa de su condición miserable. Y este es un hecho general, lo mismo en Europa que en América.

En el barrio italiano de Nueva York, la mortalidad es horrorosa, debido á la completa ausencia de condiciones higiénicas. Se pensó en destruir dicho barrio, y no faltó con médico que á ello se opusieran, debido á que, en la actualidad, encuentran su beneficio en la propagación de las enfermedades.

La ignorancia es una consecuencia de la miseria; los burgueses y los gobernantes están interesados en que el pueblo siga siendo bruto, porque así se deja explotar y dominar con más facilidad.

La prostitución, el crimen, el vicio en todas sus formas y el odio de raza, obra son de la miseria.

Si la miseria fuera un fenómeno fatal, como el rayo, no habría más remedio que aceptarla, quedándonos sólo el recurso de estudiar el modo de disminuir sus efectos, como se ha buscado, con el pararayos, la manera de disminuir los efectos del rayo; pero la miseria no es un fenómeno fatal, puesto que existen los medios de evitarla.

Si en un buque, desmantelado, sin timón y perdido en medio del océano, debido á la escasez de provisiones, los tripulantes más fuertes acuchillan á los más débiles para apoderarse de los alimentos, en vez de repartirlos equitativamente, diremos que son unos malvados; pero comprenderemos su acción, impulsada por el instinto de propia conservación.

Mas si leemos que un gran trasatlántico, de estos que hacen la travesía de continente á continente en 8 días, llevando provisiones para 100, hallándose el buque sin peligro, los tripulantes y viajeros se han acuchillado para apoderarse de los alimentos, indudablemente diremos que se habían vuelto locos.

Estos hechos guardan relación exacta con lo que sucede en la actual sociedad.

Si la naturaleza no produjera lo suficiente ni bastara el trabajo humano para satisfacer las necesidades de todos, se explicaria que los hombres se disputaran los productos, aunque lo justo seria que los repartieran equitativamente ó cuando menos, que disfrutara de ellos el que los elaborara; pero si está demostrado que en el mundo se produce lo bastante para satisfacer con creces las necesidades de todos, ¿a sin embargo nos acuchillamos unos á otros, hay que convenir que esa es una sociedad de locos.

Las estadísticas publicadas por el *Board of Trade* de los Estados Unidos, demuestran que en aquel país se produce lo suficiente para alimentar á 60 millones más de su actual población, lo cual no impide que todos los años mueran allí de hambre millares de seres humanos.

En Italia muchos campesinos se alimentan de harina de maiz, cuando pueden comer, y no es por falta de tierras, puesto que hay miles de hectáreas sin cultivar y brazos de sobras para hacer el cultivo.

Sin embargo, cuando los hambrientos piden pan, el gobierno italiano manda á los soldados que les den plomo. En Milán, 500 obreros fueron muertos en un motin motivado por el hambre. Y mientras esto sucedía, los ferrocarriles en las estaciones y los buques en los puertos, estaban cargados de granos, que no podian descargar por los crecidos derechos de entrada impuestos por el gobierno.

Resultado: la tierra está sin cultivar, se impide la entrada del trigo y el pueblo en tanto muere de hambre. ¿No es esto propio de locos?

Pero aún hay más. El trigo venía de Rusia, lo que hace suponer que allí al menos los campesinos comían, cuando en realidad estaban mucho peor que los de Italia, pues ni siquiera tenian pan; comer la harina de maiz.

En Londres pasan de 50,000 las personas que no tienen albergue, sin contar el número inmenso de los que viven en habitaciones insuficientes y malsanas; y no es esto por cierto debido á que haya escasez de albañiles ó falten los terrenos y materiales de construcción. Hay mucha gente que anda descalza ó con los zapatos rotos, porque no pueden comprar de nuevos, mientras que el zapatero permanece cruzado de brazos por falta de trabajo. Y así podrían aumentarse los ejemplos.

La miseria es una consecuencia de la abundancia y no de la escasez. Cuando hay abundancia de productos sobreviene la paralización, esto es, la crisis por sobra de producción.

Al obrero le quitan por la fuerza el fruto de su trabajo, resultando de ello que produce exclusivamente para el provecho personal de los amos.

La situación del obrero es comparable á la del burro de carga.

Un jardinero compra un burro para llevar las verduras al mercado, haciendo el cálculo que lo que gasta en la compra y manutención del animal, viene recompensado con creces por el beneficio que le proporciona. Con el mismo fin se establece un tranvía eléctrico que le permite transportar sus verduras por 5 centavos, y como ya entonces el burro es para él una carga, lo vende ó lo manda al matadero.

El burgués hace con el obrero lo que el jardinero con el burro; lo toma á su servicio cuando puede sacar beneficio de su trabajo, y cuando no, lo despide. Pero hay la diferencia del obrero al burro, que éste cuesta dinero y su muerte é inutilidad es para su dueño una pérdida sensible, en tanto que aquel no cuesta nada y el muere ó extrepamiento en nada perjudica al amo; y como consecuencia de esto el burro es mejor tratado que el obrero.

Cuando en los desastres mineros, debido á las malas condiciones en que se efectúa el trabajo, mueren centenares de obreros, los accionistas y directores no se preocupan de ello, atribuyendo la desgracia á imprudencia de los muertos y seguros de encontrar inmediatamente gente de sobras que los reemplace. En cambio mueren, si mueren mulos, toman inmediatamente sus medidas, porque éstos les cuestan dinero, y hacen responsables del desastre á los capataces ó ingenieros.

Si el obrero americano gana peso y medio, el siciliano dos pesetas y el egipcio 4 centavos, no es porque los burgueses en una parte sean mejores que en otra; la razón de esto debe buscarse en la mayor ó menor resistencia de los obreros á las exigencias del capital. El sólo límite á la explotación es la resistencia.

Los gobiernos tienen siempre tendencias á extremar la opresión, que igualmente sólo puede contrarrestarse con la resistencia. En Londres se trató de dar cierta vez un mitin en favor de Irlanda, mitin que contaba con ninguna ó muy poca simpatía entre la masa. Las autoridades trataron de impedirlo, y viendo el pueblo en ello una violación de sus derechos de libre reunión, invadió el parque, rompiendo sus puertas, arrolló á la policía y celebró el mitin. Al día siguiente el jefe de policia, ante la actitud resuelta del pueblo, trató de escusarse diciendo que no ordenes habian sido mal interpretadas por sus subordinados.

Cada día se desarrollan más los medios de producción y aumenta el número de los obreros. Cuando los productos se acumulan en los almacenes y no encuentran salida, se paraliza el trabajo.

La conquista de las Filipinas significa para los capitalistas americanos la adquisición de un nuevo mercado, por una parte, y por otra, la probabilidad de importar filipinos á América para que trabajen á menos precio que el obrero americano, ó bien llevar sus capitales allá para conseguir el mismo fin.

La lucha para mejorar el jornal encierra dificultades en la misma competencia que se hacen los trabajadores; pero, de todos modos, donde éstos luchan, su situación es mejor.

Pero si es aún inútil luchar para mejorar y hacerse respetar, no se resuelve con ello la cuestión. Para destruir la miseria, es necesario cambiar las instituciones sociales.

Supongamos por un momento, que por el sólo esfuerzo de la naturaleza y sin necesidad del trabajo humano, se produjera el trigo, se elaborara el pan, se edificaran las casas, etc. A realizarse tal milagro, podría creerse que los hombres habían llegado á la suprema felicidad de vivir sin trabajar; sin embargo, nada más ilusorio, pues siendo los productos propiedad de los que acaparan la tierra y toda la riqueza, é incapacitados los desheredados de ofrecer su trabajo para vivir, veríanse expuestos á morirse de hambre en medio de la general abundancia.

Pero si los trabajadores comprendieran que los productos de la naturaleza y la riqueza social era propiedad común y en su consecuencia tomasen posesión de ella, sería un hecho la abundancia para todos.

Y si el suelo, las minas, los instrumentos de trabajo y trasporte fueran propiedad común y todos vinieran obligados á producir para vivir, no veríamos el absurdo de que murieran de hambre millares de seres humanos en tanto los almacenes están repletos de alimentos y la tierra puede producir más que lo suficiente para todos.

En un libro publicado por el Dr. Witts, demuestra éste que el suelo de Francia puede producir para alimentar con abundancia á 60 millones de habitantes, trabajando tan sólo 56 días al año, con una jornada de 6 horas. Y Francia cuenta solamente en la actualidad 40 millones de habitantes, muchos de los cuales mueren materialmente de hambre ó lentamente por alimentación insuficiente y malsana.

Si la riqueza social fuera propiedad común, con poco trabajo podríanse satisfacer ámpliamente las necesidades de todos; y como lógica consecuencia, no existiría el vicio, el crimen y el odio, reinando la paz y el bienestar para todos.

But there is more: the grain was coming from Russia, suggesting that over there at least the peasants had enough to eat; when, in actual fact, they were much worse off than those in Italy, given that they did not even have the corn flour to eat.

In London, there are more than fifty thousand homeless people, not counting the vast number of people living in inadequate and unhealthy dwellings; and this is certainly not caused by any lack of bricklayers or shortage of land and building materials. There are many who go barefoot or wear broken shoes because they cannot afford new ones, while the shoemakers sit around with folded arms because of a lack of work. And we could continue giving examples.

Poverty is a consequence of abundance rather than of scarcity. When there is abundance of products, paralysis, which is to say a crisis of over-production, sets in.

The worker is stripped by force of the fruits of his labor, with the result that he produces exclusively for the personal benefit of the masters.

The worker's situation is comparable to that of the donkey.

A peasant buys a donkey to carry his vegetables to the marketplace, after having calculated that what it costs to buy and maintain the animal will be fully repaid by the income it will bring him. Eventually, a streetcar is built, allowing him to carry his produce to market for five cents; now that the donkey is a needless burden he either sells it on or sends it to the slaughterhouse.

The bourgeois treats the workers the same way the peasant treats the donkey; when he can profit from his labor, he hires him and when he cannot, he fires him. But there is a difference between the worker and the donkey: the donkey costs money and its death or uselessness is a significant loss to its master, while the worker costs nothing and his death or injury do not harm the master at all; the donkey is therefore treated better than the worker.

When, in a mining disaster, hundreds of workers die because of the dreadful conditions in which they are forced to work, the shareholders and directors do not worry at all and simply blame the catastrophe on the carelessness of those killed, confident that they can immediately find people to take their places. However, if the donkeys die, the owners immediately react, because donkeys cost money, and they blame the disaster on the site foreman or engineers.

If the American worker earns one and a half pesos, the Sicilian two pesetas and the Egyptian four cents, this is not because the bourgeois in one place are kinder than the bourgeois in another; the cause must be found in the greater or lesser resistance of the workers to the demands of capital. The only curb on exploitation is resistance.

Governments always tend to push oppression to extremes and this too can only be counteracted by resistance. In London, it was once attempted to hold a rally in favor of Ireland, a rally that attracted little or no support from the masses. The authorities sought to ban it, but the people, who saw this as an infringement of its rights to freely assemble, flooded the park after breaking down the gates, overwhelmed the police, and held the rally. In the face of such a determined attitude from the people, the following day the chief of police tried to make excuses by claiming that his subordinates had misunderstood his orders.

Every day the means of production are expanded and the number of unemployed grows. The basis of the current capitalist system consists of giving the worker as little as possible of the value of whatever he produces. When products are stockpiled in the warehouses and cannot find a market, work grinds to a halt.

For American capitalists, the conquest of the Philippines constitutes, on the one hand, the capture of a new market, and, on the other, the chance to import Filipinos into America to work for lower pay than American workers, or even to take their capital to the Philippines in order to achieve the same goal.

The fight for better pay is hampered by the competition between the workers themselves; however, be that as it may, wherever they fight, their situation is better.

But while it is useful to fight to improve conditions and command respect, this does not solve the question. To do away with poverty, it is required to change the social institutions.

Imagine for a moment that grain could be grown, bread made, houses built, etc. on the back of the forces of nature alone and without any need of human work. Were that miracle to take place, it might be believed that men have reached the ultimate happiness of being able to live without working; yet this would be the greatest illusion, because the products would belong to those who monopolize the land and all wealth, while the disinherited, unable to sell their labor for a living, would find themselves doomed to starve to death surrounded by general abundance.

But if the workers were to realize that the products of nature and the social wealth are the common property of all and were to take possession of them, abundance for all would become a reality.

And if the soil, the mines, the instruments of labor and the means of transport were common property and everybody was required to produce to live, we would no longer see the absurdity of thousands of human beings starving to death while the warehouses are filled with food and the land can produce more than enough for all.

A book published by Dr. Witts shows that the soil of France can produce enough to abundantly feed sixty million people, working just fifty-six days a year, at six hours a day. And France currently has only forty million inhabitants, many of whom are literally dying of hunger or slowly perishing from insufficient or inadequate nutrition.

If social wealth were common property, the needs of all could easily be met with little toil; and as a logical result, there would be no vice, crime, or hatred and there would be peace and well-being for all.

If someone, by means of some special invention, managed to bottle air and tried to sell it at five cents a bottle, we would not hesitate to oppose him, because air is an essential element of life. Nevertheless, we have allowed a minority to monopolize the land, which is as essential for life as air.

One example of the unfair expropriation of the land can be found in the Spanish occupation of Cuba, against the will of its original inhabitants; and the method we should use to seize the land from the hands of those who now control it are the same as those that were used to end Spanish rule over Cuba.

Despite this, the Cubans have managed to reap very little from the expulsion of the Spanish government, because the Spanish capitalists who exploit them remain here; and even if they managed to throw them out, too, the Cuban people will have achieved nothing so long as they remain subject to other capitalists— Cubans, Americans or of any other nationality.

Evidence of how little has really been achieved thus far can be seen with the Cuban soldiers, who shed their blood to set this land free and now, after so much struggle, find themselves obliged to sweep the streets in order not to starve.

The fact is that Cuba, no matter how free she claims to be, belongs not to the Cubans but to the privileged people who possess all her wealth.

There is something, though, that the Cubans have achieved, and that is the awareness that, having managed to drive Spanish rule out of Cuba by force, they will obtain by force whatever they aim for.

Political and economic oppression must be equally destroyed, and that requires determination and unity among the workers. It is understandable that there should be division and struggle between the oppressors and the oppressed, but not within the latter's ranks. Unfortunately, often the oppressed fight each other, misled by the oppressors who ignite feelings of division and enmity within their hearts, based on differences in nationality, race, and even profession.

The people have always been deceived by its tendency to install leaders. Such behavior needs to be abandoned. Let us get used to professing and championing ideas because of their intrinsic value rather than the value of the men who propagate them and can betray and sell them out.[192]

He concluded by inviting anyone who disagreed with the ideas set out to argue against them, a challenge no one accepted.

The large audience, which completely filled the spacious rooms of the *Centro General de Obreros*, applauded the speaker's arguments enthusiastically.

As to our notes, we have tried to produce as faithful as possible a record of the things said by comrade Malatesta, although, because of space, we have in many instances confined ourselves to summarizing his thinking.

In the next issue, we shall look at his second lecture.

---

192   According to the testimony of Adrián Del Valle, "at the end, turning his gaze to the government's delegate [Malatesta] said with subtle irony: 'The gentlemen will be delighted to see that I have respected the law—given I had no other alternative—and I spoke about everything except Anarchy.'"

Malatesta's Second Lecture: Civilization and Freedom

Translated from "Segunda conferencia Malatesta: Civilización y libertad," parts 1 and 2, *Nuevo Ideal* (Havana) 2, nos. 58 and 59 (March 29 and April 6, 1900)

In human societies, civilization and progress are characterized by the growth of freedom.

The word civilization is used today by many people as an excuse for attempts to legitimize fraud, theft, and oppression.

The Catholic priest preaching his absurd doctrine claims to be an agent of civilization and the same claim is made by the capitalist who exploits the invention of a machine in order to produce more at less cost; in civilization's name, the Italian government has tried to steal the land of the Abyssinians, the English seeks to grab the Transvaal and the Americans the Philippines; using the pretext of civilization, white people go to Africa to enslave and prey upon poor black people; and it is, for sure, always in the name of civilization that one Havana newspaper dares invoke the necessity of war on account of over-population, which is like seeking to abolish poverty by killing workers.

No, civilization does not equal the enslavement of people, and it is not so much based on mere industrial progress as on the intellectual and material development of everyone.

Civilization has known its ups and downs, stunning progress, abrupt halts and set-backs; however, its overall tendency has always been toward the good and no doubt its promoting factors will bring the people to the realization of the ideal of peace and love.

The isolated man is the weakest animal in the universe; the vast strength he possesses is entirely derived from association and cooperation, to which he owes the development of his intelligence, as is apparent from the fact that intelligence can only manifest itself through language, which is a consequence of association.

There are two kinds of association: the authoritarian and the free; the former implies the domination of one over others; the latter is founded upon mutual cooperation.

In general, when association is founded upon authoritarianism, men have made their best efforts either trying to dominate or trying to rebel, without understanding that it would be better and more convenient for everyone to cooperate voluntarily on the goals of life.

Basing association upon domination has been a consistent source of suffering, the origins of it dating back to the primitive tribes that used to fight and enslave each other in their struggle for survival. And despite the gradual development of society, the same causes of struggle remain, except that we have moved on from the crude weapons of the wild to the Mauser and the machine-gun, and from the simple forms of primitive slavery we have evolved to the most complex forms of trade and industry, so complex that the worker often does not know by whom he is being exploited.[193]

(Our comrade sets out many wonderful examples in support of his claims, which we refrain from rehearsing so as not to render this report too long).

Civilization and progress arise wherever authority is countered by rebellion, while the people among whom this does not happen remain stalled in their development.

Hence, authority causes stagnation and revolution causes progress.

Religious controversies were nothing more than battles for freedom of thought, oppressed by dogma. Protestantism was a terrific blow to Catholicism, an authoritarian religion at its heart.

For fourteen centuries science was stalled, governed by principles laid down by Aristotle, whose authority was considered incontrovertible; only when sufficiently intelligent and vigorous men countered Aristotle's obsolete principles with new principles, did science emerge from its stagnation and rapidly advance.

Every day, attempts are made to halt progress in the name of established principles and vested interests, and if they fail to achieve their purpose, this is due entirely to the innovative, critical, and revolutionary mind that seeks its own expansion outside the narrow limits of established legality.

All progress is the child of the spirit of freedom and every regression or stagnation that of authority. Every new progress is therefore a violation of the law, which is to say, of the boundary imposed by authority.

We have an example of this in Cuba, which, in order to shake off the ancient domination, had to violate Spanish law and rebel against the authority forced on it. Martí and Maceo, today rightly venerated by the Cuban people, were criminals and traitors in the eyes of Spanish law.[194]

The French Revolution was likewise a break from feudal law and a manifestation of the spirit of freedom. And it is worth noting that while that spirit manifested itself spontaneously, without the hindrance of new laws or authority, the people won respect; but as soon as a new government was established, new laws were created to dominate the people again, to such an outrageous extent that the first law passed by the republican Convention imposed the death penalty on any worker entering into a work-related association. Thus, freedom died the very same day that the government could impose itself, free of fear of the people's protests.[195]

There is a false idea shared by many, according to which revolutions are made by governments, when in actual fact these are established once the revolution

---

193   Mauser was the name of a German arms factory, famous for its rifles and semi-automatic pistols.

194   José Martí (1853–1895), poet and writer, created the Cuban Revolutionary Party in 1892; Antonio Maceo (1845–1896) was one of the leaders of the revolutionary army. They both died in the field fighting against the Spanish army.

195   The first part of the article ends here.

has run its course and they seek to limit its work, as we have seen in the French Revolution.

Probably this will be repeated in Cuba and the people who today make up the government under the protection of American intervention may well say to-morrow, if Cuba manages to achieve its independence, that it has done so thanks to them; when, in reality, it will be the result of the stance the people adopt in response to the demands of the interventionist authorities.

The people must not choose members of parliament to create laws, which result in restrictive and oppressive measures and, when they claim benefits to the workers, prove sterile and often counter-productive. Furthermore, the men whom the people, presuming their good intentions, raise into power, would quickly suc-cumb to the influence of their surroundings and end up either ruined or feeling powerless and unable to help.

Such laws in favor of workers are completely useless. Sometimes, when a law is passed that prescribes something beneficial, the workers have already secured, by their strength, what the law dictates; vice versa, when the law establishes measures that the workers have not been able to win through their efforts, it goes unheeded.

In Colorado, in the United States, the workers have fought hard for the eight-hour work day. Then the State intervened, passing a law that prescribed what the workers had already won without its help or intervention.[196]

In Pennsylvania the miners mutinied, refusing to purchase things, as they were forced to do, from the company store, where they were wickedly exploited; with their firm attitude, they managed to get the stores shut down. The pater-nalistic law-makers then passed a law banning the stores, but it oddly happened that the companies soon reopened them. The workers, relying on the law and not on their own strength, appointed lawyers to defend them and enforce the law; the result is that they wasted money and time, the stores remain open, and the miners are forced to submit to their exploitation, under the threat of losing their jobs otherwise.[197]

A few years ago the London dockers, who number many thousands, declared a strike demanding better pay and a reduction in working hours, determined not to go back to work until they had won. But they did not stop there: they declared that they did not intend to let themselves starve to death and would resort to any methods. Faced with this threat, which they appeared determined to carry through, the bourgeois and the aristocrats were overcome by fear and hastened to take out subscriptions to help them and to make pressure in favor of their demands. Thanks to their attitude those workers always had food to eat and won their strike.[198]

---

196   See "Eight Hours of Work," p. 66.
197   *La Questione Sociale* had reported on this matter in its "Fatti e opinioni" (Facts and opinions) column on January 20, 1900.
198   The great London dockers' strike took place between August and September 1889; see "About a Strike" in Volume II of these *Complete Works*.

ENRICO MALATESTA,
CÉLEBRE AGITADOR ANARQUISTA.

"Enrico Malatesta, famous anarchist agitator."
Source: *Nuevo Mundo* (Madrid), September 11, 1901

Later, those same dockers demanded the eight-hour day; but since they did not do so with the same earlier energy, they did not get what they wanted, being deceived by ambitious people who detained them by recommending to nominate members of parliament to obtain legislation in support of the eight-hour day.

Law is not just useless but even harmful, because it exerts an enervating influence. Placing their hopes in it, the workers neglect the direct and vigorous defense of their interests. In fact, the law, a truly authoritarian weapon, is made to prevent or halt rebellion, being contrary in every respect to the spirit of freedom.

Progress can only occur by constantly combating the principle of authority.

Our ideal will take root when the people have sufficient consciousness to realize it; therefore it is a foremost task to prepare and shape that consciousness.

Whatever a people hope for, it can only be achieved through struggle.

Here in Cuba there will be no shortage of people who will seek to climb to power while claiming that they seek it to work for independence and the good of the people. Such men will deceive the people, because they will only achieve what the people can bring about by themselves; not to mention that their real motive for aspiring to power is primarily their personal interests.

The work of civilization and freedom is not the work of governments but the work of the peoples, driven by conscious minorities.

Governments, champions of the interests of the privileged classes, are instead the main obstacles that systematically oppose the development of civilization and freedom.[199]

---

199   Adrián Del Valle recalled the three days after the March 3 lecture as follows:

The following day, Sunday the 4th, a lunch was held at the *La Madama* restaurant

To the Cuban People

Translated from "Al pueblo cubano," *La Discusión* (Havana), March 10, 1900[200]

As I prepare to leave this country, to which I was drawn by a powerful feeling of sympathy, permit me to send a greeting to the brave Cuban workers, white and black, born here or elsewhere, who have offered me such a warm welcome.

I have long admired the selflessness and heroism with which they fought for their country's freedom; now I have learned to appreciate them for their bright intelligence, their progressive spirit, and their truly exceptional culture for a people oppressed for so long. And I depart with the firm belief that they will soon take their place among the most

---

with Malatesta and a good number of comrades in attendance. That night he held a lecture in the nearby municipality of Regla, before an extraordinary number of people.

The third lecture in Havana, which dealt with the theme "Crime: original causes and consequences," scheduled for Monday the 5th, was suspended by the government with the excuse of "failure to respect the provisions of the law."

The workers' interest and enthusiasm to hear the persuasive words of the libertarian propagandist had worried and alarmed the authorities and the politicians, who therefore aimed to prevent him from speaking by any means, no matter whether legal or arbitrary.

Despite this, Malatesta returned to speak in public, brilliantly circumventing the government's provisions.

On Tuesday the 6th a doctor of some note, Dr. Delfín, gave a lecture on hygiene at the Circulo de Trabajadores. There was a very large turnout, not so much because of the speaker's merits as because it was known that Malatesta would be attending in the audience. When Dr. Delfín finished speaking, Malatesta asked to speak in order to refute some arguments. Needless to say Malatesta took advantage of the occasion to deliver another brilliant lecture, a possibility that the authorities had not considered.

The necessary requests were made to grant Malatesta permission to deliver the already advertised lecture, but without a positive result.

As to the March 4 lecture in Regla, correspondence carried in *El Nuevo Ideal* of March 22 reported that Malatesta "spoke for almost two hours in front of a large audience consisting of all social classes," after which, as usual, he invited the pubic to challenge him. "There were lawyers and doctors who said, 'the arguments he set out are so logical that it is better not to touch them.' But since a Don Quixote is never lacking, one gentleman did rise to his feet ... and said that he could not live without government, after which Malatesta showed him that he and everyone else would be living better."

As to the improvised talk on March 6, the March 8 evening edition of *Diario de la Marina* reports that it was interrupted by a police raid.

200   We have consulted the article's reprint included in Adrián Del Valle's retrospective article (see note 184), along with its Italian translation in *Studi Sociali* (Montevideo) of November 1, 1933.

advanced elements that fight in every country of the world for the full emancipation of humanity.

I came to Cuba to expound to the workers the ideas of a party persecuted by every Government, insulted and slandered by all who would climb onto the people's shoulders. And I knew that Cubans, themselves victims of oppression and slander, could not help but listen with sympathy to an exposition of the ideas for which countless martyrs have suffered and died; ideas for which famous scholars and artists of genius fight alongside the worthiest workers; ideas which all tyrants fight against with prisons, torture, and the guillotine; that all mercenary writers adulterate and misrepresent, but none dare confronting on the civilized terrain of debate. In any case, they would have judged these ideas for what they are worth, since they are certainly smart enough and educated enough to do so.

But the **masters** of Cuba wanted none of that.

The mercenary Press, while arguing that anarchist ideas are absurd and will never make headway with the Cubans, have twisted what little I managed to say and openly did dirty police work by demanding that I be prevented from speaking, thus confessing to the fear of truth felt by those politickers who, with the name of the homeland on their lips, strive for nothing else than their personal gain.[201]

And the present rulers, as if they wanted to prove that the anarchists are right when they say that all Governments are liberticidal by nature, and forgetting that they are in Power as a result of a successful revolution against Spanish rule, banned me from speaking by invoking a law created by the same Spanish government that, from Cuba to the Philippines, from Barcelona to Xeres, earned an infamous reputation for tyranny.[202]

This may be for the better. This way the government has made better propaganda than I could have done myself with my meager capabilities. Today, every Cuban worker who does not like being treated like a child or a slave, will feel the need to find out what this anarchy is, which strikes such fear into every kind of oppressors. And that is all I desire, because I

---

201   Some newspapers, including *El Cubano* and *The Havana Herald,* went as far as to ask that Malatesta be expelled. A correspondence from Cuba carried in *La Questione Sociale* of March 17, 1900 (see the excerpt p. 260) reads: "We know from private sources that in the upper echelons there was a great desire to arrest Malatesta, but the American authorities wanted the responsibility to be assumed by the Cuban authorities, and the Cubans did not dare do so out of fear of public opinion."

202   Regarding Barcelona see note 96; in Xeres (or Jerez) in Andalusia, a peasant revolt on January 8, 1892 was followed by indiscriminate repression, after which four anarchists were sentenced to death. Malatesta, who was in Spain at the time, was suspected of having played a role in the revolt.

am sure that, once the truth is known, all men with hearts, all who truly want justice and freedom for all, will rally under the redemptive flag of anarchy.

I just recommend workers to search for what the anarchists think in the writings of the anarchists themselves; and not in the enemy Press that, sometimes out of ignorance, sometimes with blatant bad faith, disfigures everything we say.

I myself shall, in another place, set out succinctly what I came here to tell the workers of Cuba.[203] Here I shall limit myself to express my comrades' thoughts on the issue of independence, which is being used today as an excuse to silence our propaganda.

It has been said that the anarchists are the enemies of Cuban independence; it has even been said that my presence in Cuba hurts the cause.

The truth is that anarchists, being the enemies of all Governments and claiming the right to live and grow in total freedom for all ethnic and social groups, as well as for every individual, must necessarily oppose any actual Government and side with any people that fights for their freedom. If there was any self-styled anarchist who served the Spanish Government, he was simply a traitor; and it would be just as stupid or malicious to conclude that the anarchists support the Spanish tyranny as it would be to claim that the Cubans are the enemies of Cuba's freedom just because some Cuban sold out to Spain.

The fact is that the anarchists, fighting against the existing government, do not do so to put another in its place; and it should be easy to see that if such spirit of hostility and resistance against all Governments, personified by the anarchists, had prevailed in the war of independence, today it would not be possible to impose upon the Cuban people those same Spanish laws that Martí, Maceo, Creci, and thousands of Cubans died to abolish.[204]

As for the American intervention, it is almost certain that those who use independence as an excuse to keep the workers docile and submissive and do not care about their rights, are the same people with a personal interest in the intervention continuing in order to keep foreign troops as protection against the demands of the Cuban proletariat; just as it is certain that the Americans would leave if the Cuban people were to demonstrate a firm determination to drive them out, but they would never do so at the request of the capitalists who seek their protection or of the politicians who ask them for appointments.

---

203   See "To the Cuban Workers," next article.

204   On Martí and Maceo, see note 194. Enrique Creci, one of the leading figures of Cuban anarchism, also died fighting against the Spanish army. A little over three months before Malatesta's trip to Cuba, the procession transferring his remains to Havana had triggered clashes with the police.

We anarchists want Cuba's freedom, just as we want that of all peoples: we want true freedom, though. And for this we have fought and will continue to fight.

The Cubans can count on us.

ERRICO MALATESTA.

To the Cuban Workers

Translated from "A los trabajadores cubanos," *Nuevo Ideal*
(Havana) 2, no. 57 (March 22, 1900)

Dear comrades at NUEVO IDEAL.

To you, who valiantly fight for ideals that we share; to you, who have been by my comrades in struggle for many years, I ask for hospitality to tell the Cuban workers, in few but explicit words, what the governmental arrogance has prevented me from saying and discussing in public meetings. And I am all the more happy to do so, because it gives me the opportunity to publicly express my solidarity with you, who are today the target of an unfair war waged by many of the very people for whose redemption you fight.[205]

The Cuban workers have struggled heroically for their country's independence; for it they have sacrificed their children's bread; for it they have shed rivers of blood.

It would be sad, very sad, if so much heroism and sacrifice only resulted in a change of masters, as has happened in other countries, including Italy, where the people, having shed its blood for national independence and momentarily enjoyed the thrill of victory, soon realized that domestic tyrants were as wicked as foreign ones. And this is precisely the danger that threatens Cuba, if the Cuban worker does not hasten to stop it.

The Spanish ruler has been beaten, definitively beaten; and those who try to raise the spectre of "reconquest" are simply waving an imaginary danger in front of the people in order to distract them from the real danger that threatens them.

Still, there remains the American ruler; there remain the Cuban aspiring rulers, who rely today on the occupier to keep the people down, and tomorrow will oppress them by means of their own children, as is the case in all "independent" countries of the world; and, above all, there remain the owners of the land and all Cuba's wealth, whose defense from the dispossessed workers is the fundamental task of every government.

---

205   The reference is to anti-Spanish prejudice that also divided the Cuban labor movement.

Can the Cuban people call themselves free just because the police and soldiers who will trample over their freedom and jail and shoot them when they rebel against tyranny will do so not by order and in the name of the king of Spain, but by order and in the name of the president of the United States or the president of the Cuban Republic? Is it not ironic to claim that "Cuba belongs to the Cubans," when in fact Cuba belongs to the landowners, whether they were born here or elsewhere, and the Cuban peasant will fertilize the soil so that the idle and arrogant bourgeois may enjoy and thrive?

Cuba is not an exception in the history of the world. Everywhere, as in Cuba, the government, be it native-born or coming from abroad, has been and will always be a means of seizing the product of other people's labor and of defending the thieves; everywhere, as in Cuba, private ownership of the land and of the instruments of production is and has always been the cause of the economic misery, the political subjection and the moral deterioration of the workers.

To be truly free, it is necessary to abolish not only this or that government but the very institution of government, which gives some the right and means to force their will on others; and if freedom is not to be an empty word, it is necessary to abolish the right to appropriate the work of others, and ensure that the land and all the instruments of production be freely available to all, so that everyone is guaranteed the means to live and out of the free association of equals a society organized for everyone's well-being can arise.

Everywhere the people, rebelling against the yoke and failing to understand the true cause of their suffering, have troubled to change masters, and they have always found out that the change was useless, unless, waking up to their own strength, they were able to impose respect and fear upon the new masters; it should not be forgotten, though, that the improvement is not due to the kindness of the new masters, but to the strength of popular resistance, and that such improvements only last as long as that resistance stays alive and active.

Cubans today aspire to free themselves of the intervention of the American government—which, wearing the false disguise of liberator, arrived to play the master and tyrant as if over a conquered country— and their aspiration is just and holy; to realize it, though, they must count neither on the wealthy class, which needs American protection to safely exploit the strong Cuban worker who already knows how to fight oppressors, nor on the merchants of patriotism who beg the occupier for their share of the plunder.

The Civil Governor of Havana, to justify the violence he used to prevent me from expressing my thoughts, confessed to me that it was the American sword to rule here; and he, a Cuban patriot, to maintain his position is not ashamed of turning into a tool of the foreign soldier's arrogance... unless he invokes or makes it up to cover up his own arrogance.[206]

The American occupier will leave only when the Cuban workers force it out with their moral or material resistance, which would be a great achievement for them; but let the workers not imagine that, once the Americans have been expelled, they will be free and emancipated if some new government is installed and tyrannizes in Cuba and if the proletarians continue to work for the masters' benefit, whenever it is good for the masters to make them work. The struggle will have only just begun and it will be necessary to continue it, unrelenting and without mercy, against every government and every exploiter.

Meanwhile, let the workers organize: in the economic sphere to resist the capitalists, and in the political sphere, not to send their own representatives into the government but to resist its arrogance, hamper it, create the vacuum around it, and prevent it from hiding its true nature as the enemy of the people.

As long as there are governments and owners, this is the best way of ensuring that they do as little harm as possible; and it is also the way to prepare minds and marshal strength for the revolution, which, through the expropriation of the propertied class, the socialization of wealth, and the libertarian organization of the people, without any authoritarian imposition, will give rise to a society founded upon solidarity and love.

And Cuban workers must take care not to fall into the traps laid for them by those who try to fan national and racial hatred, especially between Cubans and Spaniards.

The Spanish worker, forced by poverty or persecution into leaving his homeland, has as much reason to hate the Spanish government as the most persecuted Cubans; and has as much interest today in stopping bourgeois exploitation as any native-born Cuban worker.

Those with an interest in preserving the division between workers are the bourgeois, that is, now as ever, those who provoke hatred between Cubans and Spaniards, between whites and blacks, because they know

---

206   Concerning Malatesta's meeting with the civil governor, Adrián Del Valle reports: "At Malatesta's own request, he and I went to visit the civil governor, General Emilio Núñez, in order to get a permission. Although he received us amiably he refused to grant that permission, arguing that there was a law, dating back to Spanish times, prohibiting anarchist propaganda; so Malatesta, very subtly, pointed out to General Núñez that when he was fighting the Government of Spain he must not have found it too unpleasant to disobey the Spanish laws that now he was trying so hard to enforce." On this encounter see also "At the Workers' Circle. A Lecture by Malatesta," p. 253.

that when the workers fight against each other, they do not think about fighting the master and do not have the strength to do so.

For the worker conscious of his own interests and aspiring to something more than living in this society of wolves that survives to everyone's detriment, every other worker is a brother, while the enemy, the foreigner, is the master, the oppressor, regardless of their place of birth.

These, my friends at Nuevo Ideal, are the ideas I intended to present to my brothers, the Cuban workers, and they are the very same ideas that you have been championing, against the wind and the tide.

Carry on. These people may be deceived for a short time by those who seek to exploit them for personal purposes; but they are too clever for that deception to last indefinitely. Judging by my short experience, these are some of the people best equipped to understand our ideals and best prepared to fight for their success.

Carry on. You are planting seeds in fertile ground.

Your comrade.

Enrico MALATESTA.[207]

To the Comrades

Translated from "Ai compagni," *La Questione Sociale*
(Paterson, New Jersey) 6, new series, no. 28 (March 17, 1900)

The growing deficit that burdens our administration forces us to reduce spending.

For this reason, starting with the next issue the paper will be interlined and we will mostly stop using the *brevier*, that is, the small type in which the *Social Movement* column is now printed.

This will save us 5 dollars in composition expenses; which means that, while improving the paper's economic conditions, this measure is far from ensuring normal life.

We think there is no need to stress the severity of the situation.

We know that now our newspapers published in Italy absorb part of what the comrades can give to propaganda; and we are greatly delighted that Italian anarchists abroad have not forgotten the most important part of our work which is propaganda in Italy.

---

207   Adrián Del Valle says this of his farewell with Malatesta:

Saturday March 10 Malatesta set sail for New York. When we said our farewells on the pier, he said to me with a smile:
First Barcelona, then London, now Havana. Where will we meet next time?
I don't know—I replied—but I hope we will meet again somewhere.

But if one believes that an anarchist newspaper is useful over here—and to us this seems obvious—then we must provide it with the means to survive.

Let the comrades think this over and make an effort.

The Paris Commune

Translated from "Il Comune di Parigi," parts 1 and 2, *La Questione Sociale* (Paterson, New Jersey) 6, new series, nos. 28 and 29 (March 17 and 24, 1900)[208]

March 18, 1871

A celebrated historian, Lecky,[209] said that legend is often more truthful than history; and in so saying expresses, in a somewhat paradoxical form, a true and profound insight.

Legend is truer and more interesting than history; since, while history tries laboriously to establish hard facts about circumstances, events, and individuals, and only with difficulty manages to ascertain the truth, amid the complexity of always inadequate elements and contradictory witnesses; legend instead, being formed unconsciously and expressing, not the fact, but how people saw the fact, reveals the state of mind of a people, the innermost meaning of a historical moment.

This was the case for the revolutionary movement known as the Paris Commune, which erupted on March 18, 1871, and was suffocated in blood the following May. Even before there was a single positive fact established about it, every person interpreted it according to his own desires; and the legend that circulated throughout Europe and the world had a much greater influence than the precise knowledge of the facts could have had. The result is this: that the Paris Commune is claimed by all socialists of the world, while in reality it was not a socialist movement; that it is claimed by all anarchists, while it was not an anarchist movement.

In 1871 the minds were perfectly prepared to give the Parisian movement the significance it has been given; and most likely, if the repression

---

208   This article was the subject of a curious misunderstanding when reprinted in *Il Pensiero* of Rome on March 16, 1907. A note from the editors stated: "This study of the Paris Commune was published in 1900 in an English-language American magazine. On the occasion of the forthcoming 36th anniversary of the important event, a friend has done a translation, which we are publishing ... " The publication was in fact a faithful reprint of the original article reproduced here.

209   The main work of Irish historian William Edward Hartpole Lecky (1838–1903) was *A History of England in the Eighteenth Century*, the twelfth and final volume of which appeared in 1890.

had failed to snuff it out at birth, it really would have become what it was believed to be from the very beginning.

The reactionary force born out of the defeat of the 1848 European revolution was exhausted, and everybody sensed that the time was ripe for a new revolution.

The impotence of "liberal" principles left as a legacy to the posterity of the French Revolution at the end of the last century, had become clear; and new currents of ideas, new aspirations were exciting the masses. The "social question" had become the big question. The birth and rapid ascendancy of the International, a consequence that became a cause in turn of this situation, had given birth to hopes in some and fears in others of upcoming political and economic radical changes.

At this juncture, the Franco-Prussian war breaks out. Everything hangs in the balance; everyone anxiously watches the battlefield and makes predictions about what will happen after the war: the suspense merely increases the tension in people's minds.

As the French army is defeated and the Emperor taken prisoner, conservative and reactionary elements accept the republic as the only feasible solution for the moment, but with the firm intention either to re-establish the monarchy as soon as possible, or ensure that the republic does not really differ from the monarchy. The people, stunned by the thunder of war and discouraged by the defeats and betrayals, which continue with the republic just as with the empire, looks on wavering between hope, fear, and suspicion.

The people of Paris want to fight the besieging enemy, but are tricked, betrayed, and vanquished in partial sorties that seem, or are, organized deliberately to fail; they are subjected to a shameful surrender.

Provincial voters appoint an assembly made up of all the most reactionary elements that feudal and militaristic France contains; and this assembly, stigmatized with the name *rural*, hurries to accept all the conditions of peace imposed by Bismarck, and prepares to subject France to the rule of the saber and the aspersorium.

Enough is enough.

Revolutionary elements begin to come together; the workers of Paris, Lyon, Marseilles, are champing at the bit, due partly to profound economic uneasiness, partly to patriotic feeling offended by the treachery and incompetence of the military and civilian leadership, and partly to hatred of the monarchy whose restoration is a threat.

The government understands that to protect its reactionary work Paris needs to be disarmed. On the night of March 17–18, secretly, it sent troops to seize the cannons that the national guard has held since the days of the siege; but the attempt is discovered, the alarm is sounded; the soldiers of the national guard, startled awake, rush to defend their cannons; the women accompanying them fling themselves into the midst of the troops, beg them, insult them, embrace them; the troops turn their rifles upside down and fraternize with the people. Two generals, Thomas and Lecomte, renowned butchers, are shot, as if in a pact of blood between the rebel troops and the insurgent people.

The next morning, March 18, all of Paris is shaken by the news; the authorities flee... the insurrection is triumphant.

As news of the Paris events scatters through Europe, instinctively all revolutionaries, socialists, anarchists, and republicans who looked upon the republic as a radical transformation of the social order, all friends of progress whose generous instincts were not paralyzed by belief in religious and political dogma, all, from Bakunin, to Marx, to Garibaldi, from the methodical German workers to the enthusiastic Italian revolutionary youth, were on the side of the Parisians, on the side of the Commune. And all reactionaries, all rulers, butchers, and people's tormentors were on the side of the government that, having escaped from Paris and selected the city of Versailles as its headquarters, was called the Versailles government. It was painful to find among the latter Giuseppe Mazzini, whose hieratic instinct clouded his intellect and his heart.

Revolutionaries and reactionaries believed it was a certain thing that the social revolution had broken out in Paris, and with this persuasion they judged the movement according to their tendencies.

The legend was created in one fell swoop, and this was a fortunate circumstance, as it had an immense effect on propaganda. In every country the socialist movement (socialist in the broad sense of the term) benefited from it, and in some countries, such as Italy, it almost gave birth to the movement. So big and beneficial was that influence that the legend persisted and persists to this day, alongside the now familiar history.

But while it is good to profit from the legend, which essentially means profiting from popular tendencies that materialize by idealizing an historical reality, it is also necessary to know the actual facts as they occurred, in order to benefit from the lessons of experience.

More of that in our next issue.

March 18–May 28, 1871
Even the simplest historical facts, always being the result of a thousand different factors, variously modified by a thousand circumstances, never exactly correspond to the ideal of one party or school of thought, and cannot fit into any ideological classification. This is especially true when it involves those great social events that all needs, all interests, all feelings, all ideas existing among the people of a country, consciously or unconsciously, contribute to determine—such events are not planned and prepared by a party nor provoked by their initiative, but are spontaneously born by

circumstances and thrust themselves upon parties and men of ideas, who must then accept them as they present themselves!

The March 18 insurrection and the resulting "Commune" was one of these events.

On the eve of March 18 all advanced men and the general population of the great cities felt the need for a revolution and intensely desired one.

But what sort of revolution was this? What aims were pursued?

In the latter years of the Empire the social question was widely debated in France and there was a spreading awareness of the need for a transformation that went beyond the political constitution. All socialistic ideas and systems that had excited minds during the decade prior to 1848 and which had been snuffed out by the reaction, had been brought back into discussion. The International proclaimed the principle that the emancipation of the workers had to be the workers' own doing, and it was organizing the laboring masses outside of and in opposition to all bourgeois parties.

But the war had brought an end to that entire movement. The International in France did indeed protest the war and affirmed the solidarity between French workers and German workers, just as the German Internationalists did in turn; but patriotic prejudice prevailed, and they were not able to stop the war. The defeats of the French army, the surrender at Sedan, due to Napoleon's incompetence and cowardice, the surrender at Metz due to Bazaine's treason,[210] the surrender at Paris where treason was again suspected, the shameful peace after arrogant boasting, increasingly offended and irritated nationalist sentiment. The intentions to restore the monarchy, clearly demonstrated by the government and the assembly, ensured that nearly every revolutionary element believed that the one and only big issue of the moment was to save the republic from the danger of restoration.

Among the people of Paris the prevalent desire was to establish a truly republican government... and to redo the war on Germany to take their revenge. When suddenly, unexpectedly, following the government's flight after the failed attempt to seize the cannons that the national guard had successfully rescued from the Prussians, Paris found herself master of herself and with the need to see to her own destiny, and defend herself against the attempts at repression that the government hidden in Versailles was about to make.

The situation was faced as the circumstances allowed; but there was no understanding of the need to revolutionize society and spread the revolution beyond Paris, among the peasants, if only as the sole means of being able to win the material struggle.

---

210   François Achille Bazaine, who commanded the only organized army remaining in France, surrendered to the Prussian army.

There were certainly some who intended to develop the movement into social revolution, and the people, as in every insurrectionary movement, were animated by a more or less vague aspiration for justice and well-being. But the prevailing idea was to resist the government's high-handedness, save the republic, and avenge French *honor.*

A free Commune was proclaimed… essentially because there was no way of imposing the will of Paris over all of France; however, a Parisian government was immediately appointed, which was a government like all the rest… although during the days when Paris had remained without a government—from March 18 until elections were held on April 3— it had shown that things of public interest, better than through orders from a government, could be accomplished through the efforts of everyone concerned, through Associations and Committees that had no powers beyond those given to them by popular approval.

An attempt was made to make peace with the government provided that the existence of the republic was guaranteed; and the attempts failed only because of the criminal stubbornness of the government, of the hatred and desire for revenge against Parisians of the Bonapartist generals' (temporarily posing as republicans), and of the thirst for blood and power of the morally monstrous Adolphe Thiers, who controlled the executive power.

In the organization of the armed forces, defensively and offensively, the old military traditions were followed.

True, there was none of the scandalous salaries of other governments, but the principle of privilege and a hierarchy of salaries were respected, as these ranged from 6 thousand lire a year paid to rulers to thirty *soldi* a day paid to soldiers.

The arrangements to defend against the Commune's internal enemies were the usual police procedures of house searches, arrests, suppression of newspapers and other and worse violations of freedom.

Private ownership was rigorously respected. The rich peacefully continued to possess their wealth and, even during the scarcity of the siege, managed to carouse and mock at the misery not only of the people, but also of those fighting for the Commune. Benoît Malon, who was a member of the Commune's government (*Council*) recounts how the *Fédérés* (the name given to the soldiers of the Commune) returning from combat disheveled and bloodied through the wealthier avenues, were insulted and called *thirty-pennies* by the bourgeois seated outside the luxurious cafés, drinking and smoking.

The Commune's work (manufacturing uniforms for soldiers) was subcontracted out to entrepreneurs who had people work for little money.

The soldiers of the Commune were sent to guard the treasures of the Bank of France, from whom loans were sought with all the same formalities and guarantees used in the financial transactions of bourgeois governments.

The only undertakings of vaguely socialist leanings were (if memory does not fail us) a decree against nighttime work in bakeries; a decree (never implemented) that gave workers united in cooperatives the right to take over factories deserted by owners, *as long as they compensated the owners* upon their return; a postponement of payments on rents and debts, some meager distribution of food to the hungry, and the return, free of charge, of pawned items of minimal value:—all things that can be done (and most of which have been done repeatedly) by a bourgeois and monarchist government, in the interest itself of public "order" and the tranquility of the bourgeois.

And along with this, a great deal of declarations of principles, very advanced but never implemented; eloquent manifestos to the French people, to the peasants, to the people of the entire world, which never went beyond words; and symbolic acts, such as the demolition of the Vendôme column[211] and the burning of the guillotine, certainly of great moral value, but of no practical importance.

This is what the Paris Commune actually was.

Given the people who took part in it, given the preceding ferment of ideas that the war could interrupt but not destroy, given how the European public interpreted the movement, something that could not have failed to influence the movement itself, one can surmise that, had the movement not been so quickly drowned in blood, perhaps it would have turned into social revolution.

But was it not mainly the direction in which the movement was taken to cause the Commune's failure—even from a military point of view?

If armed bands of Parisians, prior to the tightening of the siege, had ventured into the countryside to preach expropriation and help the locals carry it out, the movement would have spread and the government would not have been able to assemble its forces and send them all against Paris.

If within Paris the bourgeoisie had been expropriated and everything made available to the people, then the entire population would have been interested in the revolution and would have defended it;—while instead, according to the reports of the Communards themselves, only a small number of inhabitants took part in the fighting, and in the last days the Commune's defenders numbered no more than ten thousand.

The Commune was defeated, and it was defeated without having done what could and should have been done to win, because the principle of authority killed its momentum.

---

211 The imperial column in Place Vendôme, topped by a statue of Napoleon and adorned with battle scenes, was considered an affirmation of militarism.

We do not intend to blame the men, who all gave admirable proof of their selflessness, devotion, heroism.

And we would be deceiving ourselves if we claimed that it was the fault of the "leaders."

The "leaders" exists only as long as the people want and tolerate them; and they are what the people allow them to be.

The problem lies within the people themselves: it is within the people that we must fight the cult of authority, the faith in the necessity and usefulness of government. Once this is done the revolution may triumph.

Let us honor the martyrs of the Paris Commune, who, even though they chose the wrong path, gave their lives for freedom.

But let us put ourselves in a position to do better than them.

[Untitled]

Translated from *La Questione Sociale*
(Paterson, New Jersey) 6, new series, no. 28 (March 17, 1900)

Upon returning to Paterson I learn that the comrades whom I designated as my representatives in my dispute with Ciancabilla have been rejected, because they were involved in the issue.[212]

I could dispute whether the comrades representing Ciancabilla are the best suited, when the agreement is that jury members must be "impartial" people and not representatives of the parties, who then agree to fill out the rest of the jury with one or more individuals agreeable to both parties; I could claim that in appointing my representatives I was guided by the same criteria that appear to have guided my opponent; I could show that the names upon which my selection settled had been put forward by my opponent's sympathizers as those expected to be appointed, without any foreseeable objection;—but none of this is important. I want the truth to come out as soon as possible; and therefore, to eliminate difficulties, I immediately entrusted two other comrades, wholly unconnected with the dispute, who have agreed to the assignment and who will contact Ciancabilla's representatives immediately.

They are:

PIETRO CANE of 223 E. 21 St., New York.

and

LUIGI RAFFUZZI of 554 W. 132 St., New York.

For now, I would have nothing more to add. But since, even at this stage in the dispute, when the most elementary delicacy would require

---

212   See the untitled note of February 24, 1900, p. 217.

that insults and insinuations be suspended and the question be left in the hands of the jury, Ciancabilla chose to use language that... does not correspond to the truth, let me point out what everybody already knows, that is, that the delay I caused in appointing my representatives was not spent on "lengthy meditations," but was due to the fact that I was far away and continually on the move, and I could not appoint my representatives without first asking them if they were willing to accept the task.[213]

ERRICO MALATESTA.

The Irreconcilable Contradiction

Translated from "La contradizione irreduttibile," *La Questione Sociale* (Paterson, New Jersey) 6, new series, no. 30 (March 31, 1900)

They write from Bari, Italy:

Our city is going through a very sad crisis.

Barrel-making, once a thriving industry, is increasingly on the decline.

The cause of this decline lies in the introduction of new fares by railroad and shipping companies, which allow for the return of empty casks at very low cost; therefrom comes a decreased consumption of barrels.

Some time ago the barrel-making masters took steps to resolve this critical condition by asking that the transportation costs of empty casks be increased.

Last Sunday, in front of the prefecture, they met to ask the authorities for help.

A committee of 12 barrel-making workers, accompanied by a public safety inspector, was received by the prefect, who promised to sort things out.[214]

How on earth will the prefect sort things out?

By ordering the railroad companies to increase again the transportation costs for empty casks? How so, if the capitalists are the ones who own the railroads, the ones who command the prefects and the prefects' masters!

And then, increasing the charge for returning barrels would drive up the price of wine.

---

213 The jury never came to a unanimous verdict. Malatesta's and Ciancabilla's representatives issued separate statements, published in *La Questione Sociale* on May 19 and 26, 1900, respectively.
214 The letter had appeared in the socialist *Avanti!* of February 24, 1900.

If the wine consumers were to turn to the prefect, would he promise to sort things out for them too?

That poor prefect must find himself in a similar position as Almighty God, to whom one person asks for rain and another for good weather. And he is not even omnipotent!

But in vain do we worry about the position of prefects, who know quite well how to dig themselves out of this puzzle... by making promises to everybody and keeping none of them.

Much more deserving of our commiseration are those poor workers who, ignorant of the root causes of their problems, let themselves be deceived and mocked to the extent that they let themselves be escorted to the prefecture by a public safety inspector, and hope that the officials will care about their fate.

The case of the barrel-makers of Bari is a typical case, which clearly shows the absurdity of capitalist society.

In similar cases there is no possible cure other than the abolition of capitalism, the radical transformation of the system of production. And every trade, every form of human activity must, sooner or later, find itself in the same case, which is already rather widespread due to the overabundance of labor.

Associations are of no help; nor are strikes and all other forms of resistance; nor cooperatives.

Whenever no one needs the labor of a worker, the worker cannot impose any agreement: he must die of hunger—more or less slowly, more or less convulsively, but die of hunger he must... unless he can break free from the current system.

And progress tends to make the labor of an ever-increasing number of workers unnecessary.

This is the ultimate, irreconcilable contradiction between capitalism and progress.

Either prevent all progress, enshrining the current castes, abolishing competition between capitalists, prohibiting any production development, any new machine, any new scientific application, and reducing workers to the status of domestic animals granted rations by their masters—in short, a regime like the one the Jesuits exercised in Paraguay;[215] or destroy capitalism and organize production not for the profit of a few, but for the greatest well-being for all.

The request of the Bari barrel-makers to increase the transportation

---

215   In the wake of Spanish colonization, between the 17th and the 18th centuries, the Jesuits acquired enormous power in Paraguay and carried out one of the greatest social engineering experiments in history, organizing the lives of hundreds of thousands of native peoples in dozens of communities (*reducciones*) planned according to the Christian doctrine.

cost of used casks, so that the wineries would find it more convenient to burn them rather than send them back, is the same as asking the barrel-makers to only send 10 out of every 100 barrels to the market and destroy the other 90 before they can be used.

Is it possible to achieve that? Of course not. Yet, the current structure of society is so absurd that it would make such a measure beneficial.

When people die of hunger because there is too much stuff, or because it is too easy to produce it, or because it is too durable, destruction might appear—and might fleetingly be—more useful than production. A fire, an earthquake might be a blessing, bringing work and bread to the unemployed.

But destruction of wealth is not how workers can emancipate themselves. And luckily the time has passed, at least in the more advanced countries, during which workers thought they could stop progress, and put as much energy into smashing up machinery as it would have required to take control of it.

We must not fight progress, but direct it to everyone's benefit.

And for that to happen workers must take possession of all the capital, all social wealth, so that it would then be in their interest that products abound and production require the least possible effort.

This is why it is necessary to make the revolution.

Labor organizing, strikes, resistance of all kinds can at a certain point in capitalist evolution improve the conditions of workers or prevent them from worsening; they can serve very well to train workers for the struggle; they are always, in capable hands, a means of propaganda;—but they are hopelessly powerless to resolve the social question. And thus they must be used in such a way as to help prepare minds and muscle for the revolution—for expropriation.

Anyone failing to grasp this, is reduced to pleading to the prefects... and being mocked.

A Good Idea from a Legislative Body

Translated from "Una buona idea in un corpo legislativo," *La Questione Sociale* (Paterson, New Jersey) 6, new series, no. 30 (March 31, 1900)

The Paris Municipal Council, given that the habit of spitting one's expectorate right and left is not only filthy and indecent, but also a cause of the spread of tuberculosis—decided to erect in the main city streets and public buildings enameled iron plaques on which is written, in large characters visible from a distance: "War on tuberculosis. The public is asked not to spit on the sidewalks."

Thus nothing more than a request. It does not read "by order of the superiors": no threat of punishment for offenders. Just how anarchists understand things!

And this anarchist approach will prove more effective than any terrifying authoritarian measure.

First of all, it will probably be better observed, since it would be rude to not consider it; while ignoring a threat of punishment is an act of courage that can lend a certain nobility even to things that are actually bad.

Moreover, those who understand its usefulness, being unable to rely upon the efforts of the municipal police, will find the need to convince others of its usefulness. And thus a measure which, presented in the form of a compulsory instruction, would have looked like ridiculous oppression and would have contributed to making hygiene and hygienists objects of hatred and ridicule, presented instead as a request and a recommendation, serves beautifully to educate the people and to spread the sense of duty that everyone has when it comes to refraining from actions that are in any way harmful to others.

Which goes to show that even a legislative body can be useful... when it renounces its power to legislate.

Cesare Batacchi Freed

Translated from "Cesare Batacchi in libertà," *La Questione Sociale* (Paterson, New Jersey) 6, new series, no. 30 (March 31, 1900)

With a decree of March 14 Cesare Batacchi has been "pardoned."

With its conventional phraseology, the sycophant press will say that the magnanimity of the king came to remedy a deplorable judicial error.

The truth is that the king and his successive governments have kept an innocent man in prison for 22 years, that they deliberately closed their eyes to the obvious proof of his innocence and resisted the popular uproar for as long as they could, and when it was no longer possible to resist they came along with a "pardon," not to fix an error, but to grant amnesty for a heinous judicial murder.

Our greetings to our very dear comrade who comes back to life.

We do not know if his long, terrible martyrdom will have left him the strength to return to the struggle. But his name will always be remembered as a very noble example of moral strength, and will ring out shame for the system and people who govern the Italy of the Savoy.

[Untitled]

Translated from *La Questione Sociale*
(Paterson, New Jersey) 6, new series, no. 31 (April 7, 1900)

Errico Malatesta leaves for Europe, grateful for the warm welcome bestowed upon him by comrades and friends.

He is sorry he was unable to achieve more than the smallest part of what he had proposed and hoped to do for propaganda in these lands; this may be due to the poverty of his abilities, but certainly not to any lack of good will. He hopes that the comrades will, through their redoubled activity, make up one thousand-fold for the feeble contribution he was able to offer them.

Bidding farewell to comrades, he hopes to meet many of them again in other more effective battles, which perhaps are not too far away.

Malatesta remains a contributor to our newspaper.

He proposes to keep us informed of the European movement, thus giving LA QUESTIONE SOCIALE that newsy character which thus far, due to the conditions under which it has been composed, it has always lacked.

Those who have to write to Malatesta should address their letters in his name to:

112, High Street, Islington, N.
London (England)

Retraction

Translated from "Ritrattazione," *La Questione Sociale*
(Paterson, New Jersey) 6, new series, no. 31 (April 7, 1900)

The one time we had said something good about a legislating body, we are immediately obliged to take it back.

Misled by an inaccurate report, we said that the Paris Municipal Council, given the harm and danger of spitting in the streets, had decided to *ask* citizens to refrain from doing so.

It appears however that this is yet another of the usual *ordinances* carrying threats of fine and imprisonment.

Certainly only the anarchists are capable of appealing to the common sense and goodwill of the people. Everybody else relies solely on fear of the police.

Yet, between a public that carelessly spits and one that does not spit for fear of the municipal cops, we still prefer the former; since, while there may perhaps be a little more tuberculosis among them, the latter group will certainly contain a greater dose of servility.

"L'Agitazione"

Translated from "'L'Agitazione,'" *La Questione Sociale*
(Paterson, New Jersey) 6, new series, no. 31 (April 7, 1900)

The 1st issue of the revived *L'Agitazione* has reached us, from Ancona.

The writer of this news, while not holding back the delight brought to him by his appreciation of it, since he was too closely linked to that newspaper during the first phase of its existence and hopes to again be of service to it in this new phase, which he wishes to be even more fortunate and productive than the first.[216]

He will however be allowed to congratulate the brave Ancona comrades who, despite the fact that nearly all the old contributors are interned or far away, have managed, with the contribution of new elements, to bring back out a newspaper that, judging from its first issue, will be better than its predecessor—thereby adding new proof to that coming from comrades elsewhere in Italy, that the Italian anarchist socialist party has already attained such maturity that it no longer has to fear to be strangled by persecution.

Already it can truly be said that for every person that falls, ten more rise up.

We reprint the news of the reappearance of *L'Agitazione* given by Messina's *L'Avvenire Sociale*,[217] because it offers an exhaustive explanation of the causes that led to the deplorable dispute between the two newspapers:

[*The excerpt from* L'Avvenire Sociale *explains how the major misunderstanding, now overcome, had arisen from the fact that* "since the method

---

216   There is a presumable gap in the original text, which seems clearly disconnected. *L'Agitazione* is the periodical that Malatesta founded and edited in Ancona in 1897–98.

217   "'L'Agitazione,'" March 16–17, 1900.

of federative organization was being championed only by L'Agitazione, *all organizing activities came together around that paper; which for those looking on from a distance, like us, produced the effect that* L'Agitazione *was almost an authoritarian center of the anarchist movement."*][218]

Direct anything relating to *L'Agitazione* to Giambattista Carboni, general delivery. Ancona (Italy).

The Right to Judge

Translated from "Il diritto di giudicare," *La Questione Sociale* (Paterson, New Jersey) 6, new series, no. 33 (April 21, 1900)[219]

Entire volumes could be written—without exhausting the subject—on errors in thought and action resulting from imperfections of language: synonyms, ambiguous terms, etc.

One instance of this is the confusion that exists regarding the question of the right to *judge*, precisely because of the double meaning of the word.

Throughout the entire course of history the minority of strong or fortunate people who have oppressed and exploited the laboring masses has little by little constructed a range of beliefs and institutions all intended to ensure, justify, and perpetuate its rule. Besides the army and other means of physical coercion, which are the first weapon and last resort of oppression, they created a "morality" tailored to their own interests, they classified as criminal anything that went against those interests, and formulated a body of laws that force, with the due penal sanctions, the oppressed to respect these principles, which they call moral and just, and that are nothing else than the interests of the oppressors. And as custodians and avengers of these laws they put in place "judges," charged with ascertaining violations and punishing the violators.

These judges, which the privileged have always commended to the public precisely because they support their privilege, have been and are one of most nefarious plagues suffered by humanity.

Through their work every rebellious thought and action has been persecuted and repressed: they are the ones who have martyred the thinkers

---

218   On the earlier controversy between *L'Avvenire Sociale* and *L'Agitazione*, see "True or False Disagreements (Between Anarchists)," p. 410 of Volume III of these *Complete Works*.

219   The issue prior to this one, namely no. 32 of April 14, 1900, which might have contained articles by Malatesta, unfortunately cannot be found. As to the present article, even though it was published after Malatesta's departure, it is the last in a series of original articles penned by Malatesta for *La Questione Sociale* and as such it was included in this volume.

who in all ages have striven to open up a little more light, a little more truth; they are the ones who have sentenced to the gallows or to life in prison those who rebel against oppression and try to conquer a little more justice for the people; they are the ones who fill the jails with scores of poor wretches who, even when they did wrong, were driven and often compelled to do it by the same social order that their punishment defends. Posing as the priests of justice, they manage to make people preserve and accept a situation that the raw violence of soldiers would be incapable of maintaining; and cloaked by a false independence from other government organs and by an even more false incorruptibility, they operate as the docile and willing instruments of the hatreds, vendettas, fears of all tyrants big and small. The fact that they are raised above others, that they can control the life, liberty, and assets of whomever falls into their hands, and that their job is to convict people, produces a moral degeneracy that turns them into a breed of monsters, deaf to any feelings of humanity, sensitive only to the horrible delight of making people suffer.

It is natural then that these judges and this institution of "justice" have been and remain targets of attack from all men who love freedom and true justice.

Add to the above the more precise understanding one has these days of the influence of heredity and social environment, which reduces to a minimum, if it does not entirely eliminate, individual moral responsibility; add the deeper knowledge of psychology that, rather than shedding light on the human mind's motives, has so far managed only to hint how tremendously complicated and difficult they are;—and one will understand why it has been said that "man has no right to judge man."

And we anarchists, who want to eliminate violence and imposition from the relationships between men, are right to protest louder than others against this right to "judge," when *judging* means *convicting* and *punishing* those who do not want to submit to the law made by the rulers.

But *judging* also means expressing one's own opinion, formulating one's own *judgment*; and this is simply the right to criticize, the right to express one's thoughts on anything and everything, which is the first foundation of freedom. To deny the right to judge, in this sense of the word, is not just denying any possibility of progress, but completely denying the intellectual and moral life of humanity.

The ease of making mistakes and the great difficulty of judging correctly, especially when dealing with the moral motives of man's actions, advise us to be cautious with our own judgments, to never adopt an attitude of infallibility, to always be ready to correct ourselves, and to judge the act with as little concern as possible to the actor, but they cannot in any way invalidate the right to judge, that is, to think and express one's own thoughts. We may make mistakes, we may be unfair in our own judgment; but the freedom to make mistakes, the freedom to assert an error is inseparable from the freedom to assert the true and just: everybody must be fully free to say and propagate whatever he pleases, as long as he does not impose his opinion by force and uses reasoning as the only weapon to support his judgments.

Some comrades were confused by the double meaning of the word judge, and on the occasion of deeds variously appreciated within the anarchist camp, they have believed they could get out of the embarrassment by saying that anarchists must not judge.

Why on earth? The anarchists, who proclaim unbounded freedom, should thus be deprived of the basic right they demand for everyone! They, who accept neither dogma nor popes and aspire to always move forward, should renounce the right and habit of criticizing one another, which is the means and guarantee of improvement!!!

Anarchists have no right to judge?! Then how on earth could they combat the current society, if they had not judged it to be bad? And the claim that one has no right to judge, is that not a judgment itself? Does it not mean judging the judger?

Ultimately, this is just a more or less unconscious hypocrisy of the mind, triggered and reinforced by the linguistic confusion we have spoken about. For, in fact, it is all about people who deny the right of judgment to those who *do not judge as they do,* and deny it to themselves when they *do not know* how to judge.

At the Workers' Circle.
A Lecture by Malatesta

Translated from "En el Círculo de Trabajadores. Conferencia Malatesta,"
El Despertar (New York) 10, no. 199 (May 1, 1900)

On the evening of March 30, comrade E. Malatesta gave a lecture at this Circle. In it he spoke of the planned Federation of cigar workers in the United States. There was also talk of Spaniards and Cubans, of Cuba and her government, and of other rather curious details.

Let us take things in order. The New York cigar workers' society had asked Malatesta to visit Tampa and a fewer other locations, if possible, during his propaganda tour of the United States, and to meet up there with the cigar workers, with the goal of spreading the Federation. And he did as was requested.

In this lecture, Malatesta reported back on his effort to fulfill the task entrusted to him.

He said that he had been in Tampa and had found the organized cigar rollers quite ready to defend their rights, but without the solidity that is required, because of certain political and patriotic divisions. He noted more or less the same in Cuba.

In Florida, he tried to give lectures recommending harmony between "Moors" and "Christians," although the outcome failed to live up to his good intentions: there are those who are determined to spread hatred and division, and it is well known that, unfortunately, this is the easiest thing to do among workers.[220] Malatesta said that, after one such call for harmony, some of the workers who were blinded by political passion, simply told him:—It is no use, Malatesta, we cannot live together with the Spaniards.

This response reveals the reason why the poor are poor. Jews and Russians in Poland, Italians and French in Europe, Turks and Christians in Greece, blacks and whites in other places, Spaniards and Cubans in Cuba, everywhere it is the same thing.

In Havana, Malatesta found the seed of the same evil. Despite this, he strove to combat it, giving good advice and arguing that slaves should not behave like children but rather like adults; but in Havana he had deal with a rebel general who now acts as a representative of the American authorities and who simply forbade him from giving any more public talks, because Malatesta was an anarchist and under a law framed by a gentleman who is now dead, anarchist propaganda is not allowed in Cuba. Malatesta was not convinced. Accompanied by some friends he paid a personal visit to the rebel general who was now representing the American authorities and asked him if it was true that he, the Italian Malatesta, who carried in his suitcase as a memento a portrait of Angiolillo, Cánovas's executioner, was banned from giving public lectures. The Cuban general answered that it was true, the ban was real and that they had no choice but to obey the American authorities.[221]

In sum, he said that the cigar workers in the United States have a rather difficult and delicate task facing them if they want to carry on with their federation; the task is to boldly and fearlessly combat the seeds of patriotic strife that the bourgeois have inoculated in them, the way the plague is inoculated in rats. The evil is not deeply rooted because, luckily, there are workers who understand, while the blind are a minority; but it could get worse.

Comrade Malatesta took his leave of the New York cigar workers (because he had to leave for Europe) by wishing them prosperity, balanced judgments, and personal integrity in the struggles against their exploiters.

. . .

---

220   On Malatesta's stay in Tampa see note 183.
221   On this meeting, see note 206.

SECTION VI
Press Clippings

Boastful Italian Anarchist

The Washington Post, no. 8480 (August 28, 1899)

ENRICO MALATESTA SAYS HE WILL ORGANIZE IN LEADING AMERICAN CITIES.

New York, Aug. 27.—Enrico Malatesta, the Italian anarchist who recently escaped from a prison in his own country and came to the United States, addressed a French anarchist meeting in Paterson, N. J., and a few hours later spoke to 200 Italian anarchists in this city.[222]

He told his hearers that the Italian and Spanish workingmen were getting ready for a revolution, and that they were organizing for a great uprising. He said that he would stay in this country about three months and organize anarchist groups in many of the leading cities.[223]

Correspondence. From W. Hoboken. Malatesta Lecture

Translated from "Corrispondenze. Da W. Hoboken. Conferenza Malatesta," *Il Proletario* (New York) 4, no. 20 (September 2, 1899)

. . .

In reporting the lecture given by Malatesta here in W. Hoboken on Friday evening of last week,[224] on the premises of *Tua* and brother, I do not want to follow the same course Paterson's *La Questione Sociale* has thus far maintained in its reports of the lectures given by our comrade Rondani . . .

A few minutes after eight, Malatesta introduced himself to the audience in a simple manner and with clear words developed the topic of the lecture, "The

---

222 The two meetings were held on August 27. The New York meeting was held at Teutonia Hall, on Third Avenue.

223 The same news had appeared in similar or identical terms in many other newspapers, including the *New York Herald, New York Sun, Evening Post, Evening Telegram* (New York), *Boston Evening Transcript, San Francisco Call, Kansas City Journal, Milwaukee Sentinel, Elmira Gazette, Geneva Daily Times* of the same date; the *Indiana State Journal* (Indianapolis) on August 30; the *Weekly Rocky Mountain News* (Denver) on August 31. Some of them also published a short biography of Malatesta. The August 29 issue of *Il Progresso Italo-Americano* summarized the New York meeting in these terms: "The audience, of about 200 people applauded the strong thinker several times, as he demonstrated the need for Spanish and Italian anarchists to be ready for a future action in their respective countries."

224 August 25.

social question," criticizing in an unassailable manner the system of present-day society and urging solidarity among workers.

...When he arrived at the end of his lecture, he tried to prove the uselessness of the political struggle.

...

Malatesta was countered by our comrades Antonio Cravello and Arturo Meunier...

There were repeated attacks from both sides, with Malatesta wanting us to believe that with the triumph of socialism there would always be an oppressive government...

Up and down the Colony (From the *Reporter's* Notebook). The Wounding of Malatesta[225]

Translated from "Su e Giù per la Colonia (Dal Taccuino del *Reporter*). Il ferimento di Malatesta," *Il Progresso Italo-Americano* (New York) 20, no. 212 (September 6, 1899)

...

Enrico Malatesta has proven he is a great soul again on this occasion. Not only has he refused to name his assailant, but he has also declared that he has forgiven him from the bottom of his heart.

"I am sure—Malatesta said—that by now he regrets his action."

...

Correspondence. Barre, Vermont

Translated from "Corrispondenze. Barre Vermont," *Il Proletario* (New York) 4, no. 25 (October 7, 1899)

The debates between our comrade Rondani and Malatesta were followed attentively by hundreds and hundreds of workers.

We are very satisfied to observe that many anarchists now accept the economic struggle to obtain immediate improvements in the field of working conditions.

Even on the political issue that is currently so urgent in Italy, Malatesta admits that it is necessary to make a joint effort to successfully overthrow the barrier to all progress which is the Monarchy.

...

---

225   See note 94.

Social Movement. From the United States. West Hoboken, N. J.

Translated from "Movimento Sociale. Dagli Stati Uniti. West Hoboken N. J." *La Questione Sociale* (Paterson, New Jersey) 5, new series, no. 12 (November 25, 1899)

On the evening of Saturday the 11th Malatesta spoke before a small crowd on the "Possibility of Anarchy."

Noteworthy was the attitude of the democratic socialists who, seemingly, made up the bulk of the small audience.

Malatesta had argued that government is useless and harmful as much in an egalitarian society, as when used as an instrument of education and emancipation.

And the socialists invited to debate the matter replied that, if the term "anarchy" were to be replaced by "socialism," they were entirely in agreement with what Malatesta had said; and they repeat as much in correspondence sent to *Il Proletario*.[226]

. . .

Social Movement. United States. Cecil [by L. Decrolière]

Translated from "Mouvement Social. États Unis. Cecil," *Germinal* (Paterson, New Jersey) 2, no. 9 (January 30, 1900)

Comrade Malatesta gave a lecture here on the 2nd of January.[227] Due to the lack of time we had had to organize it, few people attended. It is true that many workers prefer to spend their time in bars or attending cockfights.

In his address, our comrade put the capitalist system on trial and vigorously chastised the workers for their laxity, weakness, and lack of vigor in their quest for self-emancipation.

It is regrettable that our comrade had to speak in front of such a small audience, nevertheless, we hope that he gave those who listened to him something to think about.

L. DECROLIÈRE.

---

226   The correspondence to *Il Proletario,* signed "Fra Dolcino" and carried in the November 18 issue, adds no details on Malatesta's speech, except that "discussion of the chosen topic 'The possibility of anarchy' was a very easy task for Malatesta, because all he did was repeat sentences that Kropotkin wrote in *The Conquest of Bread*."

227   Cecil is a town in Pennsylvania, about fifteen and a half miles southwest of Pittsburgh.

The Havana Contracts

The Times (Washington), March 2, 1900[228]

. . .

The Italian Anarchist Malatesta, who is now here, says that the Cuban workmen have no present cause for complaint. Their hours are easy and their wages good. He adds that the time is coming when they will have recourse to anarchy to cure the evils that will arise. He urges the Cubans to boycott the Americans, not to bend the knee to the military power, and to refuse to accept any position in the government. Malatesta intends to deliver a number of speeches, but if he continues this sort of talk he will be hauled up short, as the Spanish law is very strict regarding Anarchists. Malatesta is said to have come from the United States.

. . .

Social Movement. From Abroad. Cuba

Translated from "Movimento sociale. Dall'Estero. Cuba," *La Questione Sociale* (Paterson, New Jersey) 6, new series, no. 28 (March 17, 1900)

Our comrade Errico Malatesta received the warmest welcome not just from comrades but also from the general public in Havana.

The press made a great fuss for and against him.

The government applied to him the Spanish law, which prohibits anarchist propaganda. Consequently our comrade gave his lectures without mentioning anarchy, and concluding:

"Be aware that the ideas I am expounding to you are those of a party which I cannot name, because the law, which you thought you had overthrown by fighting for Cuba's independence and driving out the Spanish tyrant, prohibits to mention anarchy."

The audience, always very numerous, laughed and applauded.[229]

. . .

---

228 The title refers to the stipulation of contracts for the construction of sewers and street paving, which is the main subject of the article.
229 On this anecdote compare note 192, p. 226.

[Untitled]

Translated from *Germinal* (Paterson, New Jersey) 2, no. 13 (March 30, 1900)

News reaching us from Cuba merely confirm our ideas on the value of governments. Not long ago, in this same place, we explained our views on the political change occurred in the Pearl of the Antilles. Just a few days ago, comrade Malatesta, back from Cuba, explained to us the autocratic way the new rulers are running the country's affairs. Our comrade was tolerated and could give lectures, but with the explicit condition that he not utter the name of the cause he championed. Even certain laws that had fallen into disuse are enforced by the Americans; laws dating back to the time of Cánovas, of sinister memory. Strange that those same laws that are no longer enforced in Spain, are enforced in Cuba today, and moreover by the very people who claimed that they wanted to set Cuba free.

. . .

Up and down the Colony.
The Departure of Errico Malatesta

Translated from "Su e Giù per la Colonia. La partenza di Errico Malatesta," *Il Progresso Italo-Americano* (New York) 21, no. 81 (April 5, 1900)

Errico Malatesta, the well-known anarchist organizer who spent nine months in these lands spreading among the Italians of the United States the ideas that he so lovingly champions, sailed yesterday for England on board the "Saint Paul" of American Line.

A few comrades were on the pier to wave goodbye. He told our reporter that he was leaving immensely satisfied with the results of his propaganda work and that it is not unlikely that he may return here again.

Have a good trip, with the hope that the police of Europe's most serene governments leave him in peace.[230]

---

230   "Most Serene Republic" (Serenissima Repubblica) was the traditional name by which the Venetian maritime republic was known.

Chronology

JANUARY	Malatesta is in *domicilio coatto* on the island of Lampedusa.
JANUARY–FEBRUARY	Receives a visit from the socialist deputy Oddino Morgari.
APRIL 26–27	Escapes from Lampedusa with two comrades.
MAY 24 (APPROX.)	After passing through Tunisia and Malta, returns to London.
JUNE 11	London lecture on "The duty of progressive parties in response to current conditions."
AUGUST	In London, anonymously publishes the pamphlet *Against the Monarchy.*
AUGUST 5	Sails from Southampton for New York, under a false name.
AUGUST 12	Arrives in Paterson (New Jersey).
AUGUST 16	First lecture in Paterson, Teatro Sociale, on "The anarchists and the current situation in Europe."
AUGUST 26	Lecture on "The social question" in West Hoboken (New Jersey), Camillo Tua beer hall.
AUGUST 27	Speaks to French anarchists in Paterson and to Italian ones in New York, Teutonia Hall.
SEPTEMBER 1	Speaks to an international gathering of anarchists in New York, East Broadway.
SEPTEMBER 3	Is wounded during a meeting in West Hoboken.
SEPTEMBER 9	The new series of Paterson's *La Questione Sociale* begins, edited by Malatesta.
SEPTEMBER 15–18	Lectures in Newark, Orange Valley, West Hoboken, and Brooklyn.
SEPTEMBER 20	Speaks at the Paterson demonstration against the Twentieth of September celebration, Proletario Hall.
SEPTEMBER 23	Malatesta's propaganda tour of the Northeastern United States begins.
SEPTEMBER 26 – OCTOBER 5	Series of five lectures in Barre (Vermont).
MID-OCTOBER	Stay in Boston (Massachusetts). Lectures on October 10, 12, and 14. Lectures also in West Quincy and Milford (October 20).

OCTOBER 24 AND 26	Lectures in Providence (Rhode Island).
START OF NOVEMBER	Malatesta is back in Paterson.
NOVEMBER 11	Lecture on "The possibility of anarchy" in West Hoboken.
NOVEMBER 15	Malatesta–Rondani debate in Paterson, Proletario Hall.
NOVEMBER 18	Lecture on "The anarchists and what they want" in Orange Valley (New Jersey), Salone Rosso.
NOVEMBER 22–25 (APPROX.)	Malatesta is in Philadelphia (Pennsylvania). Lectures given on November 24 and 25.
DECEMBER 13–16	Series of four lectures in New York, Sala Tirelli.

1900

START OF JANUARY	Malatesta is in Pennsylvania since late December: he gives lectures in Italian and French in Coupon, Pittsburgh, Yohoghany, Bishop, Federal, Cecil (January 2) and Charleroi (January 6).
LATE JANUARY	Series of lectures in Spring Valley (Illinois).
2ND HALF OF FEBRUARY	Spends time in Tampa, Florida, where he delivers daily lectures between February 18 and 20, and in Key West.
FEBRUARY 27	Arrives in Cuba.
MARCH 1	First lecture in Havana, Centro General de Obreros.
MARCH 3	Second lecture in Havana, Centro General de Obreros, on "Civilization and freedom."
MARCH 5	Lecture in Regla.
MARCH 5	The third scheduled lecture in Havana, on the topic "Crime: original causes and consequences," is prohibited by the government.
MARCH 6	Improvised talk at the Centro General de Obreros in Havana, police raid.
MARCH 10	Returns from Cuba to the United States.
MARCH 18	Speaks in Paterson to commemorate the Paris Commune.
MARCH 26	Lecture in New York on "Civilization and freedom," Colombo Hotel.
MARCH 30	Speaks at the Círculo de Trabajadores in New York.
APRIL 4	Sets sail for London.

Index of Publications

The 1900 Socialist Congresses in Paris..204
Against the Monarchy (Appeal to All Men of Progress) 16
Among the Ferocious Anarchists [by O. Morgari] 9
The Anarchist Gospel Explained by Enrico Malatesta 27
An Anarchist Programme 43
Anarchist Propaganda..218
The Anarchists and Workers' Societies 105
Anarchists Divided Among Themselves..42
Anarchists in the Labor Unions..174
Anarchist-Socialist Federation...79
The Anarchists' Task...159
Are We Socialists? 96
At the Workers' Circle. A Lecture by Malatesta 253
Boastful Italian Anarchist 257
Buffoonery 92
Cesare Batacchi Freed...248
Challenge 119
Consequences of Commercialism 202
Concerning the "Problem of Love" (The Other Side)
      [by Beniamino Mazzotta] 206
Correspondence. Barre, Vermont..258
Correspondence. From W. Hoboken. Malatesta Lecture..............................257
The Crisis of Anarchism 149
Delegation and Delegation..104
Discussion (A Reply to the "Dissidents")..69
Dreyfus's Conviction [by Charles-Albert] 108
Eight Hours of Work 66
Electoral Struggle and Direct Struggle 178
Face to Face with the *Coatti* [by O. Morgari] 3
Falsification 172
Federalism and Anarchy 208
For New York's *Il Proletario* 107
A Good Idea from a Legislative Body 247
Going Backwards like Crabs 143
The Havana Contracts 260
The Irreconcilable Contradiction..245
It's a Shame!..153
"L'Agitazione"..250
"Le Journal du Peuple" 162
A Letter from Malatesta Regarding the Arrests on Lampedusa.....................13
The Long Way and the Short Way 186

Malatesta, Anarchist. A Talk with the Italian Outlaw Who Is Here
  [by Abraham Cahan] 35
Malatesta Lectures 30, 78, 220
The Malatesta Lectures 195
Malatesta on the Problem of Love 196
Malatesta's Second Lecture: Civilization and Freedom................227
Martyrdom in Chicago. November 11, 1887..............................127
The Milan Elections. The Anarchists' Conduct 170
Minority Rights and the Ballot Box Trial 139
New Rival for John Most..35
Object Lesson 141
Oddino Morgari's "True Anarchist"...87
On a Personal Matter...184
On Behalf of Cesare Batacchi...82
Open Reply to an "Intrasigent" [by Domenico]...........................125
Our Challenge to "Il Proletario"...136
Our Correspondence. From Barre, Vermont. Malatesta Lectures
  [by S. Pallavicini]...109
Our Correspondence. London Letter [by G. Lanfranchi].................14
Our Financial Situation 123
Our Organization 130
The Paris Commune...238
Parting of the Ways..38
Personal Matter..190, 201
Police Exploits..124
The Principle of Organization...92
Provoked 174
Regarding an Escape [by O. Morgari] 8
Regarding Anarchists Who Vote...76
Remembrances of the International [by O. Morgari] 9
The "Resistance" of the Republicans...103
Retraction 249
Revolutionary Alliance 95
The Right to Judge...251
"Ruined by the Law" [by O. Morgari] 7
Setting the Record Straight [Concerning the Declarations of
  the "Dissidents"]..61
Signor Malatesta Explains...28
Social Movement. From Abroad. Cuba 260
Social Movement. From the United States. West Hoboken, N. J. ...259
Social Movement. United States...156
Social Movement. United States. Cecil [by L. Decrolière] 259
Socialism and Provincialism 165
Socialist Congress?..189
The Socialist Split in France..111
The Taxpayers' Strike in Spain...155

Them Too!...83
To All Comrades..195
To Anarchist Speculators [by Critico] 137
To Conclude...210
To the Comrades 142, 207, 237
To the Cuban People 231
To the Cuban Workers 234
Towards Anarchy...167
The Twentieth of September Celebration...74
"The Two Freedoms"..145
Unawareness and Cowardice [by Domenico Zavattero] 117
Universal Suffrage...98
Unjustified Criticism..182
[Untitled] 82, 87, 97, 120, 126, 144, 177, 192, 200, 201, 217, 217, 244, 249, 261
Up and down the Colony (From *The Reporter's* Notebook):
    The Wounding of Malatesta 258
Up and down the Colony. The Departure of Errico Malatesta 261
What Our Newspaper Will Be [Statement of the New Editorial Board] 39
What We have to Say to "Il Proletario"...152
The "Wicked Laws" in France...163

Index

A

Acciarito, Pietro, 125
Agitatore, L' (Neuchâtel), 14
Agitazione, L' (Ancona), 192, 250, 251
Altgeld, John Peter, 129
Angiolillo, Michele, 254
Aquadro, Lorenzo, 186
Arbeiter-Zeitung (Chicago), 128
Aristotle, 228
Aurora, L' (Paterson – W. Hoboken, New Jersey), 69–73, 97, 98, 144, 145, 150, 153, 174, 175, 177, 182–85, 190–96, 202, 210, 212
Avanti! (Rome), 3, 7–9, 13, 14, 87, 142, 143, 171
Avvenire Sociale, L' (Messina), 250
Avvenire, L' (Buenos Aires), 135, 172
Azzati, Angelo. *See* Terzaghi, Carlo

B

Bakunin, Mihail, 11, 150, 185, 240
Barricello, Sabino, 165
Barry, Leonora, 187
Barsotti, Carlo, 153, 177
Batacchi, Cesare, 82, 83, 124, 126, 127, 248
Bava-Beccaris, Fiorenzo, 104
Bazaine, François Achille, 241
Besso, G., 186
Bianco, S., 186
Bismarck, Otto von, 239
Bissolati, Leonida, 140
Blanc, Louis, 147
Blanqui, Louis-Auguste, 113

Boffa, Clemente, 186
Bourgeois, Léon, 112, 164
Briganti, P., 92, 108
Brisson, Henri, 112

C

Cahan, Abraham, 35
Calcagno, Pietro, 14
Cane, Pietro, 188, 244
Cánovas del Castillo, Antonio, 254, 261
Carboni, Giambattista, 251
Casale, A., 186
Casale, Giuseppe, 186
Caserio, Sante, 163
Castagneto, Carlo (pseud. Prete), 213
Castelli, Graziano, 186
Cavallo, G., 186
Cerino, A., 186
Cerino, S., 186
Cerruti, Arturo, 186
Charles-Albert. *See* Daudet, Charles Victor Albert Fernand
Ciancabilla, Giuseppe, 172, 173, 184–86, 190–96, 201, 202, 211–13, 217, 244, 245
Cianfarra, Camillo, 195, 200
Clément-Thomas, Jacques Léonard, 240
Comercio, El (Cuba), 220
Cominetti, Battista, 186
Commercial Advertiser, The (New York), 35
Costa, Andrea, 12, 73

Cravello, Antonio, 258
Cravello, Ernestina, 186
Cravello, Vittorio, 186
Creci, Enrique, 233
Crispi, Francesco, 36, 37
Critico (correspondent to *La
Questione Sociale*), 137, 138
Cubano, El (Havana), 220
Cumplowitz (marxist professor), 14

D
Daudet, Charles Victor Albert
Fernand (pseud. Charles-Albert),
108
De Felice Giuffrida, Giuseppe, 165
Decrolière, Louis, 259
Della Barile, Giovanni, 217
Despertar, El (New York), 191, 253
Deville, Gabriel, 111, 113, 116
Dewey, George, 220
Diario de la Marina, El (Havana), 220
Discusión, La (Havana), 218, 219,
231
Domenico (correspondent to *La
Questione Sociale*), 125
Dreyfus, Alfred, 108, 109, 111, 126,
127, 164, 181

E
Engel, George, 129
Engels, Friedrich, 34, 114, 116, 208
Esteve, Pedro, 34, 78, 177, 186, 190,
191, 202, 210–12, 214
Evening. *See* Raveggi, Pietro

F
Faure, Sébastien, 162, 163
Ferri, Enrico, 201
Ferro, P., 186
Fielden, Samuel, 129
Fischer, Adolph, 128, 129
Flaustier. *See* Sosset, Paul
Forno, Andrea, 125

Foschini, G., 186
Frattini, Lucia, 186
Frattini, Luigi, 186
Freedom (London), 144
Freiheit (New York), 207
Frezzi, Romeo, 125

G
Galliffet, Gaston de, 34, 109, 111,
113, 126, 165
Gallo, Firmino, 186
Garibaldi, Giuseppe, 240
Gavilli, Giovanni, 89, 90
Germani, Ferdinando, 14
Germinal (Paterson, New Jersey),
156, 191, 259, 261
Gillia, E., 186
Goldman, Emma, 38, 42
Granotti, Giuseppe, 214
Grave, Jean, 192
Guabello, Alberto, 177, 186
Guesde, Jules, 111–14, 116, 117
Gussoni, Carlo, 105

H
Humbert I (king of Italy), 108

I
Italia, L' (Rome), 83, 103, 104

J
Jaurès, Jean, 113, 114, 189
Journal du Peuple, Le (Paris), 162, 163

K
Kropotkin, Peter, 91, 112, 206, 218

L
Lafargue, Paul, 111, 113, 116
Lanfranchi, Giuseppe, 14
Lecky, William Edward Hartpole,
238
Lecomte, Claude Martin, 240

Leone, E., 149, 151, 152
Leyret (lawyer), 164
Libertaire, Le (Paris), 145, 163
Lingg, Louis, 128, 129
Loubet, Émile, 109, 164
Loyola, Ignacio de, 185

M

Maceo, Antonio, 228, 233
Magliocco, C., 186
Mainardi, S., 186
Malon, Benoît, 242
Martí, José, 228, 233
Martin, Constant, 145, 147
Marx, Karl, 11, 30, 34, 200, 208, 240
Mazzini, Giuseppe, 10, 240
Mazzotta, Beniamino, 177, 186, 206, 207
McKinley, William, 92, 174
Mercandino, Giacomo, 186
Mercandino, Giuseppe, 186
Merlino, Francesco Saverio, 104, 105
Meunier, Arturo, 258
Millerand, Alexandre, 34, 111–14, 116, 117, 143, 189
Minero Re, L., 186
Monod, Gabriel, 164, 165
Morello (lawyer), 124
Morgari, Oddino, 3, 7–9, 87, 88, 90, 91
Most, Johann, 35, 36, 38, 43, 207
Motta, Marcello, 186

N

Napoleon III (emperor of France), 241
Neebe, Oscar, 129
Neue Zeit, Die (Stuttgart), 114
New York Herald, 42
Nieuwenhuis, Ferdinand Domela, 205
Nordau, Max, 63
Nuevo Ideal (Havana), 220, 227, 234, 237

P

Pallavicini, Salvatore, 109
Pandiani, Sisinio, 171
Parsons, Albert Richard, 128, 129
Pelloux, Luigi, 104, 112, 139, 141
Perino, L., 186
Picco, Giuseppe, 186
Pietraroja, Gennaro, 14
Piva (socialist), 14
Porrino, F., 186
Porrino, M., 186
Presente e Avvenire (Rome), 149
Prete. *See* Castagneto, Carlo
Prina, Quinto, 186
Progresso Italo-Americano, Il (New York), 27, 28, 152, 153, 177, 258, 261
Proletario, Il (New York), 82, 92, 96, 97, 104, 107, 108, 110, 119, 136, 137, 152–54, 165, 171, 172, 174, 175, 177, 195, 200, 201, 257–259

Q

Quintavalle, Nicola, 217

R

Raffuzzi, Luigi, 254
Raveggi, Pietro (pseud. Evening), 186
Réveil du Nord, Le (Lille), 117
Richards, Vernon (Vero Recchioni), 43
Riscossa, La (Roma), 170, 171, 177
Rivetti, S., 186
Robespierre, Maximilien de, 90
Robino, P., 186
Roda, Cesare, 186
Rolli, G., 186
Rondani, Dino, 14, 15, 32–34, 109–11, 141, 142, 156, 158, 195, 200, 257, 258

Rospo Volante, Il (Rome), 177

S

Saint-Simon, Claude-Henri de
Rouvroy, count of, 200
Sanguinetti, B., 186, 217
Schwab, Justus, 128, 129
Sella, Guido, 186
Simone, A., 186
Socialista, Il (Lugano), 14
Sola, A., 186
Somebody (columnist for *Il
Proletario*), 177, 201
Sonnino, Sidney Costantino, 141
Sosset, Paul (pseud. Flaustier), 138
Spencer, Herbert, 200
Spies, August, 127–29

T

Tamaroglio, Amedeo, 186
Tamaroglio, Antonio, 186
Tamaroglio, Giovanni, 186
Tedeschi, Mario, 14, 15
Temps Nouveaux, Les (Paris), 108,
192
Terzaghi, Carlo (pseud. Angelo
Azzati), 213
Thiers, Marie-Joseph-Louis-
Adolphe, 242
Thomas. *See* Clément-Thomas,
Jacques Léonard
Times, The (Washington), 260
Tognetti, Enrico, 186
Torquemada, Tomás de, 90
Tribuna, La (Rome), 124
Tua, Camillo, 257
Turati, Filippo, 170

U

Unique, L' (Orléans), 196

V

Vaillant, Auguste, 163
Vaillant, Édouard, 111, 113, 114, 116,
117
Verolet, L., 186
Victor (correspondent to *Avanti!*),
142
Vineis, E., 186
Vineis, Giovanni, 186
Vittorio Emanuele di Savoia, 108

W

Waldeck-Rousseau, Pierre, 109,
111–13, 117, 143
Washington Post, The, 257
White, J. W. F., 202
Widmar, Francis, 186, 217
Witts (doctor), 225

Z

Zavattero, Domenico, 117, 118